THE IMPERIAL GUPTAS
A BIBLIOGRAPHY

THE IMPERIAL GUPTAS
A BIBLIOGRAPHY

Edited by
JAGDISH S. YADAV
NIRMALA YADAV

MANOHAR
AMERICAN INSTITUTE OF INDIAN STUDIES
NEW DELHI
1997

First published 1997

ISBN 81-7304-197-0

Published by
Ajay Kumar Jain for
Manohar Publishers & Distributors
2/6 Ansari Road, Daryaganj
New Delhi 110 002

Lasertypeset by
Apoorva Computers
B1/3, Vijagarh House, Assi
Varanasi 221 005

Printed at
Print Perfect
A-23, Mayapuri, New Delhi 110 064

Dedicated

to

M.A. Dhaky

CONTENTS

FOREWORD

The American Institute of Indian Studies is proud to present the latest in a series of scholarly bibliographies on Indian art and culture. This most recent volume, *The Imperial Guptas: A Bibliography*, has been edited and compiled by Jagdish S. Yadav, long-time Librarian at the AIIS' Center for Art and Archaeology in Varanasi and Nirmala Yadav. Together, in record time, they have combed the vast scholarly literature on the Gupta dynasty, covering such diverse topics as history, education, religion, painting and iconography.

The volume fills a major lacuna in the Indological studies. Believed by many to represent India's golden age, the Gupta period is often seen as a peaceful secure time, when even Chinese pilgrims could wander safely from *tirtha* to *tirtha*. For these reasons and others, the fourth- through sixth-century Gupta era, perhaps more than any other single historical period, has attracted tremendous scholarly attention. Yet until now there was no single bibliographic source on the Guptas. This lack was, in part, because the task was deemed overwhelming for all but the most experienced bibliographers. But Jagdish Yadav, having earlier published *Pradeep: Index to Felicitation and Commemoration Volumes* and *Cultural Heritage of Mathura: A Bibliography* was ready to take on the daunting task of a bibliography on the Guptas. He and Nirmala Yadav, who had assisted him on earlier projects, prepared the volume's 2744 entries, ferreting out sources published internationally and in India. To make the task of researching the Gupta period even easier for the user, they have provided a subject index, author index, and a key-word index.

On behalf of the American Institute of Indian Studies, I thank Jagdish and Nirmala Yadav for their hard and thorough work. Thanks to them, research on Gupta art, history and culture will be a greatly facilitated.

Catherine B. Asher
Chair
Committee on Art & Archaeology
American Institute of Indian Studies

26 August 1996

PREFACE

There is hardly any period in ancient Indian history that has engaged so much attention of scholars as the Gupta. The period still allures researchers to undertake fresh enquiries into the realm of the unknown and re-assessment of the known. The Guptas ruled over a vast empire in ancient Northern India between the fourth and the sixth century A.D. In their times, within the domains of literature and art, in political and economic spheres, no less in philosophical and metaphysical speculations, is witnessed what is believably the finest and the highest of which the ancient Indians were capable. As a result, it has been often called the "Golden Age of Indian History".

A vast amount of published literature on the Guptas covering all the major aspects — history, society, costume and jewellery, economy, religion, literature, archaeology, epigraphy, numismatics, art, iconography, sculpture, terracottas, architecture etc., exists. But there is no comprehensive bibliography of this vast published material. This bibliography aims to fill this gap.

The bibliography is divided into three parts in the following sequence :

i) Classified Subject Index

ii) Author Index

iii) Key-word Index

CLASSIFIED SUBJECT INDEX: All books and articles have been classified according to the subjects mentioned in the "Contents". Each entry in this part has been serialized for cross reference in indexes (ii) and (iii). The names of authors in each subject-group are alphabetically arranged beginning with the surname followed by name (in full or initials). If references about Guptas figure on a large number of pages in a particular book, then the information concerning the book alone is given. In case of the articles dealing with Guptas are in the collected works (Felicitation, Commemoration, Seminar-proceedings, etc.) or Journals, then fuller details including the page numbers are given. Examples of a few entries in the Classified Subject Index are presented below:

Williams, Joanna
The art of Gupta India: Empire and province. New Delhi, Heritage Publishers, 1983.

In this entry, author's surname is given first, followed by forename, title of the book, place of publication, publisher and year of publication. Since references about Guptas figure on many pages of this publication, these pages have not been mentioned in the entry.

Asher, Frederick M.
Gupta art in Eastern India. In Karl Khandalawala, ed., *The Golden age: Gupta art — empire, province and influence.* Bombay, Marg Publications, 1991: 73-80.

In this case, an article dealing with Guptas is in a collected work. Hence the complete information about the author's name, title of the article, editor of the collected work, title of the collected work, place of publication, publisher, year of publication, and the page numbers on which this article appeared are given.

Another example:

Sharma, R.C.
Gupta Sculpture from Mathura. *Bulletin of Museums & Archaeology in U.P.*, Nos. 27-28, June-December 1981: 89-109.

Here author's name, title of the article, name of the journal in which this article was published, the issue number of the journal, year of publication and pages on which this article appeared are given.

AUTHOR INDEX: An Author Index is provided to locate an author's contributions irrespective of any subject-group. The names of the authors have been alphabetically arranged by surname followed by first name. The entries have been numbered serially in Classified Subject Index and these entry numbers are mentioned against the name of each author. For example:

Joshi, M.C., 590, 1115-1116, 1614-1618, 2257, 2662.

Krishna Deva, 901, 1122, 1630, 1999-2002, 2273-2275, 2432, 2616-2618, 2665-2667.

All books and articles by M.C. Joshi and Krishna Deva are listed at serial numbers mentioned against their names in the Classified Subject Index.

KEY-WORD INDEX: The Classified Subject Index has been supplemented by a Key-word Index. Sometimes it is difficult to classify an article or a book, particularly when it deals with more than one subject. To help scholars to find an article or book on any subject covered in this bibliography, this part should prove very useful. Important key-words from the titles of the books and articles in the journals listed in this bibliography have been selected and listed in an alphabetical order. Against each key-word, serial numbers of the Classified Subject Index are given. For example:

Deogarh, 897-898, 1136, 2188, 2252-2253, 2286, 2315, 2399, 2403, 2626, 2632, 2641, 2651, 2658, 2698, 2700-2701.

Siva, 2156, 2179, 2209, 2232, 2243, 2268, 2271, 2275, 2284, 2290, 2314, 2334, 2544, 2642, 2662.

Skandagupta, 13, 19, 64, 80, 152, 165, 201, 223, 244, 290, 296, 335-336, 349-350, 375, 430, 955-956, 962, 1027, 1032, 1035, 1095, 1141, 1150, 1169, 1171-1172, 1221, 1227, 1238-1239, 1245, 1248, 1255, 1307, 1309, 1334, 1336, 1346, 1350, 1359, 1419, 1440, 1479, 1597, 1615, 1624, 1635, 1712, 1720, 1766, 1784.

Vakataka, 24, 131, 139, 141, 161, 186, 197, 218, 225-228, 238-239, 245, 362, 394, 412, 417, 451-452, 712, 980, 1089-1091, 1180, 1987, 2138, 2349.

An attempt has been made to make the bibliography as comprehensive as possible within the frame work of the above discussed structure. It is hoped, this publication will be of help to researchers working not only on any aspect of Guptas and their times but also of Indian political, social and religious history, archaeology, epigraphy, numismatics, art, iconography, sculpture, terracottas, architecture etc., in general. For any shortcomings in the book, the responsibility is entirely ours.

20 December 1996

Jagdish S. Yadav
Nirmala Yadav
Editors

ACKNOWLEDGEMENTS

We are grateful to Prof. Catherine B. Asher, Department of Art History, University of Minnesota, U.S.A., and Chair, AIIS Committee on Art and Archaeology for her support, encouragement and also for writing the Foreword. Dr. Pradeep Mahendiratta, Director-General & Vice-President, AIIS always encouraged us for such projects, we are grateful to him for his consistent encouragement and support. We are thankful to all our colleagues at the Center for their help and cooperation. We would like to record our great appreciation and thanks to Shri O.N. Pandeya and Shri V.K. Gupta for their help and cooperation. We are thankful to Dr. Ravindra Kumar for his valuable suggestions. Thanks are also due to the staff of the Libraries of Archaeological Survey of India and National Museum in New Delhi, and Bharat Kala Bhawan at Varanasi for their help. Dr. Anupama Srivastava composed the manuscript in a very short time for which we are grateful to her. We are grateful to our son Yogesh and daughter Shikha whose love and affection lies behind the completion of this work.

Jagdish S. Yadav
Nirmala Yadav

CLASSIFIED SUBJECT INDEX

HISTORY

1. **Acharya, P.**

   Ancient routes in Orissa. *Orissa Historical Research Journal*, Vol. 5, Nos. 3-4, 1955-56 : 43-50.

2. **Agarwal, K.L.**

   Gupta rule in Bundelkhand. *Journal of the Madhya Pradesh Itihasa Parishad*, No. 6, 1968 : 27-41.

3. **Agrawal, Ashvini**

   Can Kacha of the Gupta gold coins be identified with Bhasma of Aryamanjusrimulakalpa ? In A.M. Shastri and others, ed., *Vajapeya : Essays on evolution of Indian art & culture: Prof. K.D. Bajpai felicitation volume*, Vol II. Delhi, Agam Kala Prakashan, 1987 : 329-331.

4. ———.

   The Maitraka-Gupta relations—A reappraisal of D.R. Bhandarkar's view. In D.C. Bhattacharyya and Devendra Handa, ed., *Praci-Prabha : Perspectives in Indology* (*Essays in honour of Professor B.N. Mukherjee*). New Delhi, Harman Publishing House, 1989 : 127-131.

5. ———.

   The place of Ghatotkachagupta in the Gupta history. *Panjab University Research Bulletin* (*Arts*), Vol. 17, No. 1, 1986 : 141-146.

6. ———.

   The place of Kacha in Gupta chronology. *Journal of the Numismatic Society of India*, Vol. 43, pt. 1, 1981 : 71-74.

7. ———.

   Rise and fall of the Imperial Guptas. Delhi, Motilal Banarsidass, 1989.

8. **Agrawal, Jagannath**
Ayodhya from the Maurya to the Gupta period. In Lallanji Gopal, ed., *Ayodhya : History, archaeology and tradition*. Varanasi, All India Kashiraj Trust, 1994 : 61-67.

9. ______.
Ayodhya from the Maurya to the Gupta period. *Purana*, Vol. 36, No. 1, January, 1994 : 61-67.

10. ______.
Samudragupta's performance of Asvamedha sacrifice. In Hari Ram Gupta, ed., *Sir. Jadunath Sarkar commemoration volume*, Vol. II. *Essays presented to Sir Jadunath Sarkar*. Hoshiarpur, Panjab University, 1958 : 10-13.

11. ______.
The status of Govinda Gupta. *All India Oriental Conference Proceedings*, Session 24, 1968 : 339-343.

12. ______.
The status of Govinda Gupta. *Journal of Ancient Indian History*, Vol. 3, 1969-70 : 101-107.

13. ______.
The status of Skandagupta's mother. *Annals of the Bhandarkar Oriental Research Institute*, Vols. 48-49, 1968 : 325-327.

14. **Agrawala, R.C.**
Rajaputana through the ages (Saka-Kusana and Gupta periods). *Journal of the Bihar Research Society*, Vol. 41, pt. 3, September 1955 : 292-326.

15. **Agrawala, V.S.**
The Kamboja Janapada. *Purana*, Vol. 6, No. 1, 1964 : 221-229. .

16. **Ahmad, Nisar**
Ghatotkacaguptas. *Bharati*, Nos. 12-14, 1968-1971 : 331-343. .

17. ______.
Harigupta—a successor of Kumaragupta I. *Indian History Congress Proceedings*, Session 45, 1984 : 892-900.

18. ______.

On the historicity of Ramagupta. *Indian Historcal Quarterly*, Vol. 38 No. 4, December 1962 : 283-291.

19. ______.

Samudragupta II : A successor of Skandagupta. *Journal of the Bihar Research Society*, Vols. 69-70, 1983-1984 : 174-179.

20. **Aiyangar, S. Krishnaswami**

Studies in Gupta history. *Journal of Indian History*, Vol. 6, pt. 2, August 1927 : 1-61.

21. **Altekar, A.S.**

Further discussion about Ramagupta. *Journal of the Bihar and Orissa Research Society*, Vol. 15, pts. 1-2, March-June 1929 : 134-141.

22. ______.

A new Gupta king. *Journal of the Bihar and Orissa Research Society*, Vol. 14, pt.2, June 1928 : 223-253.

23. ______.

Vishnuguptas in the Gupta dynasties. *Indian History Congress Proceedings*, Session 5, 1941 : 179-181.

24. ______.

Were the Vakatakas defeated by the Guptas in c. 350 A.D. ? *Indian Culture*, Vol. 9, 1942-1943 : 99-106.

25. Ancient India : Land of mystery. Virginia. Time-Life Books, 1994.

26. **Aquique, Md.**

Notes and queries on successors of Budha Gupta. In Upendra Thakur and Yugal Kishore Mishra, ed., *The heritage of India : L.N. Mishra commemoration volume*. Bodh Gaya, L.N. Mishra Commemoration Publication Committee, 1978 : 257-265.

27. **Arokiaswamy, M.**

The Gupta dynasty and the early Pallavas of Kanchi. *Journal of Indian History*, Vol. 56, pt. 1, April 1978 : 47-109.

28. **Bajpai, K.D.**
Central India in the Gupta period. In K.D. Bajpai, ed., *The glory that was Bundelkhand : Mahendra Kumar 'Manav' felicitation volume*. Bhopal, Mahendra Kumar Manav Abhinandan Samiti, 1993 : 366-375.

29. ______.
Cultural history of India, Vol. I : Madhya Pradesh. Kanpur, Prajna Prakasan, 1985.

30. ______.
Fresh light on the problem of Ramagupta. *Indian Historical Quarterly*, Vol. 38, No. 1, March 1962 : 80-85.

31. ______.
Fresh light on the problem of Ramagupta. *Indian History Congress Proceedings*, Session 24, 1961 : 53-57.

32. ______.
Identification of Ramagupta. *Journal of Indian History*, Vol. 42, pt. 2, August 1964 : 389-393.

33. ______.
The problem of Pusyamitras. *Bulletin of Ancient Indian History & Archaeology*, No. 1, 1967 : 13-19.

34. ______.
Some problems of ancient Indian history (c. 200 B.C.-600 A.D.). *Bulletin of Ancient Indian History & Archaeology*, No. 1, 1967 : 1-6.

35. ______.
Yug-yug mein Ahicchatra. *Panchala*, Vol. 2, 1986 : 71-94 (Hindi).

36. **Banerji, Adris**
Gupta survival and influences. *Journal of the Varendra Research Museum*, Vol. 4, 1975-76 : 41-54.

37. ______.
Narasimhagupta. *Journal of the United Provinces Historical Society*, Vol. 17, pt. 2, December 1944 : 34-44.

38. **Banerji, R.D.**
The age of the Imperial Guptas.New Delhi, Ramanand Vidya Bhawan,1981.

39. ———.
The chronology of the late Imperial Guptas. *Annals of the Bhandarkar Institute*, Vol. 1, pt. 1, 1918-19 : 67-80.

40. ———.
History of Orissa, Vol. I. Calcutta, R. Chatterjee, 1930.

41. ———.
Later Guptas of Magadha. *Journal of the Bihar and Orissa Research Society*, Vol. 14, pt. 2, June 1928 : 254-265.

42. ———.
Prehistoric, ancient and Hindu India. Bombay, Blackie & Son, 1950.

43. **Banerji-Sastri, A.**
Sources of Indian History. *Journal of the Bihar and Orissa Research Society*, Vol. 27, pt. 2, June 1941 : 131-186.

44. **Barnett, L.D.**
Political history of ancient India. *Calcutta Review*, Third Series, Vol. 10, 1924 : 248-253.

45. **Barua, K.L.**
The Gupta era. *Indian Culture*, Vol. 5, No. 1, July 1938 : 114-15.

46. **Basak, Radhagovinda**
Chandra's conquest of Bengal. *Indian Antiquary*, Vol. 48, June 1919 : 98-101.

47. ———.
The history of North-Eastern India. Calcutta, Sambodhi Publications, 1967.

48. **Basham, A.L.**
The date of the end of the reign of Kumara Gupta I and the succession after his death. *Bulletin of School of Oriental and African Studies*, Vol. 17, pt. 2, 1955 : 366-369.

49. ———.
The wonder that was India. London, Sidgwick and Jackson, 1961.

50. **Bhandarkar, D.R.**
Asvamedha by Samudragupta. *Indian Culture*, Vol. 1, No. 1, July 1934 : 115-118.

51. ———.
Govindagupta and Purugupta. *Indian Culture*, Vol. 11, No. 4, April-June 1945 : 231.

52. ———.
New light on the early Gupta history. In *Malaviya commemoration volume*. Varanasi, Banaras Hindu University, 1932 : 189-211.

53. **Bhandarkar, R.G.**
The epoch of the Gupta era. *Journal of the Bombay Branch of the Royal Asiatic Society*, Vol. 17, pt. 2, 1887-1889 : 80-98.

54. ———.
A peep into the early history of India from the foundation of the Maurya dynasty to the downfall of the Imperial Gupta dynasty. In Narayana Bapuji Utgikar and Vasudev Gopal Paranjpe, ed., *Collected works of Shri R.G. Bhandarkar*, Vol. I. Poona Bhandarkar Oriental Research Institute, 1933 : 1-61.

55. ———.
A peep into the early history of India from the foundation of the Maurya dynasty to the fall of the Imperial Gupta dynasty (B.C. 322-circa 500 A.D.). *Journal of the Bombay Branch of the Royal Asiatic Society*, Vol. 20, 1897-1900 : 356-408.

56. **Bhattacharya, Amitabha**
A note on the conquest of the region of Mandasore by Kumaragupta I. *Indian History Congress Proceedings*, Session 26, pt. I, 1964 : 70.

57. ———.
A note on the expression Licchavi-Dauhitra. *Indian History Congress Proceedings*, Session 25, 1963 : 90-92.

58. **Bhattacharya, Asok Kumar**
A note on Samudragupta's Southern campaign. *Indian History Congress Proceedings*, Session 25, 1963 : 50-53.

59. **Bhattacharya, B.**
New light on the history of the Imperial Gupta dynasty. *Journal of the Bihar Research Society*, Vol. 30, pt. 1, March 1944 : 1-46.

60. ______.
New light on the history of the Imperial Guptas. *Journal of the Ganganatha Jha Research Institute*, Vol. 1, pt. 3, May 1944 : 287-291.

61. **Bhattacharya, Sibesh**
Kaca problem—A re-examination. *Journal of Indian History*, Vol. 45, pt. 3, December 1967 : 727-733.

62. ______.
Some aspects of female names in Eastern India of Gupta and post-Gupta periods. In *K.C. Chattopadhyaya memorial volume*. Allahabad, Department of Ancient History, Culture & Archaeology, 1975 : 127-136.

63. **Bhattacharyya, S.C.**
The original home of the Guptas. *Journal of the Asiatic Society of Pakistan*, Vol. 7, 1962 : 204-210.

64. **Bhattacharyya, Tarapada**
Was Anantadevi, mother of Skanda Gupta. *Journal of the Bihar Research Society*, Vol. 32, pt. 2, June 1946 : 182-183.

65. **Bhattasali, N.K.**
New lights on the history of Assam. *Indian Historical Quarterly*, Vol. 21, No. 1, March 1945 : 19-28.

66. **Bongard-Levin, G.M.**
Ancient Indian civilization. New Delhi, Arnold-Heinemann, 1985.

67. **Buddha Prakash**
Aspects of Indian history and civilization. Agra, Shiva Lal Agarwala & Co., 1965.

68. ______.
The Central Asiatic expedition of Chandragupta Vikramaditya. *Journal of the Royal Asiatic Society of Bengal, Letters*, Vol. 13, No. 1, 1947 : 31-39.

69. ______.
The Kusana invasion of India under Kumaragupta. *Indian Historical Quarterly*, Vol. 30, No. 3, September 1954 : 219-236.

70. ______.
Last days of the Gupta empire. *Annals of the Bhandarkar Oriental Research Institute*, Vol. 27, pts. 1-2, January-April 1946 : 124-141.

71. ______.
The political geography of India on the eve of Gupta ascendency. *Indian Culture*, Vol. 13, No. 2, October-December 1946 : 85-90.

72. ______.
Samudragupta's Southern expedition : A new interpretation. In *Professor K.A. Nilakanta Sastri felicitation volume*. Madras. Prof. K.A. Nilakanta Sastri Felicitation Committee, 1971 : 15-31.

73. ______.
Studies in Indian history and civilization. Agra, Siva Lal Agarwala & Co., 1962.

74. **Chakraborti, Haripada**
India as reflected in the inscriptions of the Gupta period. New Delhi, Munshiram Manoharlal, 1978.

75. **Chattopadhyay, Aparna**
A note on the Kaca problem of Gupta history. *Journal of the Oriental Institute*, Vol. 22, Nos. 1-2, September-December 1972 : 64-67.

76. **Chattopadhyay, Bhaskar**
Ayodhya in the post-Maurya period. *Purana*, Vol. 36, No. 1, January 1994 : 68-73.

77. **Chattopadhyaya, Sudhakar**
Early history of North India from the fall of the Mauryas to the death of Harsa, c. 200 B.C.-A.D. 650. Calcutta, Progressive Publications, 1958.

78. ______.
The Ephthalite invasion. *Indian History Congress Proceedings*, Session 19, 1956 : 178-181.

79. ______.
The later Imperial Guptas.*Indian Historical Quarterly*, Vol. 29, No. 2, June 1953 : 156-161.

80. **Chaudhuri, P.C.**
Ajapura of Skanda Gupta and the area around Bihar. *Journal of the Bihar and Orissa Research Society*, Vol. 19, pt. 3, September 1933 : 337-343.

81. **Chhabra, B.Ch.**
Chandragupta's abdication. *Indian Culture*, Vol. 14, No. 4, April-June 1948 : 141-150.

82. **Choudhary, Radhakrishna**
A critical reappraisal of the problem of the Hunas in India (with special reference to the later Hunas). *Journal of the Bihar Research Society*, Vol. 57, 1971 : 1-10.

83. ______.
History of Bihar. Patna, Motilal Banarsidass, 1958.

84. ______.
The Huna invasion of India. *Journal of the Bihar Research Society*, Vol. 45, 1959 : 112-142.

85. **Dabral, Shivprasad**
Uttarakhanda ka itihas, Vol. 3, Garhwal, Veer-Gatha-Prakashan, 1969 (Hindi).

86. **Daji, Bhau**
A brief survey of Indian chronology, from the first century of the Christian era to the twelfth. *Journal of the Bombay Branch of the Royal Asiatic Society*, Vol. 8, 1863-66 : 236-251.

87. **Dandekar, R.N.**
The age of the Guptas and other essays. Delhi, Ajanta Publications, 1982.

88. ______.
Some aspects of the Gupta civilization. In H.L. Hariyappa and M.M. Patkar, ed., *Professor P.K. Gode commemoration volume.* Poona, Oriental Book Agency, 1960 : 50-62.

89. **Dani, Ahmad Hasan**
Ramagupta problem—a new solution. *Journal of the Numismatic Society of India*, Vol. 26, pt. 1, 1964 : 11-14.

90. **Das, D.R.**
Bhanugupta. *Indian History Congress Proceedings*, Session 28, 1966 : 121-122.

91. **Das, Dharma Narayan**
The early history of Kalinga (A socio-economic and cultural history of coastal Orissa). Calcutta, Punthi Pustak, 1977.

92. ______.
On the theory of the Gupta rule in Kalinga. *East*, Vol. 1, No. 1, June 1967 : 164-169.

93. **Das Gupta, Kalyan Kumar**
The Malavas. *Our Heritage*, Vol. 13, pt. 2, 1965 : 1-27.

94. **Das Gupta, Nalini Nath**
The Kaca problem. *Indian Historical Quarterly*, Vol. 20, No. 4, December 1944 : 351-353.

95. ______.
On the successors of Kumaragupta I. In D.R. Bhandarkar and others, ed., *B.C. Law volume*, Part I. Calcutta, Indian Research Institute, 1945 : 617-625.

96. ______.
On Vainyagupta. *Indian Culture*, Vol. 5, No. 3, January 1939 : 297-303.

97. ______.
Rama Gupta. *Indian Culture*, Vol. 4, No. 2, October 1937 : 216-222.

98. **Deo, Jitamitra Prasad Singh**
Cultural profile of South Kosala (from early period till the rise of the Nagas and the Chauhans in 14th century A.D.). Delhi, Gian Publishing House, 1987.

99. **Dikshit, S.K.**
Candra-Gupta II, Sahasamka alias Vikramaditya and the nine jewels. *Indian Culture*, Vol. 6, No. 2, October 1939 : 191-210.

100. ______.
Candra-Gupta II, Sahasamka alias Vikramaditya and the nine jewels. *Indian Culture*, Vol. 6, No. 4, April 1940 : 377-392.

101. ______.
Some light on the chronology of the later Imperial Guptas. *Indian Culture*, Vol. 5, 1938-1939 : 425-429.

102. **Dikshitar, V.R. Ramachandra**
I-tsing's India.*Indian Historical Quarterly*, Vol. 28, No. 1, March 1952 : 7-16.

103. **Diskalkar, D.B.**
An epithet of Samudragupta.*Indian Antiquary*, Vol. 52, 1923 : 17.

104. **Diwakar, R.R.**
Bihar through the ages. Bombay, Orient Longmans, 1959.

105. **Dunbar, George**
A history of India from the earliest times to the present day, Vol. I. London, Nicholson & Watson, 1943.

106. **Dwivedi, Gautam N.**
The Western limits of the Gupta empire. *Indian History Congress Proceedings*, Session 34, Part I, 1973 : 76-79.

107. **Dwivedi, R.K.** and **Vaish, Devi Lal**
A history of the Guptas : Political & cultural. Allahabad, Technical Publishing House, 1985.

108. **Fergusson, James**
On the Saka, Samvat and Gupta Eras. A supplement to his paper on Indian chronology. *Journal of the Royal Asiatic Society of Great Britain and Ireland*, New Series, Vol. 12, 1880 : 259-285.

109. **Fleet, J.F.**
Alberuni's statement regarding the Gupta era. *Indian Antiquary*, Vol. 17, 1888 : 243-246.

110. ______.
The conquests of Samudragupta.*Journal of the Royal Asiatic Society of Great Britain and Ireland*, 1898 : 369-370.

111. ______.
The epoch of the Gupta era. *Indian Antiquary*, Vol. 15, 1886 : 189-194.

112. ______.
The Gupta-Valabhi era. *Indian Antiquary*, Vol. 20, November 1891 : 376-389.

113. ______.
A note on a matter arising out of the Gupta era. *Journal of the Bombay Branch of the Royal Asiatic Society*, Vol. 18, 1890-1894 : 71-87.

114. ______.
A note on the origin of the Gupta era. *Indian Antiquary*, Vol. 15, 1886 : 278-279.

115. ______.
The scheme and equation of the years of the Gupta era. *Indian Antiquary*, Vol. 16, 1887 : 141-154.

116. ______.
Summary of results regarding the epoch and origin of the Gupta era. *Indian Antiquary*, Vol. 17, 1888 : 359-369.

117. ______.
The use of the twelve-year cycle of Jupiter in records of the early Gupta period. *Indian Antiquary*, Vol. 17, 1888 : 331-339.

118. **Ganguly, D.C.**
The early home of the Imperial Guptas. *Indian Historical Quarterly*, Vol. 14, No. 3, September 1938 : 532-535.

119. ______.
The original home of the Imperial Guptas. *Indian Historical Quarterly*, Vol. 28, No. 4, December 1952 : 386-391.

120. ______.
The Puranas on the Imperial Guptas.*Indian Historical Quarterly*, Vol. 21, No. 2, June 1945 : 141-143.

121. ______.
Vainyagupta Dvadasaditya. *Indian Historical Quarterly*, Vol. 9, No. 3, September 1933 : 784-788.

122. ______.
Vainyagupta Dvadasaditya. *Indian Historical Quarterly*, Vol. 10, No. 1, March 1934 : 154-156.

123. **Ganguly, D.K.**
Historical geography and dynastic history of Orissa upto the rise of the Imperial Gangas. Calcutta, Punthi Pustak, 1975.

124. ______.
History and historians in ancient India. New Delhi, Abhinav Publications, 1984.

125. ______.
The Imperial Guptas and their times. New Delhi, Abhinav Publications, 1987.

126. ______.
The Ramagupta problem. *Journal of the Numismatic Society of India*, Vol. 43, pt. 2, 1981 : 97-113.

127. **Gokhale, B.G.**
The origin of the Imperial Guptas. *Journal of the Bombay Branch of the Royal Asiatic Society*, New Series, Vol. 27, Supplement, 1952 : 275-278.

128. ______.
Samudra Gupta : Life and times. Bombay, Asia Publishing House, 1962.

129. **Gokhale, Sobhana**
The present and ancient boundaries of Madhya Pradesh. *Journal of the Madhya Pradesh Itihasa Parishad*, No. 5, 1967 : 93-135.

130. **Goyal, S.R.**

Early chronology of the Gupta dynasty. *Journal of the Bihar Research Society*, Vol. 52, 1966 : 14-19.

131. ______.

Gupta aur Vakataka samrajyon ka yug. Meerut, Kusumanjali Prakashan, 1988 (Hindi).

132. ______.

Gupta samrajya. Jodhpur, Meghna Prakashan, 1993 (Hindi).

133. ______.

A history of the Imperial Guptas. Allahabad, Central Book Depot, 1967.

134. ______.

The problem of the Baladityas in the Gupta period. In Maheswar Meog and H.K. Barpujari, ed., *Professor Surya Kumar Bhuyan commemoration volume*. Gauhati, All India Oriental Conference, 1966 : 100-114.

135. ______.

Rajasthan : The original home of the later Guptas. *Bharati*, No. 15, 1971-84 : 20-28.

136. ______.

Rajasthan : The original home of the later Guptas.*Indian History Conference Proceedings*, Summaries of papers, Session 34, 1973 : 8.

137. ______.

Samudragupta and the North-West. *All India Oriental Conference Proceedings*, Session 22, Vol. 2, 1965 : 153-168.

138. **Goyal, Shankar**

Aspects of ancient Indian history and historiography. New Delhi, Harman Publishing House, 1993.

139. ______.

Chandragupta II's political influence on the Vakatakas : Epigraphical evidence re-examined. In Bhaskar Chatterjee and others, ed., *History and archaeology : Prof. H.D. Sankalia felicitation volume*. New Delhi, Ramanand Vidya Bhawan, 1989 : 351-356.

140. ______.
Gupta samrato ki samajik pratistha. *Parishad Patrika*, Vol. 25, No. 2, July 1985 : 74-80 (Hindi).

141. **Gupta, Karuna Kana**
Mr. K.P. Jayaswal on the Guptas and the Vakatakas (II). *Indian Culture*, Vol. 2, 1935-1936 : 61-66.

142. ______.
The Nagas and the Naga cult in ancient Indian history. *Indian History Congress Proceedings*, Session 3, 1939 : 214-229.

143. ______.
Some recent views on the Gupta era. *Indian Culture*, Vol. 3, No. 1, July 1936 : 47-61.

144. **Gupta, P.L.**
Can Kacha be identified with Ramagupta ? *Journal of the Numismatic Society of India*, Vol. 11, pt. 1, 1949 : 33-37.

145. ______.
The dates of the copper plates of Samudra Gupta and the Gupta era. *Journal of the Bihar Research Society*, Vol. 42, pt. 1, March 1956 : 72-75.

146. ______.
Ghatotkacagupta. *Indian Historical Quarterly*, Vol. 22, No. 4, December 1946 : 316-319.

147. ______.
The Gupta era-a re-assessment. *Journal of the Bihar Research Society*, Vol. 49, 1963 : 71-87.

148. ______.
Gupta samrajya. Varanasi, Vishwavidyalaya Prakashan, 1970 (Hindi).

149. ______.
The Imperial Guptas. 2 Vols. Varanasi, Vishwavidyalaya Prakashan, 1974-1979.

150. ______.
Kaca problem solved. *Indian Historical Quarterly*, Vol. 22, No. 1, March 1946 : 60-61.

151. ______.
The later Imperial Guptas. *Indian Historical Quarterly*, Vol. 26, No. 4, December 1950 : 253-262.

152. ______.
The legitimacy of Skandagupta's succession. *Journal of Indian History*, Vol. 40, pt. 2, August 1962 : 243-252.

153. ______.
The predecessors of the Guptas in Magadha. *Indian Culture*, Vol. II, No. 3, January-March 1945 : 137-141.

154. ______.
The rulers of the Gupta dynasty. In Karl Khandalavala, ed., *The golden age : Gupta art-empire, province and influence*. Bombay, Marg Publications, 1991 : 1-6.

155. ______.
The rulers of the Gupta dynasty. *Marg*, Vol. 42, No. 3 : 1-6.

156. ______.
Who ruled in Saurashtra after the Western Kshatrapas ? *Bharatiya Vidya*, Vol. 18, Nos. 3-4, 1958 : 83-89.

157. **Gupte, Y.R.**
Gupta chronology. *Journal of Indian History*, Vol. 4, pt. 3, December 1925 : 118-119.

158. **Hall, Fitz-Edward**
Letter to the Secretary of the Asiatic Society of Bengal, on some recent statements touching certain of the Gupta kings and others. *Journal of the Asiatic Society of Bengal*, Vol. 30, 1861 : 383-388.

159. ______.
Note on Budhagupta. *Journal of the Asiatic Society of Bengal*, Vol. 30, 1861 : 139-150.

160. **Heras, H.**
Kacha Gupta and Rama Gupta. *Journal of the Bihar Research Society*, Vol. 34, pts. 1-2, March & June 1948 : 19-27.

161. ______.
Relations between Guptas, Kadambas and Vakatakas. *Journal of the Bihar and Orissa Research Society*, Vol. 12, pt. 4, December 1926 : 455-463.

162. ______.
Two controversial events in the reign of Samudra Gupta. *Annals of the Bhandarkar Oriental Research Institute*, Vol. 9, pts. 2-4, 1928 : 83-90.

163. **Hoernle, A.F. Rudolf**
Some problems in ancient Indian history. *Journal of the Royal Asiatic Society of Great Britain and Ireland*, 1909 : 89-144.

164. **Jagan Nath**
Are Govindagupta and Kumaragupta identical ? *Indian Culture*. Vol. 12, No. 3, January-March 1946 : 167-169.

165. ______.
Are Skandagupta and Purugupta identical ? *All India Oriental Conference Proceedings*, Session 13, pt. 2, 1946 : 426-429.

166. ______.
Early history of the Maitrakas of Valabhi. *Indian Culture*. Vol. 5, 1938-1939 : 407-414.

167. ______.
Govindagupta, a new Gupta emperor. *Indian Historical Quarterly*, Vol. 22, No. 4, December 1946 : 286-290.

168. ______.
Govindagupta : A new Gupta emperor. *Indian History Congress Proceedings*, Session 9, 1946 : 78-82.

169. ______.
Identification of Sandrakottos. *Journal of the Panjab University Historical Society*, Vol. 10, April 1947 : 26-34.

170. ______.
The Kaliyugarajavrttanta and the Imperial Guptas. *Indian History Congress Proceedings*, Session 7, 1944 : 119-124.

171. ______.
The Kaliyugarajavrttanta and the Imperial Guptas. *Journal of the Bihar Research Society*, Vol. 31, pts. 1-2, March & June 1945 : 28-33.

172. ______.
The location of the T-china temple and the original home of the Imperial Guptas. *Indian Historical Quarterly*, Vol. 22, No. 1, March 1946 : 28-33.

173. ______.
A new Gupta emperor, Govindagupta. In *Bharata-Kaumudi : Studies in Indology in honour of Dr. Radha Kumud Mookerji,*, part II. Allahabad, The Indian Press, 1947 : 1083-1088.

174. ______.
The political situation in Magadha in the third century A.D. *Journal of the United Provinces Historical Society*, Vol. 12, pt. 2, December 1939 : 101-106.

175. ______.
The predecessors of the Guptas in Magadha. *Indian History Congress Proceedings*, Session 11, 1948 : 93-100.

176. ______.
Samudragupta's Asvamedha . *All India Oriental Conference Proceedings*, Session 16, , Vol. 2, 1951 : 209-212.

177. ______.
Some observations on the character and achievements of Chandragupta II Vikramaditya. *Journal of Indian History*, Vol. 19, pt. 2, August 1940 : 158-170.

178. ______.
Some observations on the reign of Chandragupta II Vikramaditya. *New Indian Antiquary*, Vol. 2, 1939-40 : 685-694.

179. ______.
Some historical illusions. *Journal of Indian History*, Vol. 21, pt. 3, 1942 : 155-172.

180. **Jain, Kailash Chand**
Malwa through the ages (from the earliest time to 1305 A.D.). Delhi, Motilal Banarsidass, 1972.

181. **Jamsedjee, Ardeseer**
The Sudarsana or lake beautiful of the Girnar inscriptions, B.C. 300-A.D. 450. *Journal of the Bombay Branch of the Royal Asiatic Society*, Vol. 18, 1890-1894 : 47-55.

182. **Jayaswal, K.P.**
Airikina and Sanchi. *Indian Antiquary*, Vol. 61, 1932 : 159-160.

183. ______.
Alipura of Gupta history. *Indian Antiquary*, Vol. 62, 1933 : 119.

184. ______.
Chandra-Gupta II (Vikramaditya) and his predecessor. *Journal of the Bihar and Orissa Research Society*, Vol. 18, pt. 1, March 1932 : 17-36.

185. ______.
Chronology and history of Nepal, 600 B.C. to 880 A.D. *Journal of the Bihar and Orissa Research Society*, Vol. 22, pt. 3, September 1936 : 161-264.

186. ______.
History of India, c. 150 A.D. to 350 A.D. (Naga-Vakataka imperial period). *Journal of the Bihar and Orissa Research Society*, Vol. 19, pts. 1-2, March-June 1933 : 1-222.

187. ______.
An Imperial history of India in a Sanskrit text (c. 700 B.C.-c. 770 A.D.) with a special commentary on later Gupta period. Lahore, Motilal Banarsidass, 1934.

188. ______.
Nepal chronicles on the caste of the Guptas. *Journal of the Bihar and Orissa Research Society*, Vol. 22, pt. 2, June 1936 : 108-110.

189. **Jayaswal, Prashant Kumar**
Guptakalin Licchviyo ka raajnitik itihas. *Parishad Patrika*, Vol. 6, No. 1, April 1966 : 56-65 (Hindi).

190. ______.
Guptakalin Pundavardhanbhukti aur Purnia. *Parishad Patrika*, Vol. 7, No. 1, April 1967 : 23-26 (Hindi).

191. **Joshi, Maheshwar P.**
Candragupta II Vikramaditya vis-a-vis the Kalki incarnation. *Rtam*, Vol. 10, 1978-1979 : 47-50.

192. **Joshi, Narendra Prakash**
New light on the Gupta era and the chronology of early Gupta kings. *Vishveshvaranand Indological Journal*, Vol. 14, pt. 2, 1976 : 245-260.

193. **Karimi, S.M.**
Pataliputra : Its origin, growth and decay; a study in historical geography. *Journal of the Bihar Research Society*, Vols. 67-68, 1981-82 : 50-58.

194. **Khosla, Sarla**
Gupta civilization. New Delhi, Intellectual Publishing House, 1982.

195. **Kibe, M.V.**
The historical facts of the personality and reign of Vikramaditya. *Bharatiya Vidya*, Vol. 9, 1948 : 341-356.

196. ———.
Who was the founder of the Vikrama era. *Journal of the Ganganatha Jha Research Institute*, Vol. 1, pt. 4, August 1944 : 417-422.

197. **Krishnaswamy Iyengar, S.**
The Vakatakas in Gupta history. *Quarterly Journal of the Mythic Society*, Vol. 15, No. 2, 1925 : 153-164.

198. **Kulkarni, S.D.**, ed.
Beginnings of life, culture and history. Bombay, BHISHMA, 1988.

199. **Kulke, Hermann** and **Rothermund, Dietmar**
A history of India. New Delhi, Manohar Publications, 1986.

200. **Lakshminarayana, V.**
The contemporaneity of Samudragupta and Augustus Caesar of Rome and the problem of epoch of the Gupta era. *Indian History Congress Proceedings*, Session 7, 1944 : 136-143.

201. ______.
A note on the identity of Purugupta and Skandagupta. *Indian History Congress Proceedings*, Session 6, 1943 : 86-89.

202. ______.
Were the Guptas contemporaneous with the Kusanas ? *Journal of the Ganganatha Jha Research Institute*, Vol. 2, pts. 2-3, February- May 1945 : 159-166.

203. **Lakshminarayan Rao, N.**
Who was the Gupta contemporary of the Kadamba king Kakustharman ? *Indian Historical Quarterly*, Vol. 9, No. 1, March 1933 : 197-201.

204. **Law, B.C.**
Ayodhya in ancient India. *Journal of the Ganganatha Jha Research Institute*, Vol.1, pt. 4, August 1944 : 423-443.

205. **Lunai, B.N.**
Gupta samrajya ka rajanitik evam sanskritik itihas. Indore, Kamal Prakashan, 1980 (Hindi).

206. **Mahadule, Hira Lal**
Maharaj Srigupta Adiraj. *Prachya Pratibha*, Vol. 7, 1979 : 105-119 (Hindi).

207. **Mahalingam, T.V.**
Aditya and Vikramaditya. *Journal of Indian History*, Vol. 36, pt. 3, December 1958 : 369-374.

208. **Maity, S.K.**
Cultural heritage of ancient India. New Delhi, Abhinav Publications, 1983.

209. ______.
Gupta civilization : A study. Calcutta, Sanskrit Pustak Bhandar, 1974.

210. ______.
The Imperial Guptas and their times. New Delhi, Munshiram Manoharlal, 1975.

211. **Majmudar, M.R.**
Historical and cultural chronology of Gujarat. Baroda, M.S. University of Baroda, 1960.

212. **Majumdar, A.K.**
Concise history of ancient India. 3 Vols. New Delhi, Munshiram Manoharlal, 1977-1983.

213. **Majumdar, R.C.**
An advanced history of India. Madras, Macmillan, 1988.

214. ——.
The Classical age. Bombay, Bharatiya Vidya Bhavan, 1962. (History and culture of the Indian people, Vol. 3).

215. ——.
A forged purana-text on the Imperial Guptas. *Indian Historical Quarterly*, Vol. 20, No.4, December 1944 : 345-350.

216. ——.
History of ancient Bengal. Calcutta, G. Bharadwaj & Co., 1971.

217. ——.
Literary reference to Samudragupta. *Indian Historical Quarterly*, Vol. 9, No. 4, December 1933 : 930-933.

218. ——.
Note on the genealogy and chronology of the Vakatakas. *Journal of the Royal Asiatic Society of Bengal, Letters*, Vol. 12, 1946 : 1-5.

219. ——.
Original home of Imperial Guptas. *Journal of the Bihar Research Society*, Vol. 38, pts. 3-4. September & December 1952 : 410-418.

220. ——.
The original home of the later Guptas. In Bindeshwari Prasad Sinha, ed., *Comprehensive history of Bihar*, Vol. I, pt. II. Patna, K.P. Jayaswal Research Institute, 1974 : 683-690.

221. ——.
The revised chronology of the lost Gupta emperors. *Indian Antiquary*, Vol. 47, June 1981 : 161-167.

222. ______.
The successors of Kumaragupta I. *Journal & Praceedings of the Asiatic Society of Bengal*, New Series, Vol. 17, 1921 : 249-255.

223. ______.
The successors of Skanda-Gupta. *Journal of the United Provinces Historical Society*, Vol. 18, 1945 : 70-73.

224. ______.
Vainya gupta Dvadasaditya. *Indian Historical Quarterly*, Vol. 9, No.4, December 1933 : 989-991.

225. ______.
The Vakataka queen Prabhavati Gupta. *All India Oriental Conference Proceedings*, Session 13, pt. 2, 1946 : 423-425.

226. ______.
The Vakataka queen Prabhavati Gupta. *Bharatiya Vidya*, Vol. 11, Nos. 1-2, 1950 : 1-3.

227. **Majumdar, R.C.** and **Altekar, A.S.,** ed.
Bharatiya jana ka itihas : Vakataka Gupta yug. Delhi, Motilal Banarsidass, 1968 (Hindi).

228. ______.
The Vakataka-Gupta age (circa 200-500 A.D.). Lahore, Motilal Banarsidas, 1946.

229. **Majumdar, R.C.** and **Dasgupta, K.K.,** ed.
A comprehensive history of India, Vol. 3, 2 pts. New Delhi, Peoples Publishing House, 1981-82.

230. **Mankad, D.R.**
Alexander and the Guptas. *Journal of the Gujarat Research Society*, Vol. 10, No. 4, October 1948 : 284-285.

231. ______.
Kaliyugarajavrttanta and Bhavisyottarapurana. *Journal of the Bihar Research Society*, Vol. 32, pts. 3-4, September & December 1946 : 319-327.

232. ______.
Samudragupta in the Puranas. *All India Oriental Conference Proceedings*, Session 13, pt. 2, 1946 : 417-422.

233. ______.
Studies in puranic history, genealogies and chronology in modern times. *Purana*, Vol. 4, No. 1, 1962 : 3-22.

234. **Mehta, Ganga Prasad**
Chandragupta Vikramaditya. Allahabad, Hindustan Akademi, 1932 (Hindi).

235. **Mirashi, V.V.**
An ancient dynasty of Khandesh. *Nagpur University Journal*, No. 10, 1944 : 1-8.

236. ______.
Candragupta Vikramaditya and Govinda. *Indian Historical Quarterly*, Vol. 10, No. 1, March 1934 : 48-53.

237. ______.
Dr. D.R. Bhandarkar on the epoch of the Gupta era. In K.V. Ramesh and others, ed., *Indian history and epigraphy : Dr. G.S Gai felicitation volume*. Delhi, Agam Kala Prakashan. 1990 : 122-124.

238. ______.
D.R. Bhandarkar on the relations of the Guptas and Vakatakas. In Ajay Mitra Shastri, ed., *The age of Vakatakas*. New Delhi, Harman Publishing House, 1992 : 57-61.

239. ______.
D.R. Bhandarkar on the relations of the Guptas and Vakatakas. In M.S. Nagaraja Rao, ed., *Kusumanjali : New interpretation of Indian art & culture : Sh. C. Sivaramamurti commemoration volume*. Vol. I. Delhi, Agam Kala Prakashan, 1987 : 85-88.

240. ______.
Did Candragupta II become a Vanaprastha ? *Vishveshvaranand Indological Journal*, Vol. 20, 1982 : 176-183.

241. ______.
Further light on Ramagupta. *Indian Antiquary*, Vol. 62, 1933 : 201-205.

242. ______.
New light on a period in Gupta history. In V.V. Mirashi, *Indological research papers*, Vol. 1. Nagpur, Vidarbha Samshodhan Mandal, 1982 : 65-77.

243. ______.
New light on a period in Gupta history. *National Museum Bulletin*, Nos. 4-6 : 19-23.

244. ______.
New light on the reigns of Kumaragupta and Skandagupta. In Vijay Shankar Srivastava, ed., *Cultural Contours of India : Dr. Satya Prakash felicitation volume*. New Delhi, Abhinav Publications, 1981 : 101-106.

245. ______.
A note on Sohoni's theory about the original territory of the Vakatakas. *Journal of Indian History*, Vol. 49, 1971 : 143-147.

246. ______.
The Ramagupta problem re-examined. In V.V. Mirashi, *Indological research papers*, Vol. 1. Nagpur, Vidarbha Samshodhan Mandal, 1982 : 56-64.

247. ______.
The Ramagupta problem re-examined. *Journal of the Epigraphical Society of India*, Vol. 3, 1976 : 26-34.

248. ______.
Ramagupta—samasya : Puna: parikshan. *Vidarbha Samshodhan Mandal Varshik*, Vol. 19, 1976 : 98-115 (Matathi).

249. ______.
Some aspects of the Ramagupta problem. *Journal of the Oriental Institute*, Vol. 19, Nos. 1-2, September-December 1969 : 139-151.

250. ______.
Were the Maharajas of Khandesh the feudatories of the Guptas. *Indian Historical Quarterly*, Vol. 23, No. 2, June 1947 : 156-159.

251. **Mirchandani, B.D.**
Sind and the White Huns and identification of Hiuen Tsiang's Sin-Tu kingdom. *Journal of the Asiatic Society of Bombay*, New Series, Vols. 39-40, 1964-65 : 61-93.

252. **Mitra, Debala**
An examination of some traditions about the origin of certain eras. *Indian History Congress Proceedings*, Session 16, 1953 : 61-62.

253. **Mitra, Kalipada**
On the identification of Devagupta & Harigupta. *Jaina Antiquary*, Vol. 21, No. 2, December 1955 : 12-14.

254. **Mittal, A.C.**
Mandsaur. *Journal of the Oriental Institute*, Vol. 13, No. 3, March 1964 : 260-280.

255. **Modi, Jivanji Jamshedji**
The early history of the Huns and their inroads in India and Persia. *Journal of the Bombay Branch of the Royal Asiatic Society*, Vol. 24, 1915-17 : 539-595.

256. **Mookerjee, Dhirendra Nath**
Chandra Gupta and Bhadrabbahu. *Journal of Indian History*, Vol. 20, pt. 3, December 1941 : 249-274.

257. ———.
The contemporaneity of Candragupta and Kaniska. *Indian History Congress Proceedings*, Session 3, 1939 : 411-418.

258. ———.
Contemporaneity of Candragupta and Kaniska. *Poona Orientalist*, Vol. 5, 1940-41 : 197-204.

259. ———.
The contemporaneity of Samudragupta and Augustus Caesar of Rome. *Annals of the Bhandarkar Oriental Research Institute*, Vol. 22, 1941 : 264-271.

260. ———.
The genealogy and chronology of the early Imperial Guptas. *Indian History Congress Proceedings*, Session 5, 1941 : 176-179.

261. ______.
The genealogy and chronology of the early Imperial Guptas. *Journal of Indian History*, Vol. 21, pts. 1-2, April & August 1942 : 34-56.

262. ______.
The Gupta era. *Bharatiya Vidya*, Vol. 5, 1944 : 96-114.

263. ______.
The Gupta era. *Journal of Indian History*, Vol. 17, pt. 3, December 1938 : 293-313.

264. ______.
The Gupta era. *Journal of Indian History*, Vol. 20, pt. 1, April 1941 : 71-84.

265. ______.
The identify of the Gupta and the Vikramaditya eras. *Journal of Indian History*, Vol. 18, pt. 1, April 1939 : 64-69.

266. ______.
The Valabhi rulers and the Gupta era. *Indian History Congress Proceedings*, Session 3, 1939 : 419-432.

267. **Mookerji, Radha Kumud**
Chandragupta II Vikramaditya. In *Vikrama-smriti grantha*. Gwalior, Scindhia Oriental Institute, 1945 : 197-214 (Hindi).

268. ______.
Chandragupta II Vikramaditya (c. 376-414 A.D.). In *Vikrama volume*. Ujjain, Scindia Oriental Institute, 1948 : 323-359.

269. ______.
Character of Samudragupta from his inscriptions and coins. *Indian Culture*, Vol. 9, Nos. 2-3, October 1942-March 1943 : 177-179.

270. ______.
The Gupta empire. Delhi, Motilal Banarasidass, 1969.

271. ______.
Later Gupta history and chronology. *Journal of Indian History*, Vol. 4, pt. 2, August 1925 : 17-28.

272. ______.
Later Guptas of Magadha. *Journal of the Bihar and Orissa Research Society*, Vol. 15, pts. 1-2, March-June 1929 : 251-258.

273. **Moti Chandra**
Kashi ka itihas. Varanasi, Vishwavidyalaya Prakashan, 1985 (Hindi).

274. **Mukherjee, Dhirendra Nath**
The Gupta era. *Indian Historical Quarterly*, Vol. 8, No. 1, March 1932 : 85-92.

275. **Mukherjee, S.N.**
The tradition of Rama Gupta and the Indian nationalist historians. *East and West*, New Series, Vol. 13, No. 1, March 1962 : 49-52.

276. **Munshi, K.M.**
The golden age of the Imperial Guptas. *Bharatiya Vidya*, Vol. 3, pt. 2, May 1942 : 113-125.

277. ______.
Organic periods in Indian history. *Bharatiya Vidya*, Vol. 2, pt. 1, November 1940 : 1-22.

278. **Nag, Kalidas**
History and culture of Bengal. Calcutta, Chuckervertti, Chatterjee & Co., 1963.

279. **Narain, A.K.**
Gupta empire. In Ainslie T. Embree, ed., *Encyclopedia of Asian History*, Vol. 2. New York, Charles Scribner's Sons, 1988 : 10-13.

280. **Narayanan, M.G.S.**
A reappraisal of Samudra Gupta's digvijaya. In B.N. Mukherjee and others, ed., *Sri. Dinesacandrika : Studies in Indology ; Shri D.C. Sircar festchrift*. Delhi, Sundeep Prakashan, 1983 : 283-293.

281. **Negi, J.S.**
Some points in early Gupta history. In J.S. Negi, *Some Indological studies*, Vol. I. Allahabad, Panchananda Publications, 1966 : 167-174.

282. **Newton**
On the Sah, Gupta and other ancient dynasties of Kattiawar and Guzerat. *Journal of the Bombay Branch of the Royal Asiatic Society*, Vol. 7, 1861-63 : 1-36.

283. **Nigam, M.L.**
Cultural history of Bundelkhand (3rd c. B.C. to A.D. 650). Delhi, Sundeep Prakashan, 1983.

284. **Nilakanta Sastri, K.A.** and **Srinivasachari, G.**
Advanced history of India. Bombay, Allied Publishers, 1970.

285. **Ojha, Kailash Chandra**
An analysis of the Ramagupta tradition. *Journal of the Bihar Research Society*, Vol. 37, pts. 1-2, March & June 1951 : 39-47.

286. ———.
Was Kacha a brother of Samudragupta ? *Journal of the Numismatic Society of India*, Vol. 12, pt. 2, 1950 : 170-175.

287. **Pai, M. Govinda**
The Gupta and the Valabhi eras. *Journal of Indian History*, Vol. 11, pt. 2, August 1932 : 175-189.

288. ———.
The Gupta and the Valabhi eras. *Journal of Indian History*, Vol. 12, pt. 2, August 1933 : 215-240.

289. **Pandey, Deen Bandhu**
Dhruvaswamini. *Shodh Patrika*, Vol. 25, No. 1, 1974 : 5-10. (Hindi).

290. **Pandey, H.**
Dates of Skanda-Gupta and his successors. *Journal of the Bihar and Orissa Research Society*, Vol. 4, pt. 3, September 1918 : 344-350.

291. **Pandey, M.S.**
A fresh study of the early Gupta chronology & Lichchhavi Gupta relationship. *Journal of the Bihar Research Society*, Vol. 46, 1960 : 117-120.

292. ———.

Original home of the Imperial Guptas. *Journal of the Bihar Research Society*, Vol. 54, 1968 : 141-150.

293. **Pandey, Rajbali**

Prachin Bharat. Varanasi, Vishwavidyalaya Prakashan, 1974 (Hindi).

294. **Panigrahi, Krishna Chandra**

New light on the early history of Bhubanesvara. *Journal of the Asiatic Society, Letters*, Vol. 17, No. 2, 1951 : 95-115.

295. **Panikkar, K.M.**

A survey of Indian history. Bombay, Asia Publishing House, 1966.

296. **Panna Lall**

The dates of Skandagupta and his successors. *Journal of the Royal Asiatic Society of Great Britain and Ireland*, 1919 : 260-262.

297. ———.

Some problems in Gupta chronology. *Journal of the Bihar and Orissa Research Society*, Vol. 4, pt. 4, December 1918 : 412-417.

298. **Parabrahma Sastry, P.V.**

Re-appraisal of Samudragupta's Southern expedition. *Puratan*, No. 4, 1986 : 45-54.

299. **Pathak, Haldhar**

Cultural history of the Gupta period based on epigraphic and numismatic records. Delhi, Bharatiya Publishing House, 1978.

300. **Pathak, K.B.**

New light on the Gupta era and Mihirakula. *Indian Antiquary*, Vol. 46, 1917 : 287-296.

301. ———.

New light on Gupta era and Mihirakula. *Indian Antiquary*, Vol. 47, 1918 : 16-22.

302. ______.
New light on Gupta era and Mihirakula. In *Commemorative essays*. Delhi. Nag Publishers, 1977 : 195-222.

303. ______.
A passage in the Jain Hrivamsa relating to the Guptas. *Indian Antiquary*, Vol. 15, 1886 : 141-143.

304. **Paul, Promode Lal**
The early history of Eastern India, Vol. I. Delhi, Sharada Prakashan, 1990.

305. **Prasad, S.N.**
Dhruvadevi ki jaati. *Journal of the Ganganatha Jha Research Institute*, Vol. 26, pts. 1-3, January-July 1970 : 757-762 (Hindi).

306. **Pusalkar, A.D.**
Early history of Maharashtra. *Adyar Library Bulletin*, Vol. 25, 1961 : 381-396.

307. **Rai, U.N.**
Gupta-raajvansh tatha uska yug. Allahabad, Lokbharati Prakashan, 1977 (Hindi).

308. **Rajaguru, Satyanarayan**
The Gupta rule in Kalinga. *Orissa Historical Research Journal*, Vol. 1, No. 2, 1952 : 31-42.

309. ______.
The Mana-samvat of Orissa. *Orissa Historical Research Journal*, Vol. 4, Nos. 1-2, 1955 : 6-10.

310. **Rajpurohit, Bhagwati Lal**
Chandragupta ke putra ka sachiv : Subandhu. *Parishad Patrika*, Vol. 25, No. 2, July 1985 : 29-32 (Hindi).

311. **Ramadas, G.**
Kingdoms of the Deccan (mentioned in the Allahabad pillar inscription of Samudragupta). *Indian Historical Quarterly*, Vol. 1, No. 4, December 1925 : 679-689.

312. **Rao, Gurty Venket**
The problems of the Baladityas in the Gupta period. *Indian History Congress Proceedings*, Session 15, 1952 : 51-56.

313. **Rao Sahib, C.S.K.**
Sri-Gupta. *Quarterly Journal of the Mythic Society*, Vol. 24, No. 3, 1934 : 218-223.

314. **Rath, Asoka Kumar**
Did the Guptas rule over Orissa ? *Indian Historical Quarterly*, Vol. 38, Nos. 2-3, June & September 1962 : 213-221.

315. **Rawlinson, H.G.**
India : A short cultural history. London, The Cresset Press, 1954.

316. **Ray, H.C.**
The line of Krsnagupta. *Indian Culture*, Vol. 8, Nos. 2-3, October 1941-March 1942 : 133-136.

317. **Ray, S.C.**
The Gupta phase at Nalanda. *Indian History Congress Proceedings*, Session 17, 1954 : 78-83.

318. **Ray Chaudhuri, H.C.**
The decline of the early Gupta empire. *Calcutta Review*, Vol. 35, 1930 : 36-44.

319. ______.
The Gupta empire in the sixth and seventh centuries A.D. *Journal & Proceedings of the Asiatic Society of Bengal*, New Series, Vol. 16, 1920 : 313-326.

320. ______.
The Guptas in the land of Kuntala. *Indian History Congress Proceedings*, Session 2, 1938 : 43-47.

321. ______.
The order of succession of the later Imperial Guptas. *All India Oriental Conference Proceedings*, Session 2, 1922 : 335-338.

322. ______.
Political history of ancient India. Calcutta, University of Calcutta, 1953.

323. ______.
The successor of Kumar Gupta I. *Indian Historical Quarterly*, Vol. 8, No. 2, June 1932 : 352.

324. **Raychoudhry, S.C.**
Social, cultural and economic history of India (Ancient times). Delhi, Surjeet Publications, 1978.

325. **Roy, U.N.**
A fresh investigation of the Imperial Gupta Capital. In J.S. Jha, ed., *K.P. Jayaswal commemoration volume*. Patna, K.P. Jayaswal Research Institute, 1981 : 361-372.

326. ——.
Govind Gupta ka ek abhinav mulyankan. In Sita Ram Chaturvedi and others, ed., *Dr. Rajbali Pandey Smriti granth*. Deoria, Dr. Rajbali Pandey Smriti Granth Prakashan Samiti, Kalanidhi Prakashan, 1976 : 176-188 (Hindi).

327. ——.
Pataliputra in the Gupta age. In C.R.P. Sinha and others, ed., *Archaeology and art (Krishna Deva felicitation volume)*, Part II. New Delhi, Ramanand Vidya Bhawan, 1990 : 519-526.

328. **Sahai, Bhagwant**
Ancient history of Bihar (600 B.C. to 1200 A.D.). In Bhagwant Sahai and Sachidanand Sahay, ed., *Bihar past and present*. Patna, Bihar Historical Society, 1981 : 4-11.

329. **Sahi, M.D.N.**
Early Huna invasion of Peshawar in the light of Fa-hien's account and its significance. *Journal of Indian History*, Vol. 52, pt. 1, April 1974 : 89-99.

330. **Saletore, B.A.**
Samudra Gupta's conquest of Kottura. *Annals of the Bhandarkar Oriental Research Institute*, Vol. 26, pts. 1-2, January-April 1945 : 120-141.

331. **Saletore, R.N.**
Life in the Gupta age. Bombay, The Popular Book Depot, 1943.

332. **Sankar, K.G.**
The epoch of the Gupta era. *New Indian Antiquary*, Vol. 3, 1940-41 : 419-428.

333. **Saraswati, Bandana**
The Sanakanikas, the Kakas, etc., the Western Kshatrapas and the Guptas. *Indian History Congress Proceedings*, Session 26, pt. 1, 1964 : 69.

334. **Sarkar, Bijoy Nath**
Finger-posts of Bengal History. *Indian Historical Quarterly*, Vol. 7, No. 3, September 1931 : 435-457.

335. **Sarma, I.K.**
Skandagupta Kramaditya of the Gupta dynasty. *Bharati*, Nos. 12-14, 1968-1971 : 165-183.

336. ———.
The succession and early career of Skandagupta Kramaditya of the Gupta dynasty. *Journal of the Andhra Historical Research Society*, Vol. 33, pts. 2-4, 1973-74 : 37-55.

337. **Sastri, Sakuntala Rao**
Parama-Bhagavata Samudragupta. *Indian Culture*, Vol. 10, No. 2, October-December 1943 : 78-79.

338. **Schwartzberg, Joseph E.**, ed.
A historical atlas of South Asia. Chicago, University of Chicago Press, 1978 : 178-179.

339. **Sengupta, P.C.**
The Gupta era. *Journal of the Royal Asiatic Society of Bengal, Letters*, Vol. 8, 1942 : 41-56.

340. **Sethi, R.K.**
Maharaja Ghatotkacha, builder of the Gupta empire. *Journal of the Madhya Pradesh Itihasa Parishad*, No. 7, 1969 : 51-53.

341. **Sethna, K.D.**
Hiuen-Tsang on the time of the Imperial Guptas. In K.C. Varma and others, ed., *Rtambhara : Studies in Indology (Acharya Udaya Vira Shastri felicitation volume)*. Ghaziabad, Society for Indic Studies, 1986 : 45-50.

342. ———.
The location of Kamboja. *Purana*, Vol. 6, No. 1, 1964 : 207-214.

343. ——.
Megasthenes and the Indian chronology as based on the Puranas. *Purana*, Vol. 10, No. 1, 1968 : 35-53.

344. ——.
Megasthenes and the problem of Indian chronology as based on the Puranas. *Purana*, Vol. 10, No. 2, 1968 : 124-147.

345. **Shah, U.P.**
Some aspects of the Ramagupta problem—a reply to Mm. Mirashi. *Journal of the Oriental Institute*, Vol. 19, Nos. 1-2, September-December 1969 : 152-156.

346. ——.
Vikramaditya—saga—1. *Journal of the Oriental Institute*, Vol. 4, No. 1, September 1954 : 69-84.

347. **Sharma, Braj Bhanu**
Gupta-samrat Kach. *Shodh Patrika*, Vol. 25, No. 2, 1974 : 17-23 (Hindi).

348. **Sharma, Dasharatha**
The Dharana Gotra of the Guptas. *Journal of the Bihar and Orissa Research Society*, Vol. 20, pt. 2, 1934 : 225.

349. ——.
The legitimacy of Skandagupta's succession. *Journal of Indian History*, Vol. 43, pt. 1, April 1965 : 219-225.

350. ——.
The legitimacy of Skandagupta's succession. *Journal of Indian History*, Vol. 37, pt. 2, August 1959 : 145-152.

351. ——.
The origin and original home of the Imperial Guptas. *Journal of the Bihar Research Society*, Vol. 39, pt. 3, September 1953 : 265-268.

352. ——.
Puranas shed new light on Gupta history. *Journal of the Ganganatha Jha Research Institute*, Vol. 7 , pt. 1, November 1949 : 61-65.

353. ______., ed.
Rajasthan through the ages, Vol. I. Bikaner, Rajasthan State Archives, 1966.

354. ______.
The Saka rival of Ramagupta. *Indian Culture*, Vol. 5, No. 3, January 1939 : 328-330.

355. ______.
The significance of Candragupta II's title Cakravikrama. *Journal of the Ganganatha Jha Research Institute*, Vol. 7 , pts. 2-4, 1950 : 311-312.

356. ______.
Some new light from the Skanda-Purana on the Dharana gotra of the Guptas. *Purana*, Vol. 7, No. 1, 1965 : 183-185.

357. **Sharma, M.J.**
The identification of Kacha : A fresh study. *Journal of the Epigraphical Society of India*, Vol. 1, 1974 : 75-84.

358. **Sharma, Ram Padarth**
Samudragupta ki Viddatsabha. *Parishad Patrika*, Vol. 22, No. 2, July 1982 : 84-87 (Hindi).

359. **Sharma, R.S.**
Indian feudalism : c. 300-1200. Calcutta, University of Calcutta, 1965.

360. **Shashi Kant**
Political and cultural history of mid-North India. Delhi, Neha Prakashan, 1987.

361. **Shastri, Ajay Mitra**
Candragupta II Vikramaditya and king Pramati of the Matsya-Purana. *Nagpur University Journal*, (Humanities), Vol. 17, No. 2, April 1976 : 150-157.

362. ______.
Fresh epigraphic evidence on the Vakatakas. *Nagpur University Journal*, (Humanities), Vol. 35, 1984-85 : 130-164.

363. ——.
King Pramati of the Matsya-Purana : A re-appraisal. *Nagpur University Journal*, (*Humanities*), Vol. 18, No. 2, October 1967 : 140-144.

364. ——.
The puranic king Pramati : some reflections. *Purana*, Vol. 33, No. 1, 1991 : 25-59.

365. **Shastri, H.G.**
The genealogy and chronology of the Gupta sovereigns. *Journal of the Oriental Institute*, Vol. 27 , Nos. 3-4, March-June 1978 : 86-94.

366. ——.
Some interesting results of recent research in the ancient history of Gujarat. *All India Oriental Conference Proceedings*, Session 32, 1985 : 359-367.

367. **Shastri, Parmanandan**
Vaisali ki aithasik samriddhi tatha uske patan ka mula karan. *Journal of the Bihar Research Society*, Buddha Jayanti Special Issue, Vol. 2, 1956 : 475-491.

368. **Shelat, Bharati Kirtikumar**
The chronological systems of Gujarat (from early times upto 1304 A.D.). Ahmedabad, Pranav Shelat, 1987.

369. **Shrimali, Krishna Mohan**
History of Pancala to c. A.D. 550, 2 Vols. New Delhi, Munshiram Manoharlal, 1983-1985.

370. **Shukla, Dinesh Chandra**
Early history of Rajasthan. Delhi, Bharatiya Vidya Prakashan, 1978.

371. **Shukla, G.D.**
The age of the Imperial Guptas : Resurgence of Hindu culture. In R.K. Sharma and others, ed., *Krsna-smrti : Studies in Indian art and archaeology ; Prof. K.D. Bajpai commemoration volume*. New Delhi, Aryan Books International, 1995 : 309-318.

372. **Shukla, Vimal Chandra**
Gupton ka varna : Punarvichaar. *Kosala*, Vol. 2, 1979-1980 : 35-40 (Hindi).

373. **Singh, Arvind Kumar**
Gupta Adirajya. In S.N. Rai and others, ed., *Bharatiya Itihas Sankalan Samiti Patrika*, Vol. 2 : *Prayag kshetriya itihas vishesank*. Varanasi, Bharatiya Itihas Sankalan Samiti, Uttar Pradesh, 1984 : 175-183 (Hindi).

374. **Singh, G.P.**
Early Indian historical tradition and archaeology. New Delhi, D.K. Printworld, 1994.

375. **Singh, Jai Prakash**
History and coinage of Skandagupta Kramaditya. Varanasi, Banaras Hindu University, 1976.

376. ——.
Observation on Kumaragupta I. *Journal of the Andhra Historical Research Society*, Vol. 37, 1978 : 1-14.

377. **Singh, Sheo Bahadur**
Panchala Janpad : Ek etihasik samiksha. *Panchala*, Vol. 1, No. 1, 1986 : 19-23 (Hindi).

378. **Sinha, B.P.**
Art of war in ancient Bihar. In Bindeshwari Prasad Sinha, ed., *Comprehensive history of Bihar*, Vol. 1, pt. II. Patna, K.P. Jayaswal Research Institute, 1974 : 691-706.

379. ——.
Bearing of numismatic on the history of the later Imperial Guptas. *Journal of the Bihar Research Society*, Vol. 34, pts. 3-4, September & December 1948 : 18-26.

380. ——.
Capital of the Gupta empire. In Bindeshwari Prasad Sinha, ed., *Comprehensive history of Bihar*, Vol. 1, pt. II. Patna, K.P. Jayaswal Research Institute, 1974 : 652-658.

381. ——.
Causes of the downfall of the Gupta empire. In Bindeshwari Prasad Sinha, ed., *Comprehensive history of Bihar*, Vol. 1, pt. II. Patna, K.P. Jayaswal Research Institute, 1974 : 670-675.

382. ______., ed.
Comprehensive history of Bihar, Vol. 1, pt. II. Patna, K.P. Jayaswal Research Institute, 1974.

383. ______.
The decline of the kingdom of Magadha (cir. 455-1000 A.D.). Patna, Motilal Banarsidass, 1954.

384. ______.
Dynastic history of Magadha cir. 450-1200 A.D. New Delhi, Abhinav Publications, 1977.

385. ______.
Gupta empire. In Bindeshwari Prasad Sinha, ed., *Comprehensive history of Bihar*, Vol. 1, pt. II. Patna, K.P. Jayaswal Research Institute, 1974 : 1-113.

386. ______.
Gupta era and chronology of the Guptas. In Bindeshwari Prasad Sinha, ed., *Comprehensive history of Bihar*, Vol. 1, pt. II. Patna, K.P. Jayaswal Research Institute, 1974 : 659-669.

387. ______.
Kumara Gupta III. *Journal of the Bihar Research Society*, Vol. 36, pts. 3-4, September & December 1950 : 57-68.

388. ______.
Original home of Imperial Guptas. *Journal of the Bihar Research Society*, Vol. 37, pts. 3-4, September & December 1951 : 138-144.

389. ______.
Original home of Imperial Guptas. *Journal of the Bihar Research Society*, Vol. 38, pts. 3-4, September & December 1952 : 419-428.

390. ______.
Readings in history and culture. Delhi, Sundeep Prakashan, 1978.

391. ______.
Twilight of the Imperial Guptas. Delhi, National Centre for Oriental Studies, 1993.

392. **Sircar, D.C.**
The Bhavishyottara Purana and early Gupta history. *Journal of the Numismatic Society of India*, Vol. 6, 1944 : 34-36.

393. _____.
End of Gupta empire. In Hari Ram Gupta, ed., *Sir Jadunath Sarkar commemoration volume*, Vol. II : *Essays presented to Sir Jadunath Sarkar*. Hoshiarpur, Panjab University, 1958 : 343-347.

394. _____.
Further notes on the Vakatakas. *Journal of the Royal Asiatic Society of Bengal, Letters*, Vol. 13, No. 2, 1947 : 75-79.

395. _____.
Ghatotkacagupta. *Indian Historical Quarterly*, Vol. 24, No. 1, March 1948 : 71-72.

396. _____.
Govindagupta. *Indian Historical Quarterly*, Vol. 24, No. 1, March 1948 : 72-75.

397. _____.
Gupta rule in Orissa. *Indian Historical Quarterly*, Vol. 26, No. 1, March 1950 : 75-79.

398. _____.
Kamboja. *Purana*, Vol. 6, No. 1, 1964 : 215-220.

399. _____.
Kumaragupta I and his feudatory Bandhuvarman. In Bhagwant Sahai, ed., *History and culture : B.P. Sinha felicitation volume*. New Delhi, Ramanand Vidya Bhawan, 1987 : 212-214.

400. _____.
The Maukharis and the later Guptas. *Journal of the Royal Asiatic Society of Bengal, Letters*, Vol. 11, No. 2, 1945 : 69-74.

401. _____.
Samudra Gupta's Asvamedha sacrifice. *Journal of Indian History*, Vol. 13, pt. 1, April 1934 : 35-40.

402. ——.
Some great women of India. *Bharatiya Vidya*, Vol. 15, No. 3, 1956 : 5-27.

403. ——.
Some problems of early Indian history. *Journal of the Royal Asiatic Society of Great Britain and Ireland*, 1976 : 130-135.

404. **Sitholey, B.S.**
Was Kacha a Gupta monarch ? *Journal of the Numismatic Society of India*, Vol. 12, pt. 1, 1950 : 38-40.

405. **Smith, Bardwell L.**, ed.
Essays on Gupta culture. Missouri, South Asia Books, 1983.

406. **Smith, V.A.**
The conquests of Samudra Gupta. *Journal of the Royal Asiatic Society of Great Britain and Ireland*, 1897 : 859-910.

407. ——.
Revised chronology of the early or Imperial Gupta dynasty. *Indian Antiquary*, Vol. 31, 1902 : 257-266.

408. ——.
Samudra Gupta. *Journal of the Royal Asiatic Society of Great Britain and Ireland*, 1897 : 19-33.

409. **Sohoni, S.V.**
Govindagupta. *Journal of the Bihar Research Society*, Vol. 55, 1969 : 90-96.

410. ——.
Govindagupta. *Journal of the Ganganatha Jha Kendriya Sanskrit Vidyapeetha*, Vol. 32 , 1976 : 1-10.

411. ——.
Guptas, Kadambas, Pallavas and Kalidasa. *Annals of the Bhandarkar Oriental Research Institute*, Vol. 60, 1979 : 1-40.

412. ______.
Notes on Vakataka history. *Journal of the Bihar Research Society*, Vol. 58, 1972 : 95-104.

413. ______.
Recent data on Gupta and post-Gupta history. *Journal of the Bihar Research Society*, Vols. 65-66, 1979-80 : 189-211.

414. ______.
Samudragupta ki viddatsabha. *Parishad Patrika*, Vol. 22, No. 2, July 1982 : 76-83 (Hindi).

415. ______.
Samudragupta's expedition against Persia (356-362 A.D.). *Annals of the Bhandarkar Oriental Research Institute*, Vol. 38, pts. 3-4, 1957 : 217-224.

416. ______.
Transfer of power to Samudra Gupta. *Quarterly Journal of the Mythic Society*, Vol. 76, Nos. 1-2, 1985 : 23-28.

417. ______.
Vakaraka Rudrasena I and Samudragupta. In Ajay Mitra Shastri, ed., *The age of Vakatakas*. New Delhi, Harman Publishing House, 1992 : 37-45.

418. ______.
Western front of Chandragupta II and Kumaragupta I. *Journal of the Bihar Research Society*, Vol. 42, pts. 3-4, September-December 1956 : 396-406.

419. **Soundara Rajan, K.V.**
Glimpses of Indian culture—history and archaeology. Delhi, Sundeep Prakashan, 1980.

420. **Srivastava, A.L.**
Political significance of the legand Lichchhavayali. *Journal of the Numismatic Society of India*, Vol. 36 , 1974 : 57-61.

421. **Srivastava, B.N.**
Sasanka, king of Gauda. *Bulletin of the U.P. Historical Society*, No. 3, 1965.

422. ———.
Sasanka, the king of Gauda. *Journal of the U.P. Historical Society*, New Series, Vol. 10, pt. 1, 1962 : 27-55.

423. **Srivastava, Kamal Shankar**
History of Magadha (from 6th century B.C. to 12th century A.D.). Varanasi, Sangeeta Prakashan, 1995.

424. **Stapleton, H.E.**
A `line of time' for Northern Bengal. *Journal and Proceedings of the Asiatic Society of Bengal*, New Series, Vol. 28, 1932 : 131-145.

425. **Sullere, Sushil Kumar**
Madhya Pradesh ke pracheen raajvansha. *Parishad Patrika*, Vol. 19, No. 2, July 1979 : 54-59 (Hindi).

426. **Sundararaman, R.P.**
A new epoch for the Gupta era. *Journal of Indian History*, Vol. 16, pt. 2, August 1937 : 132.

427. **Swaminathan, K.D.**
India and Japan : Early cultural contacts. *Journal of the Institute of Asian Studies*, Vol. 5, No. 1, September 1987 : 19-50.

428. **Thakur, Upendra**
History of Mithila (circa 3000 B.C.-1556 A.D.). Darbhanga, Mithila Institute, 1956.

429. ———.
The second phase of the Huna invasion of India. *Journal of Indian History*, Vol. 44, pt. 1, April 1966 : 67-92.

430. ———.
Skandagupta and Hunas. *Journal of the Bihar Research Society*, Vol. 47, 1961 : 72-88.

431. ———.
Some problems of Huna history. *Journal of the Ganganatha Jha Research Institute*, Vol. 26 , pts. 1-3, January-July 1970 : 695-702.

432. **Thakur, Vijay Kumar**
A Marxist view of ancient Indian history. *Journal of the Bihar Research Society*, Vol. 62, 1976 : 238-261.

433. ——.
Periodisation of Indian History : The transition from ancient to medieval times. *Journal of the Bihar Research Society*, Vol. 62, 1976 : 109-137.

434. ——.
The place of Kacha in Gupta chronology. *Journal of the Numismatic Society of India*, Vol. 39, 1977 : 108-113.

435. **Thapar, Romila**
Asokan India and the Gupta age. In A.L. Basham, ed., A cultural history of India. Oxford, Clarendon Press, 1975 : 38-50.

436. **Thibut, G.**
Some remarks on General Cunningham's new method of fixing the initial point of the Gupta era. *Indian Antiquary*, Vol. 11, 1882 : 321-324.

437. **Thomas, Edward**
The epoch of the Guptas. *Journal of the Royal Asiatic Society of Great Britain & Ireland*, New Series, Vol. 13, 1881 : 524-551.

438. ——.
Record of the Gupta dynasty. Varanasi, Indological Book House, 1973.

439. **Trautmann, Thomas R.**
Licchavi-Dauhitra. *Journal of the Royal Asiatic Society of Great Britain & Ireland*, 1972 : 2-15.

440. **Tripathi, R.P.**
Studies in political and socio-economic history of early India. Allahabad, Neeraj Prakashan, 1981.

441. **Tripathi, Rama Shankar**
History of ancient India. Delhi, Motilal Banarsidass, 1981.

442. ——.
Samrat Samudragupta. In *Vikrama-smriti grantha*. Gwalior, Scindhia Oriental Institute, 1945 : 183-196 (Hindi).

443. **Trived, Dev Sahai**
Ramagupta aur Chandragupta. *Parishad Patrika*, Vol. 14, No. 4, January 1975 : 30-33 (Hindi).

444. ———.
Sikandar aur Samudragupta. *Parishad Patrika*, Vol. 26, No. 4, January 1987 : 170-187 (Hindi).

445. **Tyagi, Vishnu Dutt**
Kachagupta. *Parishad Patrika*, Vol. 16, No. 2, July 1976 : 62-71 (Hindi).

446. **Upadhyay, Basudeva**
Prayaga—the capital of the Guptas. *Journal of the Bihar Research Society*, Vol. 57, 1971 : 11-20.

447. **Upadhyaya, Ram Bihari**
History of ancient Ayodhya. *Journal of the Ganganatha Jha Kendriya Sanskrita Vidyapeetha*, Vol. 45, 1989 : 1-15.

448. **Upadhyaya, Vasudeva**
Gupta—Kuntal sambandh. *Nagri Pracharini Patrika*, Vol. 43, No. 1, Samvat 1995 : 93-97 (Hindi).

449. ———.
Gupta samarajya ka itihas, Vol. Allahabad, Indian Press, 1969 (Hindi).

450. **Vaidya, C.V.**
Harsha and his times. *Journal of the Bombay Branch of the Royal Asiatic Society*, Vol. 24, 1915-17 : 236-276.

451. **Vajpeyi, Raghavendra**
The Nandivardhana Branch of the Vakatakas : Its relations with the Imperial Guptas—A reappraisal of evidence. *Journal of Indian History*, Vol. 63, 1985 : 129-141.

452. The Vakatakas in Gupta history. *Journal of Indian History*, Vol. 6, pt. 3, April 1938 : 13-26.

453. **Vasudevan, Geeta**
The Sarabhapuriyas : Case study of a central Indian kingdom in the Gupta period. *Quarterly Journal of the Mythic Society*, Vol. 78, Nos. 1-2, 1987 : 77-101.

454.. **Venkatachalam, Kota**
Indian eras. *Journal of the Andhra Historical Research Society*, Vol. 21, 1950-52 : 1-40.

455. **Vidyalankar, Jayachandra**
Bharatiya itihas ka unmilan, Vol. I, Allahabad, Hindi Bhawan, 1970 (Hindi).

456. ———
Bharatiya itihas ki mimansa athva Bharatiya Rashtra ka vikas hras aur punaruthan. Allahabad, Hindi Bhawan, 1960 (Hindi).

457 . **Von Pochhammer, Wilhelm**
India's road of Nationhood : A political history of the subcontinent. New Delhi, Allied Publishers, 1981.

458. **Vyas, K.B.**
The Vikramaditya problem : A fresh approach. *Annals of the Bhandarkar Oriental Research Institute*, Vol. 27, pts. 3-4, July-October 1946 : 209-236.

459. **Waston, Francis**
A concise history of India. London, Thames and Hudson, 1974.

460. **Wilberforce-Bell, H.**
The history of Kathiawad from the earliest times. New Delhi, Ajay Book Service, 1980.

461 **Zelliot, Eleanor**
Gupta history and literature : A bibliographic essay. In Bardwell L. Smith, ed., *Essays on Gupta culture*. Missouri, South Asia Books, 1983, 285-309.

SOCIETY

462. **Dandekar, R.N.**
Society in the age of the Guptas.*Journal of Indian History*, Vol. 40, pt. 3, December 1962 : 537-550.

463. **Dhavalikar, M.K.**
Coinage and cultural life. *Journal of the Numismatic Society of India*, Vol. 35, 1973 : 184-195.

464. **Dutt, Romesh Chunder**
A history of civilisation in ancient India based on Sanskrit literature. Delhi, Vishal Publishers, 1972.

465. **Dwivedi, Gautam N.**
Tribal communities in the Gupta age. *Indian History Congress Proceedings*, Session 35, 1974 : 86-88.

466. **Mazumdar, Biman Behari**
Resurgence of women in the Gupta age. *Indian History Congress Proceedings*, Session 30, 1968 : 94.

467. **Mukerjee, Sandhya**
Glimpses of Society as depicted in Indian art c. 300 A.D.- c. 600 A.D. In Govind Chandra Pande, ed., *Indian art & culture*. Allahabad, Raka Prakashan, 1994 : 217-223.

468. **Om Prakash**
Food and drinks in ancient India. Delhi, Munshiram Manoharlal, 1961.

469. **Pande, G.C.**
Population in ancient India. *Journal of the Bihar Research Society*, Vol. 45, 1959 : 381-390.

470. **Parui, Sasanka Sekhar**
Life of widows in the Gupta period. *Journal of Ancient Indian History*, Vol. 9, 1975-76 : 79-96.

471. _____
The philosophy of caste with special reference to the Gupta age. *Orissa Historical Research Journal,* Vol. 9, Nos. 3-4, 1960 : 83-96.

472. **Rawlinson, H.G.**
Foreign influence in the civilization of ancient India 900 B.C.-400 A.D. *Journal of the Bombay Branch of the Royal Asiatic Society*, Vol. 23, 1909-14 : 217-238.

473. **Saletore, R.N.**
Chandragupta II Vikramaditya ke rajya-kaal ka samajik jiwan. In *Vikram-smriti grantha*. Gwalior, Scindhia Oriental Institute, 1945 : 223-232 (Hindi).

474. **Shachi Kant**
Defining Vaisyas : A history in early Indian social formation. *Journal of the Bihar Research Society*, Vols. 69-70, 1983 -1984 : 83-109.

475. **Sharma, R.S.**
Politico-legal aspect of the caste system. *Journal of the Bihar Research Society*, Vol. 39, pt. 3, September 1953 : 306-330.

476. _____
Sudras in ancient India. Delhi, Motilal Banarsidass, 1980.

477. **Shastree, Siddhanta**
Horse-sacrifices in the Kali age. *Vishveshvaranand Indological Journal*. Vol. 13, 1975 : 351-360.

478. **Sinha, B.P.**
Resilence of the Hindu society (Ancient India). *Journal of the Bihar Puravid Parishad*, Vol. 3, 1979 : 127-148.

479. **Sircar, D.C.**
Aspects of marriage in North Indian society. *Our Heritage*, Vol. 26, pt. 2, 1978 : 1-8.

480. _____
Aspects of marriage in North Indian society. *Our Heritage*, Vol. 27, pt. 1, 1979 : 9-24.

481. ——

Caste in North India in the Gupta and post-Gupta ages. *Our Heritage*, Vol. 27, pt. 2, 1979 : 37-48.

482. ——

Caste in North India in the Gupta and post-Gupta ages. *Our Heritage*, Vol. 28, pt. 1, 1980 : 49-64.

483. **Thakur, Vijay Kumar**

Some facets of prostitution in ancient India *Journal of the Bihar Research Society*, Vol. 59, 1973 : 235-246.

484. **Vishnoi, Savita**

Economic status of women in ancient India. Meerut, Kusumanjali Prakashan, (1987).

COSTUME AND JEWELLERY

485. **Agrawal, R.C.**
`Makarkanthi' va Rajasthan ke takshankar. *Maru Bharati*, Vol. 10, No. 4, January 1963 : 53-54 (Hindi).

486. **Alkazi, Roshen**
Ancient Indian costume. New Delhi, Art Heritage, 1983.

487. **Ayyar, Sulochana**
Costumes and ornaments as depicted in the sculptures of Gwalior Museum. Delhi, Mittal Publications, 1987.

488. ———.
Foreign influence on the costumes and ornaments of ancient India. *Prachya Pratibha*, Vol. 4, No. 2, July 1976 : 107-117.

489. **Biswas, A.**
Indian costumes. New Delhi, Publication Dividion, 1985.

490. **Deo, S.B.**
A note on the `Makarika' ornament. *Journal of the Oriental Institute*, Vol. 16, No. 2, December 1966 : 164-165.

491. **Ghurye, G.S.**
Indian costume. Bombay, Popular Prakashan, 1966.

492. **Giri, Kamal**
Bharatiya shringar. Delhi, Motilal Banarsidass, 1987 (Hindi).

493. **Harle, J.C.**
A Gupta ear-ring. In Leelananda Prematilleke and others, ed., *Senarat Paranavitana commemoration volume*. Leiden, E.J. Brill, 1978 : 78-80.

494. **Mitterwallner, Gritli Von**
The silver bowl from Swat ; its Brahmi inscription and Gupta ornament. In M.S. Nagaraja Rao, ed., *Kusumanjali : New interpretation of Indian art & culture ; Sh. C. Sivaramamurti commemoration volume*; Vol. II. Delhi, Agam Kala Prakashan, 1987 : 355-368.

495. **Mohapatra, Ramesh Prasad**
Fashion styles of ancient India (A study of Kalinga from earliest times to sixteenth century A.D.). Delhi, B.R. Publishing Corporation, 1992.

496. **Moti Chandra**
Bharatiya veshbhusha. *Nagari Pracharini Patrika*, Vol. 49, Samvat 2001 : 329-376 (Hindi).

497. ______.
Costumes, textiles, cosmetics & coiffure in ancient and medieval India. Delhi, Oriental Publishers, 1973.

498. ______.
The history of Indian costume from the 3rd century A.D. *Journal of the Indian Society of Oriental art*, Vol. 12, 1944 : 1-97.

499. **Moti Chandra** and **Doshi, Saryu**
Costumes through the ages. *Marg*, Vol. 33, No. 1 : 19-58.

500. **Pandey, Indu Prabha**
Dress and ornaments in ancient India. Delhi, Bharatiya Vidya Prakashan, 1988.

501. **Pandey, Shyam Kumar**
Dress and ornaments as depicted in the art of Chhattisgarh. *Prachya Pratibha*, Vol. 6, No. 2, July 1978 : 111-122.

502. **Pandeya, Om Prakash**
Pracheen murtiyon mein vastra-sajja evam alankaran. *Parishad Patrika*, Vol. 27, 1987-1988 : 39-46 (Hindi).

503. **Sahay, S.N.**
Dress and ornaments of Mithila. *Journal of the Bihar Research Society*, Vols. 63-64, 1977-1978 : 509-539.

504. **Sahay, Sachidanand**
Indian costume, coiffure and ornament. New Delhi, Munshiram Manoharlal, 1975.

505. **Shastri, Ajay Mitra**
Gems in the Gupta age : A literary view. *Orissa Historical Research Journal*, Vol. 35, Nos. 1-2, 1989-90 : 81-98.

506. **Tiwari, Pushpa**
Prachin Bharatiya abhushan. Allahabad, Kitab Mahal, 1992 (Hindi).

ECONOMY

507. **Altekar, A.S.**
Land-ownership during the Gupta-Pallava period. In Rasiklal C. Parikh and others, ed., *Acharya Dhruva samarak grantha*, Part III. Ahmedabad, Gujarat Vidya-Sabha, 1946 : 127-135.

508. **Banerjee, Manabendu**
Religious horoscope of the Bengal land-grants of the time of the Gupta monarchs. In *A corpus of Indian studies : Essays in honour of Professor Gaurinath Sastri*. Calcutta, Sanskrit Pustak Bhandar, 1980 : 353-368.

509. **Choudhary, Radhakrishna**
Ownership of land in ancient India. *Journal of the Bihar Research Society*, Vol. 53, 1967 : 27-52.

510. ———.
Some aspects of socio-economic history of North-Eastern India on the basis of epigraphic sources (c. 320-711 A.D.). *Indian History Congress Proceedings*, Session 16, 1953 : 71-78.

511. **Dandekar, R.N.**
Some aspects of the Gupta civilization : Economic conditions. *Bulletin of the Deccan College Research Institute*, Vol. 20, 1960 : 108-115.

512. **Darian, Steven G.**
Commerce on the Ganges between the Mauryan and the Gupta period. *Journal of the Ganganatha Jha Kendriya Sanskrit Vidyapeetha*, Vol. 33, pt. 1, January-March 1977 : 1-9.

513. **Das, Sudhir Ranjan**
Types of land in North-Eastern India (from 4th century to 7th century A.D.). *Indian History Congress Proceedings*, Session 9, 1946 : 82-87.

514. **Dhadwal, Nandita**
Gupta era trade connections between Bengal and mainland Southeast Asia and China. *Indica*, Vol. 29, No. 1, March 1992 : 9-17.

515. **Jain, Beena**
Guild organization in Northern India (from earliest times to 1200 A.D.). Delhi, Pratibha Prakashan, 1990.

516. **Jain, Beena and Avasthi, R.**
Ancient North Indian guilds as Banks. *Pragdhara*, No. 2, 1991-92 : 163-166.

517. **Jain, Purushottam Chandra**
Labour in ancient India (from the Vedic age upto the Gupta period). New Delhi, Sterling Publishers, 1971.

518. **Jha, D.N.**
Assessment of land revenue in post-Maurya and Gupta times (c. 200 B.C. - A.D. 600). *Journal of the Bihar Research Society*, Vol. 46, 1960 : 228-232.

519. ______.
Forced labour in post-Maurya and Gupta times. In B.P. Sinha and others. ed., *Dr. Satkari Mookerji felicitation volume*. Varanasi, Chowkhamba Sanskrit Series Office, 1969 : 443-445.

520. ______.
Forced labour in post-Maurya and Gupta times. *Indian History Congress Proceedings*, Session 28, 1966 : 94-96.

521. ______.
Revenue system in post-Maurya and Gupta times. Calcutta, Punthi Pustak, 1967.

522. ______.
Studies in early Indian economic history. Delhi, Anupama Publications, 1980.

523. **Kaw, R.K.**
Peeps into agriculture in ancient India. *Vishveshvaranand Indological Journal*. Vol. 9, pt. 1, 1971 : 164-178.

524. **Mazumdar, B.P.**
A glimpse of economy of ancient and early medieval Bihar. In Bhagwant Sahai and Sachidanand Sahay, ed., *Bihar past and present*. Patna, Bihar Historical Society, 1981 : 53-55.

525. **Mehra, K.L.**
History of masa-pulse in India and its cultural significance. *Vishveshvaranand Indological Journal*. Vol. 8, 1970 : 217-226.

526. ———.
History of masura-pulse in India and its cultural significance. *Vishveshvaranand Indological Journal*. Vol. 10, 1972 : 131-139.

527. ———.
History of mudga-pulse in India and its cultural significance. *Vishveshvaranand Indological Journal*. Vol. 13, 1975 : 190-197.

528. ———.
History of sesame in India and its cultural significance. *Vishveshvaranand Indological Journal*. Vol. 5, pt. 1, 1967 : 94-107.

529. **Mookerji, Radha Kumud**
Indian shipping : A history of sea-borne trade and maritime activity of the Indians from the earliest times. Allahabad, Kitab Mahal, 1962.

530. **Moti Chandra**
Sarthavaha. Patna, Bihar-Restrabhasha-Parishad, 1953 (Hindi).

531. ———.
Trade and trade routes in ancient India. New Delhi, Abhinav Publications, 1977.

532. **Mukherjee, Munmun**
Industries in ancient India as reflected in the early inscriptions (200 B.C. to 550 A.D.). *Proceedings of the All India Oriental Conference*, Session 34, 1989 : 164-169.

533. **Niyogi, Puspa**
Economy of land of ancient Bengal as known from land grants (c. 400-1200 A.D.). *Journal of Ancient Indian History*. Vol. 14, 1983-84 : 270-284.

534. **Om Prakash**
India's foreign trade between c. 300 B.C. and A.D. 1000 : Assumptions and issues. *Indian History Congress Proceedings*, Session 43, 1982 : 110-114.

535. **Pandey, L.P.**
Development of horticulture and Botony in the Gupta period onward. *Journal of Indian History*. Vol. 63, 1985 : 33-62.

536. **Pandey, Lalta Prasad**
Famines in ancient India. *Journal of Indian History*. Vol. 53, pt. 1, April 1975 : 25-32.

537. **Puri, B.N.**
Irrigation and agricultural economy in ancient India. *Annals of the Bhandarkar Oriental Research Institute*. Vols. 48-49, 1968 : 383-390.

538. **Sahay, S.N.**
Textile industry in ancient India. *Journal of the Bihar Research Society*, Vol. 59, 1973 : 115-131.

539. **Sharma, R.S.**
Coins and problems of early Indian economic history. *Journal of the Numismatic Society of India*, Vol. 31, pt. 1, 1969 : 1-8.

540. ———.
Economic and social condition under the Guptas. In Bindeshwari Prasad Sinha, ed., *Comprehensive history of Bihar*, Vol. 1, pt. II, Patna. K.P. Jayaswal Research Institute, 1974 : 166-176.

541. ———.
Light on early Indian society and economy. Bombay, P.C. Manaktala and Sons, 1966.

542. ———.
A survey of land system in India from c. 200 B.C. to A.D. 650. *Journal of the Bihar Research Society*, Vol. 44, pts. 3-4, September-December 1958 : 225-234.

543. **Singh, Hari Sahai**
Institution of money-lending. *Journal of the Ganganatha Jha Kendriya Sanskrit Vidyapeetha*, Vols. 38-39, 1982 : 109-124.

544. **Singh, Y.B.**
Some taxes of Gupta and post-Gupta period—an explanation. *Prachya Pratibha*, Vol. 8, 1980 : 51-55.

545. **Sircar, D.C.**
Media of exchange in ancient and medieval India. *Journal of Ancient Indian History*. Vol. 10, 1976-77 : 1-51.

546. **Sridharan, K.**
A maritime history of India. New Delhi, Publications Division, 1965.

547. **Srivastava, Arun Kumar**
Liquor industry in ancient India. *Journal of the Bihar Puravid Parishad*, Vol. 3, 1979 : 63-72.

548. **Srivastava, Satya Prakash**
India under the Guptas (A study in economical life). *Indian History Congress Proceedings*, Session 7, 1944 : 127-132.

549. **Thakur, Jai Naraian**
Pracheen Bharat mein khanij vyavasaya. *Parishad Patrika*, Vol. 15, No. 2, July 1975 : 87-93 (Hindi).

550. **Thakur, Vijay Kumar**
Forced labour in the Gupta period. *Indian History Congress Proceedings*, Session 38, 1977 : 145-151.

551. ———.
Historiography of Indian feudalism towards a model of early medieval Indian economy. Patna, Janaki Prakashan, 1989.

552. **Tripathi, L.K.**
Coins as source of economic history. *Journal of the Numismatic Society of India*, Vol. 33, pt. 1, 1971 : 1-14.

553. **Yadava, A.L.**
Agricultural implements and technique in the Gupta period. *Journal of the Bihar Research Society*, Vols. 65-66, 1979-80 : 341-354.

554. ______.
Irrigation in Northern India during the Gupta period. *Journal of the Bihar Research Society*, Vol 62, 1976 : 53-57.

RELIGION

555. **Banerji, Adris**
Schism and Sarnath (A study on different sects occuping Sarnath). *Indian History Congress Proceedings*, Session 7, 1944 : 90-103.

556. **Chatterjee, Ashoke**
The bhumi-khanda in the Bengal recension of the Padma-Purana—a critical survey. *Purana*, Vol. 7, No. 2, 1965 : 262-275.

557. **Das, H.C.**
Religions of Orissa. *Orissa Historical Research Journal*, Vol. 30, Nos. 2-4, 1984 : 91-147.

558. **Goswami, Kunja Govinda**
Religious toleration in the Gupta period. *Indian Historical Quarterly*, Vol. 13, No. 2, June 1937 : 323-328.

559. **Hazra, Kanai Lal** .
Vaisnavism and the non-Brahmanical faiths of ancient India : The Ajivikas, Jainism and Buddhism. *Journal of the Department of Pali*, Vol. 5, 1989-90 : 88-98.

560. **Majumdar, Bhakta Prasad**
Religion and philosophy (275-550 A. D.). In Bindeshwari Prasad Sinha, ed., *Comprehensive history of Bihar*, Vol. 1, pt. II. Patna, K.P. Jayaswal Research Institute, 1974 : 122-165.

561. **Misra, Bhaskar Nath**
Religious life in the Gupta period. *Journal of United Provinces Historical Society*, Vol. 19, 1946 : 61-77.

562. **Narain, A.K.**
Religious policy and toleration in ancient India with particular reference to the Gupta age. In Bardwell L. Smith, ed., *Essays on Gupta culture*. Missouri, South Asia Books, 1983 : 17-51.

563. **O'flaheerty, Wendy Doniger**
The image of the heritage in the Gupta puranas. In Bardwell L. Smith, ed., *Essays on Gupta culture*. Missouri, South Asia Books, 1983 : 107-127.

564. **Shah, Kirit K.**
Ancient Bundelkhand : Religious history in socio-economic perspective. Delhi, Gian Publishing House, 1988.

565. **Singh, Jai Prakash**
The religious leanings of the Guptas. In Lallanji Gopal and others, ed., *D.D. Kosambi commemoration volume*. Varanasi, D.D. Kasambi Commemoration Commitee, 1977 : 73-103.

566. **Singhai, Champalal**
Gupta samraton ka dharma-sambhav. *Shraman*, Vol. 23, No. 6, April 1972 : 18-20 (Hindi).

567. **Sinha, Piyush Kamal**
Religious history of Banaras as gleaned from archaeological discoveries (200 B.C. -300 A.D.). *Journal of the Bihar Research Society*, Vols. 74-75, 1988-89 : 56-66.

568. **Shrivastava, M.C.P.**
The history of the worship of Sakti in Mithila. *Journal of the Bihar Research Society*, Vols. 63-64, 1977-78 : 540-562.

569. **Srivastava, Satya Prakash**
Religion under the Gupta age (inscriptions and coins). *Indian History Congress Proceedings*, Session 6, 1943 : 116-124.

570. **Tahsildar Singh**
Secularised religion of Gupta kings : Reflections from contemporary inscriptions. *Bharatiya Vidya*, Vol. 40, No. 4, 1981 : 9-16.

571. **Tripathi, R.R.**
Guptakala mein Saryupaar ke dharmik vishwas. In T.P. Verma and others, ed., *Bharatiya Itihas Sankalan Samiti Prakashan*. Vol. 5, *Yug yugin Saryupaar*. Varanasi, Bharatiya Itihas Sankalan Samiti, 1987 : 87-90 (Hindi).

572. **Tripathi, Rama Shankar**
Religious toleration under the Imperial Guptas. *Indian Historical Quarterly*. Vol. 15, No. 1, March 1939 : 1-12.

573. ———.
Religous toleration under the Imperial Guptas. *Indian History Congress Proceedings*, Session 2, 1938 : 63-70.

574. **Verma, Birendra**
Social and religious history of ancient Bihar. In Bhagwant Sahai and Sachidanand Sahay, ed., *Bihar past and present*. Patna, Bihar Historical Society, 1981 : 12-15.

HINDU

575. **Agrawala, R.C.**
Goddess worship in ancient Rajasthan. *Journal of the Bihar Research Society*, Vol. 41, pt. 1, March 1955 : 1-12.

576. ———.
Pracheen shilalekho va murtikala ke aadhar par purva madhyakaleen Rajasthan mein Shakti-pujan. *Maru Bharati*, Vol. 3, No. 1, April 1955 : 23-29.

577. **Agrawala, V.S.** and **Moti Chandra**
Yaksha worship in Varanasi : Matsyapurana (ch. 180). *Purana*, Vol. 1, No. 2, 1959-60 : 198-201.

578. **Akhouri, Gayatri**
Saivism in inscriptions of Bihar. *Journal of the Bihar Puravid Parishad*, Vol. 6, 1982 : 137-148.

579. **Bajpai, K.D.**
Impact of Vaisnavism on ancient art of Central India. In Ratan Parimoo, ed., *Vaisnavism in Indian art and culture*. New Delhi, Books & Books, 1987 : 319-327.

580. ———.
Sri Krsna ka veer roop. *Bulletin of Museums & Archaeology in U.P.*, Nos. 21-24, June 1978-December 1979 : 59-66 (Hindi).

581. **Bhandarkar, D.R.**
Was there any Vaishnava sect in existance in the Gupta period. *Indian Culture*, Vol. 15, 1948-1949 : 4-5.

582. **Brajesh Krishna**
The concept of Visvarupa : An appraisal. *Kurukshetra University Research Journal*. (*Arts and Humanities*), Vol. 13, 1979 : 3-8.

583. ______.
The development of Vaisnavism in ancient Panjab. *Journal of the Ganganatha Jha Kendriya Sanskrit Vidyapeetha*, Vol. 41, 1985 : 19-26.

584. **Chaturvedi, S.N.**
Early Gupta emperors and Bhagvatism. In Govind Chandra Gupta, ed., *Indian art & culture*. Allahabad, Raka Prakashan, 1994 : 203-209.

585. **Chaturvedi, Shailnath**
Gupta samarat evam Bhagwat dharma. In Sita Ram Chaturvedi and others, ed., *Dr, Rajbali Pandey smriti granth*. Deoria, Dr. Rajbali Pandey Smriti Granth Prakashan Samiti, Kalanidhi Prakashan, 1976 : 173-175 (Hindi).

586. **Dehejia, Vidya**
Rama : Hero and avatar. *Marg*, Vol. 45, No. 3 : 1-14.

587. **Goswami, Kunja Govinda**
Vaisnavism. *Indian Historical Quarterly*, Vol. 31, No. 2, June 1955 : 109-133.

588. **Hazra, K.L.**
Studies in Sun-worship in ancient India. *Journal of the Department of Pali*, Vol. 3, 1985-86 : 35-40.

589. **Jash, Pranabananda**
The cult of Sri Lakshmi in Eastern India as reflected on the coins. *Journal of the Numismatic Society of India*, Vol. 43, pt. 2, 1981 : 114-120.

590. **Joshi, M.C.**
Sakta-tantrism in the Gupta age. In B.Datta and others, ed., *Aruna-Bharati : Profesor A.N. Jani felicitation volume (Essays in contemporary Indological research)*. Baroda, Prof. A.N. Jani Felicitation Volume Committee, 1983 : 77-81.

591. **Moti Chandra**
Studies in the cult of the Mother goddess in ancient India. *Prince of Wales Museum Bulletin*, No. 12, 1973 : 1-47.

592. **Rana, R.S.**
Dharma as depicted in ancient Indian inscriptions. *Bharatiya Vidya*, Vol. 50, 1990 : 87-99.

593. **Sahai, Bhagwant**
The Pasupatas in Bihar. *Journal of the Bihar Puravid Parishad*, Vols. 4-5, 1980-81 : 319-331.

594. **Sankalia, H.D.**
The antiquity of image worship in India. *Bharati*, New Series, No. 2, 1984 : 1-20.

595. **Singh, R.C.**
Worship of Vasudeva-Krsna in ancient India based on archaeological evidences. *Bulletin of Museums & Archaeology in U.P.*, Nos. 21-24, June 1978-December 1979 : 37-42.

596. **Singh, Sheo Bahadur**
Devi through the ages. *Kurukshetra University Research Journal* (*Arts and Humanities*), Vol. 6, No. 2, 1972 : 3-5.

597. **Sinha, C.R.P.**
Foot-prints of Visnu from Bihar. *Journal of the Bihar Puravid Parishad*, Vols. 4-5, 1980-81 : 316-318.

598. **Sinha, Harendra Prasad**
Sun worship in Bihar. *Journal of the Bihar Puravid Parishad*, Vol. 2, 1978 : 239-245.

599. **Srivastava, V.C.**
The solar cult as revealed by the Gupta and post-Gupta inscriptions. *Bharatiya Vidya*, Vol. 27, 1967 : 41-48.

600. **Stein, Burton**
Mahanavami : Medieval and modern kingly ritual in South India. In Bardwell L. Smith, ed., *Essays on Gupta culture*. Missouri, South Asia Books, 1983 : 67-90.

601. **Tiwari, J.N.**
Goddess cults in ancient India (with special reference to the first seven centuries A.D.). Delhi, Sundeep Prakashan, 1985.

602. ——.
Worship of the Sun. *Purana*, Vol. 32, No. 1, 1990 : 193-217.

BUDDHIST

603. **Choudhary, Radhakrishna**
Some aspects of Budhism as gleaned through Indian art. *Journal of the Bihar Research Society*, Buddha Jayanti Special Issue, Vol. 1, 1956 : 47-65.

604. **Gokhale, B.G.**
Buddhism in the Gupta age. In Bardwell L. Smith, ed., *Essays on Gupta culture*. Missouri, South Asia Books, 1983 : 129-153.

605. **Hazra, Kanai Lal**
The rise and decline of Buddhism in India. New Delhi, Munshiram Manoharlal, 1995.

606. ——.
Royal patronage of Buddhism in ancient India. Delhi, D.K. Publications, 1984.

607. **Niyogi, Puspa**
Dynastic and regional affiliations of Buddhism in ancient Bengal. *Journal of Ancient Indian History*, Vol. 9, 1975-76 : 120-167.

608. **Pahadiya, S.M.**
Buddhism among different people of Malwa. *Bharatiya Vidya*, Vol. 30, 1970 : 81-88.

609. **Pathak, K.B.**
On Buddhamitra, the teacher of Vasubandhu. *Indian Antiquary*, Vol. 41, October 1912 : 244.

610. **Sengupta, Sudha**
Buddhism in the classical age. (c. 400-750 A.D.). Delhi, Sundeep Prakashan, 1985.

611. **Sharma, Arvind**
The disappearance of Buddhism from India as a historical conundrum. *Pasjab University Research Bulletin (Arts).* Vol. 6, No. 1, 1975 : 61-74.

612. **Thakur, Upendra**
A brief survey of Buddhism and traces of Buddhist remains in Mithila. *Journal of the Bihar Research Society*, Buddha Jayanti Special Issue, Vol. 2, 1956 : 428-449.

613. **Verma, B.S.**
Buddhism in Bihar from c. 300 A.D. to 1000 A.D. *Journal of the Bihar Research Society*, Buddha Jayanti Special Issue, Vol. 2, 1956 : 450-470.

JAINA

614. **Chakraborty, Lalita**
Jainism in early Bengal Eastern India. *Jinamanjari.* Vol. 3, No. 2, October 1991 : 68-75.

615. **Deo, S.B.**
Jainism in Indian history. *Jain Journal,* Vol. 6, No. 4, April 1972 : 175-208.

616. **Giri, Kapil Dev**
Varanasi aur Jaina dharma. *Prajna,* Vol. 18, pt. 2, 1973 : 86-92 (Hindi).

617. **Jain, Ramesh Chandra Chandrarao**
Gupta kaleem Jainadharma. *Jain Siddhanta Bhaskar*, Vol. 15, No. 1, July 1948 : 32-38. (Hindi).

618. Jainism in Madhya Pradesh. *Jain Journal*, Vol. 3, No. 4, April 1969 : 175-182.

619. Jainism in Uttar Pradesh. *Jain Journal*, Vol. 3, No. 4, April 1969 : 183-189.

620. **Mittal, Amar Chand**
Gupta kaal mein Jaina dharma. *Shraman*, Vol. 10, No. 6, April 1959 : 16-22 (Hindi).

621. **Mukherjee, S.C.**
Some reflections on Jainism in ancient Bengal. *Jain Journal*, Vol. 28, No. 4, April 1994 : 155-160.

622. **Mukherji, S.C.**
Cultural heritage of Bengal in relation to Jainism. *Jain Journal*, Vol. 24, No. 1, July 1989 : 25-34.

623. **Tiwari, Binod Kumar**
Existence of Jainism in Eastern U.P. during Gupta period. *Jaina Antiquary*, Vol. 35, No. 2, December 1982 : 13-19.

624. ———.
Rise and decline of Jainism in Bihar (from c. 600 B.C. to A.D. 1200). *Jaina Antiquary*, Vol. 38, No. 1, June 1985 : 32-35.

POLITY AND ADMINISTRATION

625. **Agrawala. V.S.**
Samant. *Journal of the Uttar Pradesh Historical Society*. Vols. 24-25, 1951-1952 : 277-280 (Hindi).

626. **Apte, B.K.**
Means and modes of warfare under the Mauryas and the Guptas. *Indian History Congress Proceedings*, Session 18, 1955 : 78.

627. **Bagchi, Night Queen**
Sovereignty in ancient India. *Prajna*, Vol. 16, pt. 2, 1971 : 195-200.

628. **Choudhary, Radhakrishna**
Feudal obligations in ancient India. *Journal of the Bihar Puravid Parisad*, Vols. 4-5, 1980-81 : 229-235.

629. ———.
Pracheen Bharatiya shasan ki rooprekha. *Parishad Patrika*, Vol. 9, No. 1, April 1969 : 44-48 (Hindi). *Indian History Congress Proceedings*, Session

630. **Dandekar, R.N.**
The system of government under the Guptas. *Bharatiya Vidya*, Vols. 20-21, 1960-61 : 340-354.

631. **Dikshitar, V.R. Ramachandra**
The Gupta polity. Delhi, Motilal Banarsidass Publishers, 1993.

632. **Ganguly, D.K.**
Aspects of ancient Indian administration. New Delhi, Abhinav Publications, 1979.

633. ———.
The *Yuvaraja* in ancient India. *Indian History Congress Proceedings*, Session 32, Vol. 1, 1970 : 69-75.

634. **Ghoshal, U.N.**
New light on the Gupta administrative system—The significance and application of the term *Kumaramatya*. *All India Oriental Conference Proceedings*, Session 6, 1930 : 211-216.

635. ———.
A note on some administrative terms in ancient India. In *Dr. S. Krishnaswami Aiyangar commemoration volume*. Madras, 1936 : 30-32.

636. ———.
On the working of village assemblies, economic guilds, religious congregations and other assemblies during the Gupta period. *Journal of the Asiatic Society*, Vol. 1, No. 2, 1959 : 177-182.

637. **Gopal, Lallanji**
Samanta—Its varying significance in ancient India. *Journal of the Royal Asiatic Society of Great Britain and Ireland*, 1963 : 21-37.

638. **Goswami, Kunja Gobinda**
Appointment of ministers and high officials in ancient India. *Indian Historical Quarterly*, Vol. 29, No. 2, June 1953 : 129-132.

639. **Gurmaita, Bhuvaneshwar Prasad**
Varnaratnakar mein kathit Rajyadhikariyo ka parichyatamak vivechan. *Journal of the Bihar Research Society*, Vol. 51, pt. 1, 1965 : 125-151 (Hindi).

640. **Maity, S.K.**
Studies in the Gupta administration. *Journal of the Asiatic Society*, Vol. 1, No. 3, 1959 : 221-231.

641. **Mookerji, Radha Kumud**
Indian administration in the age of the Guptas : From inscriptions. *Journal of Indian History*, Vol. 3, 1924 : 262-270.

642. **Nilakanta Sastri, K.A.**
The conception of empire in ancient India. *Indian History Congress Proceedings*, Session 3, 1939 : 265-279.

643. **Pandey, A.K.**
Policing in ancient India—an ageless system. *Journal of the Bihar Research Society*, Vols. 67-68, 1981-82 : 78-88.

644. **Punia, Dharmapal Singh**
Women and public administration in ancient India. *Bharatiya Vidya*, Vol. 38, 1978 : 29-35.

645. **Puri, B.N.**
The Gupta administration. Delhi, B.R. Publishing Corporation, 1990.

646. ———.
Hereditary appointments in ancient Indian administration. *Indian History Congress Proceedings*, Session 25, 1963 : 53-59.

647. ———.
The term *Dandanayaka* and *Mahadandanayaka* in the Hindu administrative machinery. *Indian History Congress Proceedings*, Session 6, 1943 : 190.

648. **Purohit, Sohan Krishna**
Pracheen Bharatiya raajnitik jivan mein istriya ki bhumika. *Parishad Patrika*, Vol. 23, No. 2, July 1983 : 133-143. (Hindi).

649. **Rai, Mangala**
Pracheen Bharat mein Zila Shasan. Delhi, Janaki Prakashan, 1983 (Hindi).

650. **Sharma, Dasharatha**
The significance of two old historical titles. *Indian Historical Quarterly*, Vol. 27, No. 4, December 1951 : 337-339.

651. **Sharma, R.S.**
Gupta administration. In Bindeshwari Prasad Sinha, ed., *Comprehensive history of Bihar*, Vol. 1, pt. II. Patna, K.P. Jayaswal Research Institute, 1974 : 114-121.

652. **Singh, Rajpal**
Guptakaleen danda-vyavastha ka muladhar `Brispatismriti' *Parishad Patrika*, Vol. 24, No. 2, July 1984 : 109-114 (Hindi).

653. **Sinha, B.P.**
Elephants in ancient Indian army. *Indian History Congress Proceedings*, Session 18, 1955 : 51-57.

654. **Sohoni, S.V.**
Pracheen Bharat mein raajdharma aur tyagapath. *Parishad Patrika*, Vol. 23, No. 1, April 1983 : 19-24. (Hindi).

655. **Srivastava, Satya Prakash**
Political life under the Guptas (on the basis of epigraphic and numismatic evidence). *Indian History Congress Proceedings*, Session 5, 1941 : 174-176.

656. **Srivastava, Shail**
Pracheen Bharatiya gramya shasan ka pramukh adhikari "Gramani". *Shodh Patrika*, Vol. 22, No. 1, 1971 : 19-26. (Hindi).

657. **Thakur, Vijay Kumar**
Role of guilds in ancient urban administration. *Journal of the Numismatic Society of India*, Vol. 49, 1987 : 70-76.

658. ——.
Role of guilds in ancient Indian urban administration (c. 200 B.C. - A.D. 600). *Bharati*, New Serties, No. 3, 1985 : 66-73.

659. **Thapliyal, U.P.**
Foreign impact on ancient Indian polity. *Journal of the Bihar Research Society*, Vol. 61, 1975 : 55-59.

660. **Thaplyal, K.K.**
Kumaramataya - a review. *Bharati*, Nos. 12-14, 1968-1971 : 307-319.

661. **Vajpeyi, Raghavendra**
Gupta perception of Indian reality and feudalism. *Indian History Congress Proceedings*, Session 48, 1987 : 95-102.

EDUCATION

662. **Banerjee, Manabendu**
Educational system as we know from the inscriptions of the Imperial Guptas. *Journal of the Oriental Institute*, Vol. 35, Nos. 3-4, March-June 1986 : 257-264.

663. **Heras, H.**
The Royal patrons of the University of Nalanda. *Journal of the Bihar and Orissa Research Society*, Vol. 14, pt. 1, 1928 : 1-23.

664. **Jha, Renuka Kumari**
Guptakaal ki shikshan paddati. *Journal of the Bihar Research Society*, Vols. 63-64, 1977-78 : 584-592 (Hindi).

665. **Mookerji, Radha Kumud**
The University of Nalanda. *Journal of the Bihar Research Society*, Vol. 30, pt. 2, June 1944 : 126-159.

666. **Sankalia, H.D.**
The University of Nalanda. Delhi, Oriental Publishers, 1972.

667. **Shrivastava, M.C.P.**
Education in ancient India. In Bhagwant Sahai and Sachidanand Sahay, ed., *Bihar past and present*. Patna, Bihar Historical Society, 1981 : 56-59.

668. **Verma, B.S.**
Education, science and literature in the Gupta age. In Bindeshwari Prasad Sinha, ed., *Comprehensive history of Bihar*, Vol. 1, pt. II. Patna, K.P. Jayaswal Research Institute, 1974 : 177-192.

LITERATURE

669. **Agnihotri, P.D.**
Learning and literature in ancient Madhya Pradesh. *Journal of the Madhya Pradesh Itihasa Parishad,* No. 8, 1970 : 30-52.

670. **Agrawal, Ashvini**
Prof. (Jagannath) Agrawal on the literary sources of the Gupta history. In Dharmendra Kumar Gupta, ed., *Prof. Jagannath Agrawal felicitation volume : Recent studies in Sanskrit and Indology*. Delhi, Ajanta Publications, 1982 : XXIV-XXVI.

671. **Agrawal, Jagannath**
The date of dramatist Visakhadatta. *Vishveshvaranand Indological Journal*, Vol. 4, pt. 1, 1966 : 53-64.

672. ——.
Echoes of Gupta history in Sanskrit dramas. *Journal of the Oriental Institute*, Vol. 15, Nos. 3-4, March-June 1966 : 475-578.

673. **Agrawala, V.S.**
Art evidences in Kalidasa. *Journal of the United Provinces Historical Society*, Vol. 22, 1949 : 81-93.

674. ——.
Kalidasa and Sanskrit Buddhist literature. *Journal of the Uttar Pradesh Historical Society*, Vol. 23, 1950 : 189-195.

675. ——.
Sanskrit literature dealing with art, architecture and sculpture, etc. *Journal of the United Provinces Historical Society*, Vol. 17, pt. 1, July 1944 : 6-12.

676. **Ahmad, Nisar**
Does Mujmalu-T-Tawarikh speak about Ramagupta's episode ? *Journal of the Oriental Institute*, Vol. 13, No.1, September 1963 : 26-30.

677. **Bajpai, K.D.**
Contribution of ancient Madhya Pradesh to Sanskrit learning. *Journal of the Ganganatha Jha Kendriya Sanskrit Vidyapeetha,* Vol. 40, 1984 : 1-31.

678. **Banerjee, Manabendu**
Devicandragupta : A study from historical point of view. *Anviksa,* Vol. 11, 1988 : 17-25.

679. **Basak, Radhagovinda**
Historical basis and model for Kalidasa's description of Raghu's conquests. *All India Oriental Congress Proceedings,* Session 2, 1922, : 325-334.

680. **Bhattacharyya, D.C.**
Kalidasa in the light of Gupta art. *Marg,* Vol. 42, No. 3 : 49-52.

681. **Bhimasankara Rao, S.**
Historical importance of the Puranas. *Quarterly Journal of the Andhra Historical Research Society.* Vol. 2, No. 2, October 1927 : 81-90.

682. **Brahman, K.S.N.**
The date of Kalidasa. *Sri Venkateswara University Oriental Journal,* Vol. 1, 1958 : 75-88.

683. **Buddha Prakash**
Samudragupta and Candragupta Vikramaditya as Sanskrit poets. *Vishveshvaranand Indological Journal.* Vol. 9, pt. 1, 1971 : 75-84.

684. **Burrow, T.**
The date of Syamilaka's Padataditaka. *Journal of the Royal Asiatic Society of Great Britain and Ireland,* 1946 : 46-53.

685. **Chakravarti, Monmohan**
Kalidasa and the Guptas. *Journal of the Royal Asiatic Society of Great Britain and Ireland,* 1904 : 158-161.

686. **Charpentier, Jarl**
Date of the Mudraraksasa. *Indian Historical Quarterly,* Vol. 7, No. 3, September 1931 : 629.

687. **Chattopadhyay, Aparna**
Mujmalu-T-Tawarikh & the Ramagupta problem of Gupta history. *Journal of the Oriental Institute*, Vol. 18, No. 4, June 1969 : 331-336.

688. **Chattopadhyaya, K.**
The date of the Kaumudimahotsava. *Indian Historical Quarterly*, Vol. 14, No. 3, September 1938 : 582-606.

689. **Choudhary, Radhakrishna**
Kalidasa and Gupta art. *Journal of the Bihar Research Society*, Vol. 42, pt. 1, March 1956 : 36-46.

690. **Chhabara, B. Ch.**
Gupta samrat aur Vishnu-sahastranama. *Nagari Pracharini Patrika*, Vol. 54, No. 1, Samvat 2006 : 1-12 (Hindi).

691. **Das Gupta, C.C.**
A note on the interpretation of the Devi-Candragupta. *Annals of the Bhandarkar Oriental Research Institute*. Vol. 39, 1958 : 136-141.

692. ______.
A note on the interpretation of the Devi-Candragupta. *Indian History Congress Proceedings*, Session 19, 1956 : 79-84.

693. **Gaur, R.C.**
Kadambari as a source for contemporary administrative history. *Journal of the Royal Asiatic Society of Great Britain and Ireland*, No. 1, 1978 : 21-30.

694. **Gupta, Dharmendra Kumar**
The historical background of Dandin's prose romances. *Journal of Indian History*, Vol. 54, pt. 2, August 1976 : 305-318.

695. **Gyani, Siva Datt**
The date of the Puranas. *Purana*, Vol. 1, No. 2, 1959-60 : 213-219.

696. **Hoernle, A.F. Rudolf**
A note on the British collection of Central Asian antiquities. *Indian Antiquary*, Vol. 29, 1990 : 63-73.

697. **Jain, K.C.**
Kalidasa Court poet not of Vikramaditya but of Chastana, founder of Saka era. *Indian History Congress Proceedings*, Session 48, 1987 : 52.

698. **Jamkhedkar, Arvind**
Dvitiya Chandraguptache kavitva—ek punavichar. *Vidarbha Samshodhana Mandal Varshik*, Vol. 16, 1973 : 142-146 (Marathi).

699. **Jawahar Lal, G.**
When did Kalidasa flourish ? *Journal of Andhra Historical Research Society*, Vol. 31, 1965-1966 : 61-73.

700. **Jayaswal. K.P.**
The book on Political Science by Sikhara, Prime Minister of Chander-Gupta II. *Journal of the Bihar and Orissa Research Society*, Vol. 18, pt. 1, March 1932 : 37-39.

701. **Jayaswal, Kashi Prasad**
The date of the Mudra-Rakshasa and the identification of Malayaketu. *Indian Antiquary*, Vol. 52, 1913 : 265-267.

702. **Kantawala, S.G.**
Puranas and Indian history and culture—an overview. *Purana*, Vol. 34, No. 1, 1992 : 5-13.

703. **Kedar, T.J.**
Kalidasa : His birth-place and date. *Nagpur University Journal*, No. 5, 1939 : 1-22. .

704. ———.
Kalidasa—His date and birth-place — Part-II. *Nagpur University Journal*, No. 6, 1940 : 1-30.

705. **Konow, Sten**
The Devicandragupta and its author. *Journal of the Bihar and Orissa Research Society*, Vol. 23, pt. 4, December 1937 : 444-451.

706. **Kunjunni, Raja K.**
The date of Kalidasa. *Adyar Library Bulletin*, Vol. 57, 1993 : 75-85.

707. **Madan, A.P.**
Was the dramatist Visakhadatta : A contemporary of Dantidurga. *Vishveshvaranand Indological Journal*, Vol. 20, 1982 : 81-90.

708. **Mahadule, Hira Lal**
Dattabhatt ka Mandasore abhilekh tatha Dhruvaswamini ki Vaishali-mudra ka rahasya. *Prachya Pratibha*, Vol. 11, 1983 : 159-166 (Hindi).

709. **Mazumdar, B.C.**
The date of Kalidasa. *Journal of the Bihar and Orissa Research Society*, Vol. 2, pt. 3, 1916 : 388-390.

710. ______.
The date of Kalidasa. *Journal of the Royal Asiatic Society of Great Britain and Ireland*, 1909 : 731-739.

711. **Miller, Barbara Stoler**
Microcosms of a complex world : Classical drama in the Gupta age. In Bardwell L. Smith, ed., *Essays on Gupta culture*. Missouri, South Asia Books, 1983 : 157-175.

712. **Mirashi, V.V.**
Some royal poets of the Vakataka age. *Indian Historical Quarterly*, Vol. 21, No. 3, September 1945 : 193-201.

713. **Mishra, Mamta**
Aspects of education and learning as gleaned from the Chaturbhandi. *Bulletin of Museums & Archaeology in U.P.*, No. 39, June 1987 : 37-39.

714. **Ojha, Kailash Chandra**
The Arya-Manjusri-Mula-Kalp on Candragupta I. *Indian Historical Quarterly*, Vol. 27, No. 2, June 1951 : 170-173.

715. ______.
Kaumudi-Mahotsava : Its historical interpretation. *Indian Historical Quarterly*, Vol. 32, No. 4, December 1956 : 417-424.

716. **Pandey, A.N.**
Anachronisms in the Raghuvamsa. *Journal of the Ganganatha Jha Kendriya Sanskrit Vidyapeetha*, Vol. 41, 1985 : 173-181.

717. **Pandurangi, K.T.**
Is Raghuvamsa complete ? *Quarterly Journal of the Mythic Society*, Vol. 75, No. 1, 1984 : 81-93.

718. **Pathak, K.B.**
Kalidasa and the Hunas of the Oxus Valley. *Indian Antiquary*, Vol. 41, November 1912 : 265-267.

719. ———.
Kumaragupta, the patron of Vasubandhu. *Journal of the Bombay Branch of the Royal Asiatic Society*, Vol. 23, 1909-14 : 185-187.

720. ———.
On the date of Kalidasa. *Journal of the Bombay Branch of the Royal Asiatic Society*, Vol. 19, 1895-97 : 35-43.

721. **Raghavacharyulu, K.**
Kaumudimahotsava and Gupta history. *Journal of Andhra Historical Research Society*, Vol. 6, pts. 3-4, 1932 : 139-141.

722. **Rajpurohit, Bhagwati Lal**
`Devichandragupta' tatha Kiratarjuniya ka samantar adhyayan. *Parishad Patrika*, Vol. 16, No. 1, April 1976 : 27-37.

723. **Ramanujan, A.K.** and **Cutler, Norman**
From classicism to Bhakti. In Bardwell L. Smith, ed., *Essays on Gupta culture*. Missouri, South Asia Books, 1983 : 177-214.

724. **Ramaswami Shastri, K.S.**
King Pravarasena and Kalidasa. *All India Oriental Conference Proceedings,* Session 7, 1933 : 99-108.

725. **Ramulu, A.**
The times of Kalidasa—an epigraphical approach. *Bulletin of the Deccan College Post-Graduate & Research Institute*, Vols. 51-52, 1991-92 : 655-658.

726. **Roy, S.N.**
Some notes and observations on the puranic account of the Imperial Guptas. *Purana*, Vol. 12, No. 2, 1970 : 265-285.

727. **Sankara, K.G.**
Notes on the Yasodharman theory of Kalidasa's date. *Journal of the Bihar and Orissa Research Society*, Vol. 6, pt. 3, September 1920 : 327-336.

728. **Sarasvati, A. Rangasvami**
Devichandraguptam or Chandragupta Vikramaditya destruction of the Saka Satraps (A glimpse into Gupta history from Sanskrit literature). *Indian Antiquary*, Vol. 52, 1923 : 181-184.

729. ———.
Further glimpses into Gupta literary history. *Quarterly Journal of the Mythic Society*, Vol. 15, No. 3, 1925 : 268-276.

730. ———.
Further glimpses into Gupta literary history. *Quarterly Journal of the Mythic Society*, Vol. 16, No. 2, 1925 : 93-103.

731. **Satya Vrat**
A note on the date of Mudraraksasa. *Vishveshvaranand Indological Journal*, Vol. 22, 1984 : 214-217.

732. **Sharma, Dadu Ram**
`Dhruvaswamini' : Nari mukti ki jayadundubhi. *Parishad Patrika*, Vol. 29, Nos. 1-2, April-July 1989 : 153-162 (Hindi).

733. **Sharma, Dasharatha**
The Candragupta of Vamana's Kavyalankara-sutras. *Indian Historical Quarterly*. Vol. 10, No. 4, December 1934 : 761.

734. ———.
Gupta samrat aur Vishnu-sahastranama. *Nagari Pracharini Patrika*, Vol. 55, No. 3, Samvat 2007 : 201-208 (Hindi).

735. ———.
The Kaumudimahotsava and the date of Kalidasa. *Indian Historical Quarterly*, Vol. 10, No. 4, December 1934 : 763-766.

736. ———.
The puranas on the Imperial Guptas. *Indian Historical Quarterly*. Vol. 30, No. 4, December 1954 : 374-378.

737. **Sharma, Jawahar Lal**
The dat of Bhagavata Purana. *Purana*, Vol. 20, No. 1, 1978 : 66-70.

738. **Sharma, Sudarshan Kumar**
Mahendra Natha of Kalidasa : A reappraisal. *Journal of the Ganganatha Jha Kendriya Sanskrit Vidyapeetha*, Vol. 41, 1985 : 67-80.

739. **Shashi Bala**
A Sanskrit manuscript of the Gupta period at the Horyuji monastery in Japan. In S. Bhaskaran Nair, ed., *Bharati-Bhanam (light of Indology) being Dr. K.V. Sharma felicitation volume*. Hoshiarpur, V.V.B. Institute of Sanskrit and Indological Studies, 1980 : 309-314.

740. ———.
A Sanskrit manuscript of the Gupta period at the Horyuji monastery in Japan. *Vishveshvaranand Indological Journal*, Vol. 18, 1980 : 309-314.

741. **Shastri, Ajay Mitra**
Chandragupta II Vikramaditya as a poet. *Indian History Congress Proceedings*, Session 27, 1965 : 109-113.

742. ———.
Chandragupta II Vikramaditya as a poet. *Prachya Pratibha*, Vol. 12, 1984 : 85-92.

743. ———.
The date of Varahamihara. *Vidarbha Samshodhana Mandal Varshik*, Vol. 4, 1961 : 26-46

744. ———.
Dvitiya Chandragupta Vikramadityache kavitva. *Vidarbha Samshodhana Mandal Varshik*, Vol. 9, 1966 : 94-100 (Marathi).

745. **Shastri, Hara Prasad**
Kalidasa—His age. *Journal of the Bihar and Orissa Research Society*, Vol. 2, pt. 1, 1916 : 31-44.

746. **Sircar, D.C.**
Inscriptional evidences relating to the development of classical Sanskrit. *Indian Historical Quarterly*. Vol. 15, No. 1, March 1939 : 38-46.

747. **Sohoni, S.V.**
Historical data about the date of Kalidasa. In A.M. Shastri and others, ed., *Vajapeya : Essays on evolution of Indian art & culture; Prof. K.D. Bajpai felicitation volume*, Vol. II. Delhi, Agam Kala Prakashan, 1987 : 333-338.

748. ———.
Kalidasa and Candragupta Vikramaditya—evidence from Vikramorvasiyam. In S.K. Maity and others, ed., *Studies in Orientology : Essays in memory of Prof. A.L. Basham*. Agra, Y.K. Publishers, 1988 : 365-369.

749. ———.
Kalidasa and relationship between Gupta and Naga dynasties. *Prachya Pratibha*, Vols. 9-10, 1981-82 : 11-21.

750. ———.
Kalidasa and Sarabhapura kingdom in South Kosala. *Quarterly Journal of the Mythic Society*, Vol. 74, No. 4, 1983 : 376-394.

751. ———.
Kalidasa, Hala Satavahana and Candragupta II. *Journal of the Bihar Research Society*, Vol. 41, pt. 2, June 1955 : 229-244.

752. ———.
The mudra of `Raksasa' in Visakhadatta's Mudrarakasam. *Journal of the Bihar Research Society*, Vol. 41, pt. 4, December 1955 : 491-498.

753. ———.
The mudra of `Raksasa' in Visakhadatta's Mudrarakasam. *Journal of the Numismatic Society of India*, Vol. 18, pt. 2, 1956 : 198-204.

754. ———.
On Visakhadatta's Devicandragupta. *Annals of the Bhandarkar Oriental Research Institute*. Vol. 62, 1981 : 169-192.

755. ——.
Prasasti of Samudragupta in purana texts. *Journal of the Oriental Institute*, Vol. 35, Nos. 3-4, March-June 1986 : 219-229.

756. ——.
Samudragupta's vidvatsabha—verse 3 in Harisena's prasasti. In K.C. Varma and others, ed., *Rtambhara : Studies in Indology* (*Acharya Udaya Vira Shastri felicitation volume*). Ghaziabad, Society for Indic Studies, 1986 : 78-82.

757. ——.
Vasubandhu, Dignaga, Vikramaditya, Nicula and Kalidasa. *Journal of the Bihar Research Society*, Buddha Jayanti Special Issue, Vol. 1, 1956 : 301-318.

758. **Srikantha Sastri, S.**
Date of the Mudra-raksasa. *Indian Historical Quarterly*, Vol. 7, No. 1, March 1931 : 163-169.

759. **Thakur, Upendra**
`Dhruvaswamini' ka Ramagupta : Etihasik samiksha. *Prishad Patrika*, Vol. 29, Nos. 1-2, April-July 1989 : 142-152 (Hindi).

760. **Thomas, F.W.**
The root gup and the Guptas. *Journal of the Royal Asiatic Society of Great Britain and Ireland*, 1909 : 740-743.

761. **Tripathi, Jay Shankar**
Kya Kalidasa kisi samrat ke ashrit thea. *Prishad Patrika*, Vol. 14, No. 2, July 1974 : 9-16 (Hindi).

762. **Tripathi, R.P.**
The historicity of the Malavikagnimitram—a re-examination. *Journal of the Ganganatha Jha Kendriya Sanskrit Vidyapeetha*, Vol. 34, pts. 3-4, July-December 1978 : 53-59.

763. **Trivedi, Ratilal Mohanlal**
Kalidasa's Vikramorvasiyam—A historical drama. *All India Oriental Congress Proceedings*, Summaries of Papers, Session 17, 1953 : 46.

764. **Upadhyaya, B.S.**
On some ancient place names in Kalidasa. *Journal of the United Provinces Historical Society*, Vol. 17, pt. 2, December 1944 : 4-26.

ARCHAEOLOGY

765. **Agrawala, V.S.**

Pottery designs from Ahichchhatra. *Lalit Kala,* Nos. 3-4 : 74-81.

766. **Altekar, A.S.** and **Mishra, Vijayakanta**

Report on Kumrahar excavations 1951-1955. Patna, K.P. Jayaswal Research Institute, 1959.

767. Ancient site and temple, Konhara Ghat, district Vaishali, Bihar. *Indian Archaeology : A Review,* 1977-78 : 77.

768. Ancient site, Hajipur, district Vaishali, Bihar. *Indian Archaeology : A Review,* 1977-78 : 77.

769. **Bajpai, K.D.**

New archaeological discoveries in Vidisa. *Journal of the Madhya Pradesh Itihasa Parishad,* No. 2, 1960 : 19-21.

770. ———.

New light on the history of Eran. *Journal of the U. P. Historical Society,* New Series, Vol. 8, pt. 2, 1960 : 47-53.

771. ———.

Tumain : A historical site of Central India. *Bharati,* New Series, No. 1, 1983 : 21-24.

772. **Banerji, Adris**

Rare and unique antiquities from Rajghat. *Journal of the Asiatic Society,* Vol. 7, Nos. 1-2, 1965 : 89-93.

773. **Barat, P.C.**

Ancient history of Baran. *Journal of the United Provinces Historical Society,* Vol. 9, pt. 1, April 1936 : 55-69.

774. **Bhowmik, S.K.**

Monuments of archaeological importance in Saurashtra. *Bulletin of the Museum and Picture Gallery, Baroda,* Vol. 23, 1971 : 71-83.

775. **Brajmohan Kumar**
Archaeology of Pataliputra and Nalanda. New Delhi, Ramanand Vidya Bhawan, 1987.

776. **Broadley, A.M.**
The Buddhistic remains of Bihar, *Journal of the Asiatic Society of Bengal*, Vol. 41, pt. 1, 1872 : 209-312.

777. **Chanchala**
The fruit and seed remains from ancient Hulaskhera, district Lucknow, U.P. (c. 700 B.C. - 500 A.D.). *Pragdhara,* No. 2, 1991-92 : 65-80.

778. **Chhabra, B.Ch.**
Antiquities from Jhusi and other sites. *Lalit Kala,* No. 9 : 11-15.

779. **Choudhury, R.D.**
Gupta influence in Kamarupa as known from archaeological evidence. *Indian History Congress Proceedings*, Session 38, 1977 : 742-746.

780. **Cunningham, A.**
Archaeological Survey of India, Vol. 3 : Report for the year 1871-72.

781. ———.
Archaeological Survey of India, Vol. 9 : Report of a tour in the Central Provinces in 1873-74 and 1874-75 : 16-31, 41-45.

782. ———.
Archaeological Survey of India, Vol. 10 : Report of tours in Bundelkhand and Malwa in 1874-75 and 1876-77.

783. ———.
Archaeological Survey of India, Vol. 11 : Report of tours in the Gangetic Provinces from Badaon to Bihar in 1875-76 and 1877-87 : 17-21.

784. ———.
Archaeological Survey of India, Vol. 16 : Report of tours in North and South Bihar in 1880-81.

785. ———.
Archaeological Survey of India, Vol. 17 : Report of a tour in the Central Provinces and Lower Gangetic Doab in 1881-82.

786. ———.
Archaeological Survey of India, Vol. 20 : Report of a tour in Eastern Rajputana in 1882-83 : 105.

787. **Dilip Kumar**
Archaeology of Vaisali. New Delhi, Ramanand Vidya Bhawan, 1986.

788. Early historical and medieval site, Sahan, district Mainpuri, Uttar Pradesh. *Indian Archaeology : A Review,* 1981-82 : 103.

789. Excavation at Agroha, district Hissar, Haryana. *Indian Archaeology : A Review,* 1978-79 : 68-69.

790. Excavation at Agroha, district Hissar, Haryana. *Indian Archaeology : A Review,* 1980-81 : 15-16.

791. Excavation at Ahichchhatra, district Bareilly, Uttar Pradesh. *Indian Archaeology : A Review,* 1964-65 : 39-42.

792. Excavation at Aphsad, district Nawadah, Bihar. *Indian Archaeology : A Review,* 1973-74 : 10-11.

793. Excavation at Aphsad, district Nawadah, Bihar. *Indian Archaeology : A Review,* 1977-78 : 16-17.

794. Excavation at Aphsad, district Nawadah, Bihar. *Indian Archaeology : A Review,* 1983-84 : 14.

795. Exploration at Atranjikhera, district Etah, Uttar Pradesh. *Indian Archaeology : A Review,* 1960-61 : 35.

796. Excavation at Ayodhya, district Faizabad, Uttar Pradesh. *Indian Archaeology : A Review,* 1979-80 : 76-77.

797. Excavation at Besnagar, district Vidisha, Madhya Pradesh. *Indian Archaeology : A Review,* 1963-64 : 16-17.

798. Excavation at Bharatpur, district Burdwan, West Bengal. *Indian Archaeology : A Review,* 1973-74 : 32-33.

799. Excavation at Bhardwaj Ashram, district Allahabad, Uttar Pradesh. *Indian Archaeology : A Review,* 1978-79 : 56.

800. Excavation at Bhardwaj Ashram, district Allahabad, Uttar Pradesh. *Indian Archaeology : A Review,* 1982-83 : 71.

801. Excavation at Bhitari, district Ghazipur, Uttar Pradesh. *Indian Archaeology : A Review,* 1968-69 : 38-39.

802. Excavation at Bhitari, district Ghazipur, Uttar Pradesh. *Indian Archaeology : A Review,* 1969-70 : 41.

803. Excavation at Bhitari, district Ghazipur, Uttar Pradesh. *Indian Archaeology : A Review,* 1971-72 : 47.

804. Excavation at Chandraketugarh, district 24- Parganas, West Bengal. *Indian Archaeology : A Review,* 1960-61 : 39-40.

805. Excavation at Chandraketugarh, district 24- Parganas, West Bengal. *Indian Archaeology : A Review,* 1961-62 : 62-63.

806. Excavation at Chandraketugarh, district 24- Parganas, West Bengal. *Indian Archaeology : A Review,* 1962-63 : 49-50.

807. Excavation at Chandraketugarh, district 24- Parganas, West Bengal. *Indian Archaeology : A Review,* 1963-64 : 63-65.

808. Excavation at Chechar, district Vaishali, Bihar. *Indian Archaeology : A Review,* 1988-89 : 9.

809. Excavation at Chirand, district Saran, Bihar. *Indian Archaeology : A Review,* 1980-81 : 9-10.

810. Excavation at Dangwada, district Ujjain, Madhya Pradesh. *Indian Archaeology : A Review,* 1979-80 : 54-55.

811. Excavation at Eran, district Sagar, Madhya Pradesh. *Indian Archaeology : A Review,* 1961-62 : 24-25.

812. Excavation at Eran, district Sagar, Madhya Pradesh. *Indian Archaeology : A Review,* 1963-64 : 15-16.

813. Excavation at Erich, district Jhansi, Uttar Pradesh. *Indian Archaeology : A Review*, 1989-90 : 100-101.

814. Excavation at Gilaulikhera, district Morena, Madhya Pradesh. *Indian Archaeology : A Review*, 1981-82 : 33-34.

815. Excavation at Gilaulikhera, district Morena, Madhya Pradesh. *Indian Archaeology : A Review*, 1983-84 : 51-52.

816. Excavation at Harsh-ka-Tila, Thanesar, district Kurukshetra, Haryana. *Indian Archaeology : A Review*, 1988-89 : 21-24.

817. Excavation at Harsh-ka-Tila, Thanesar, district Kurukshetra, Haryana. *Indian Archaeology : A Review*, 1989-90 : 27-32.

818. Excavation at Hulas, district Saharanpur, Uttar Pradesh. *Indian Archaeology : A Review*, 1978-79 : 60-61.

819. Excavation at Hulaskhera, district Lucknow, Uttar Pradesh. *Indian Archaeology : A Review*, 1978-79 : 39-40.

820. Excavation at Hulaskhera, district Lucknow, Uttar Pradesh. *Indian Archaeology : A Review*, 1979-80 : 77.

821. Excavation at Hulaskhera, district Lucknow, Uttar Pradesh. *Indian Archaeology : A Review*, 1980-81 : 71.

822. Excavation at Hulaskhera, district Lucknow, Uttar Pradesh. *Indian Archaeology : A Review*, 1981-82 : 71-72.

823. Excavation at Hulaskhera, district Lucknow, Uttar Pradesh. *Indian Archaeology : A Review*, 1982-83 : 98-99.

824. Excavation at Hulaskhera, district Lucknow, Uttar Pradesh. *Indian Archaeology : A Review*, 1983-84 : 88-89.

825. Excavation at Hulaskhera, district Lucknow, Uttar Pradesh. *Indian Archaeology : A Review*, 1985-86 : 82.

826. Excavation at Kaseri, district Meerut, Uttar Pradesh. *Indian Archaeology : A Review*, 1969-70 : 43.

827. Excavation at Khokhrakot, district Rohtak, Haryana. *Indian Archaeology : A Review,* 1986-87 : 34-36.

828. Excavation at Kolhua, district Vaishali, Bihar. *Indian Archaeology : A Review,* 1989-90 : 11-13.

829. Excavation at Mainahai, district Allahabad, Uttar Pradesh. *Indian Archaeology : A Review,* 1963-64 : 41-42.

830. Excavation at Mangalkot, district Burdwan, West Bengal. *Indian Archaeology : A Review,* 1987-88 : 111-114.

831. Excavation at Mangalkot, district Burdwan, West Bengal. *Indian Archaeology : A Review,* 1988-89 : 90-91.

832. Excavation at Mangalkot, district Burdwan, West Bengal. *Indian Archaeology : A Review,* 1989-90 : 108-110.

833. Excavation at Manwan, district Sitapur, Uttar Pradesh. *Indian Archaeology : A Review,* 1969-70 : 44.

834. Excavation at Masaon, district Ghazipur, Uttar Pradesh. *Indian Archaeology : A Review,* 1964-65 : 42-43.

835. Excavation at Masaon, district Ghazipur, Uttar Pradesh. *Indian Archaeology : A Review,* 1967-68 : 46-47.

836. Excavation at Nagari, district Chitorgarh, Rajasthan. *Indian Archaeology : A Review,* 1962-63 : 19-20.

837. Excavation at Nandur, district Raisen, Madhya Pradesh. *Indian Archaeology : A Review,* 1982-83 : 40.

838. Excavation at Pagara, district Dhar, Madhya Pradesh. *Indian Archaeology : A Review,* 1980-81 : 32-33.

839. Excavation at Purana Qila, Delhi. *Indian Archaeology : A Review,* 1969-70 : 4-6.

840. Excavation at Purana Qila, Delhi. *Indian Archaeology : A Review,* 1970-71 : 8-10.

841. Excavation at Raja Vishal-ka Gadh, district Vaishali, Bihar. *Indian Archaeology : A Review,* 1988-89 : 9.

842. Excavation at Rajbadidanga, district Murshidabad, West Bengal. *Indian Archaeology : A Review,* 1963-64 : 62-63.

843. Excavation at Rajghat, district Varanasi, Uttar Pradesh. *Indian Archaeology : A Review*, 1960-61 : 35-39.

844. Excavation at Rajghat, district Varanasi, Uttar Pradesh. *Indian Archaeology : A Review*, 1963-64 : 58.

845. Excavation at Runija, district Ujjain, Madhya Pradesh. *Indian Archaeology : A Review*, 1980-81 : 39.

846. Excavation at Sanghol, district Ludhiana, Punjab. *Indian Archaeology : A Review*, 1968-69 : 25-26.

847. Excavation at Sanghol, district Ludhiana, Punjab. *Indian Archaeology : A Review*, 1969-70 : 31-32.

848. Excavation at Sanghol, district Ludhiana, Punjab. *Indian Archaeology : A Review*, 1977-78 : 43-44.

849. Excavation at Sanghol, district Ludhiana, Punjab. *Indian Archaeology : A Review*, 1986-87 : 69-71.

850. Excavation at Sankara, district Aligarh, Uttar Pradesh. *Indian Archaeology : A Review*, 1960-61 : 32-33.

851. Excavation at Sonkh, district Mathura, Uttar Pradesh. *Indian Archaeology : A Review*, 1969-70 : 42-43.

852. Excavation at Sravasti, district Bahraich, Uttar Pradesh. *Indian Archaeology : A Review*, 1986-87 : 76.

853. Excavation at Sravasti, district Bahraich, Uttar Pradesh. *Indian Archaeology : A Review*, 1987-88 : 106-108.

854. Excavation at Sravasti, district Bahraich, Uttar Pradesh. *Indian Archaeology : A Review*, 1988-89 : 82-84.

855. Excavation at Sringaverpur, district Allahabad, Uttar Pradesh. *Indian Archaeology : A Review*, 1977-78 : 54-56.

856. Excavation at Sringaverpur, district Allahabad, Uttar Pradesh. *Indian Archaeology : A Review*, 1978-79 : 57-59.

857. Excavation at Sringaverpur, district Allahabad, Uttar Pradesh. *Indian Archaeology : A Review*, 1979-80 : 74.

858. Excavation at Sringaverpur, district Allahabad, Uttar Pradesh. *Indian Archaeology : A Review,* 1981-82 : 66-67.

859. Excavation at Sringaverpur, district Allahabad, Uttar Pradesh. *Indian Archaeology : A Review,* 1983-84 : 84-85.

860. Excavation at Sringaverpur, district Allahabad, Uttar Pradesh. *Indian Archaeology : A Review,* 1984-85 : 85-86.

861. Excavation at Sunet, district Ludhiana, Punjab. *Indian Archaeology : A Review,* 1983-84 : 67-70.

862. Excavation at Taradih, district Gaya, Bihar. *Indian Archaeology : A Review,* 1981-82 : 10-12.

863. Excavation at Taradih, district Gaya, Bihar. *Indian Archaeology : A Review,* 1982-83 : 16-25.

864. Excavation at Taradih, district Gaya, Bihar. *Indian Archaeology : A Review,* 1983-84 : 12-13.

865. Excavation at Taradih, (Bodh-Gaya), district Gaya, Bihar. *Indian Archaeology : A Review,* 1985-86 : 7-9.

866. Excavation at Taradih, (Bodh-Gaya), district Gaya, Bihar. *Indian Archaeology : A Review,* 1986-87 : 23-24.

867. Excavation at Taradih, (Bodh-Gaya), district Gaya, Bihar. *Indian Archaeology : A Review,* 1987-88 : 9-11.

868. Excavation at Taradih, (Bodh-Gaya), district Gaya, Bihar. *Indian Archaeology : A Review,* 1988-89 : 6-7.

869. Excavation at Thanesar, district Kurukshetra, Haryana. *Indian Archaeology : A Review,* 1987-88 : 28-31.

870. Excavation at Tumain, district Guna, Madhya Pradesh. *Indian Archaeology : A Review,* 1972-73 : 15-16.

871. Excavation at Virabhadra Temple-site, Rishikesh, district Dehradun, Uttar Pradesh. *Indian Archaeology : A Review,* 1973-74 : 28-30.

872. Excavations : Kumrahar, district Patna, Bihar. *Indian Archaeology : A Review,* 1953-54 : 9-10.

873. Exploration and excavations—Madhya Pradesh. *Puratan*, Vol. 1, 1984 : 89-115.

874. Exploration in district Ajmer, Rajasthan. *Indian Archaeology : A Review*, 1962-63 : 18.

875. Exploration in districts Basti, Deoria and Gorakhpur, Uttar Pradesh. *Indian Archaeology : A Review*, 1963-64 : 45.

876. Exploration in districts Bhairwa and Taulihawa, Nepal. *Indian Archaeology : A Review*, 1961-62 : 70-72.

877. Exploration in district Bhilawara, Rajasthan. *Indian Archaeology : A Review*, 1980-81 : 55.

878. Exploration in district Fatehpur, Uttar Pradesh. *Indian Archaeology : A Review*, 1979-80 : 77.

879. Exploration in district Junagadh, Gujarat. *Indian Archaeology : A Review*, 1967-68 : 13.

880. Exploration in district Mandasor, Madhya Pradesh. *Indian Archaeology : A Review*, 1965-66 : 22.

881. Exploration in district Murshidabad, West Bengal. *Indian Archaeology : A Review*, 1971-72 : 50.

882. Exploration in district Sangrur, Punjab. *Indian Archaeology : A Review*, 1974-75 : 37.

883. Exploration in district Saran, Bihar. *Indian Archaeology : A Review*, 1962-63 : 6.

884. Exploration in district 24-Parganas, West Bengal. *Indian Archaeology : A Review*, 1965-66 : 59-60.

885. Exploration in district 24-Parganas, West Bengal. *Indian Archaeology : A Review*, 1971-72 : 51.

886. Exploration in district Udaipur, Rajasthan. *Indian Archaeology : A Review*, 1961-62 : 44-45.

887. Exploration in district Ujjain, Madhya Pradesh. *Indian Archaeology : A Review*, 1979-80 : 53-54.

888. **Garg, Lalit Mohan**
Navadevakula. *Journal of the Uttar Pradesh Historical Society*, Vol. 23, 1950 : 175-188.

889. Gupta and later remains, Nachna, district Panna, Madhya Pradesh. *Indian Archaeology : A Review,* 1962-63 : 69.

890. Gupta inscription, Than, district Surendranagar, Gujarat. *Indian Archaeology : A Review,* 1989-90 : 123.

891. **Handa, Devendra**
Sunet : An ancient city of Panjab. *Vishveshvaranand Indological Journal*, Vol. 8, 1970 : 172-176.

892. **Hargreaves, H.**
Excavations at Sarnath. *Archaeological Survey of India Annual Report*, 1914-15 : 97-131.

893. **Hartel, Herbert**
Excavations at Sonkh (Mathura district) 1969-70. *Bulletin of Museums & Archaeology in U.P.*, Nos. 5-6, June-December 1970 : 1-4.

894. ______.
Excavations at Sonkh : 2500 years of a town in Mathura district. Berlin, Dietrich Reimer Verlag, 1993.

895. **Heras, H.**
A note on the excavations at Nalanda and its history. *Journal of the Bombay Branch of the Royal Asiatic Society*, New Series, Vol. 2, No. 2, 1926 : 214-218.

896. **Husain, Shahanara**
Paharpur and its material contents. *Journal of the Asiatic Society of Pakistan*, Vol. 6, 1961 : 1-10.

897. **Jain, Jyoti Prasad**
Deogarh aur uska kala vaibhav. *Jain Siddhanta Bhaskar*, Vol. 22, No. 1, June 1955 : 11-22 (Hindi).

898. **Joshi, N.P.**
Two days with the scholar at Deogarh. In Devendra Handa and Ashvini Agrawal, ed., *Ratna-Chandrika : Panorama of Oriental studies (Shri R.C. Agrawala festschrift)*. New Delhi, Harman Publishing House, 1989 : 167-174.

899. **Kala, S.C.**
Antiquities from Jhusi in the Allahabad Museum. *Journal of Indian Museums*, Vols. 14-16, 1958-60 : 1-9.

900. **Krishna, C.**
A small scale archaeological excavations at Sarangapur. *Puratan*, Vol. 7, 1989 : 14-17.

901. **Krishna Deva** and **Mishra, Vijayakanta**
Vaisali excavations : 1950. Vaisali, Vaisali Sangh, 1961.

902. **Krishnamurthy, C.** and **Gururaja Rao, B.K.**
Recent trends in Indian archaeology. *Archaeological Society of South India Transactions* for the year 1959-60 : 79-98.

903. **Margabandhu, C.** and **Gaur, G.S.**
Sanghol excavations 1987 : Some new evidences. *Puratattva*, No. 17, 1986-87 : 1-4.

904. **Marshall, J.H.**
Excavations at Bhita. *Archaeological Survey of India Annual Report*, 1911-12 : 29-94.

905. **Marshall, J.H.** and **Konow, S.**
Sarnath. *Archaeological Survey of India Annual Report*, 1906-07 : 68-101.

906. **Marshall, John**
Monuments of Snachi : Their exploration and conservation. *Archaeological Survey of India Annual Report*, 1913-14 : 1-39.

907. **Mukhopadhyay, Samir Kumar**
On the downfall of the city of Bhita. *Monthly Bulletin of the Asiatic Society*, Vol. 5, No. 5, May 1970 : 6.

908. **Narain, A.K.**
Excavations at Rajghat (1957-58 ; 1960-65). Varanasi, Banaras Hindu University, 1976-1978. 4 pts.

909. **Narain, R.B.**
Archaeological excavations at Masaon (Ghazipur district), 1965. *Bulletin of Museums & Archaeology in U.P.*, No. 1, March 1968 : 30-32.

910. **Nautiyal, K.P.**
The archaeology of Kumaon (including Dehradun). Varanasi, Chaukhamba Amarabharati Prakashan, 1969.

911. **Oertel, F.O.**
Excavations at Sarnath. *Archaeological Survey of India Annual Report*, 1904-05 : 59-104.

912. **Page, J.A.**
Nalanda excavations. *Journal of the Bihar and Orissa Research Society*, Vol. 9, pt. 1, 1923 : 1-22.

913. **Paul, R.K.**
Ahicchatra as known through archaeology. *Panchala*, Vol. 2, 1986 : 47-54.

914. **Prakash, V.** and **Roy, T.N.**
Sites and monuments of U.P. *Bulletin of the U.P. Historical Society*, No. 4, 1965.

915. **Purushottam Singh**
Early historical archaeology of Uttar Pradesh—Recent discoveries. *Journal of the Bihar Research Society*, Vols. 65-66 : 1979-80 : 132-154.

916. **Rai, Subhash** and **Sharma, Jagmohan**
Hulaskhera ke Sunga-Kusana-Guptakalin masale ka vaigyanik adhyayana. *Dhyanam*, Vol. 4, 1984 : 49-52 (Hindi).

917. **Rana, R.S.**
A new light on Jhusi culture in Allahabad, U.P. *Puratattva*, No. 17, 1986-87 : 60.

918. **Rao, S.R.**
Excavations at Amreli : A Kshatrapa-Gupta town. *Bulletin Museum & Picture Gallery, Baroda*, Vol. 18, 1966.

919. ——.
Recent exploration in Gujarat and Kathiawad. *All India Oriental Conference Proceedings*, Session 17, 1953 : 342-348.

920. **Roy, Sita Ram**
Ceramic industries of Bihar in the Gupta period. *Indian History Congress Proceedings*, Session 32, Vol. 1, 1970 : 50-53.

921. ______.
A note on ceramic industry in Bihar. *Marg*, Vol. 14, No. 3, June 1961 : 55-56.

922. **Sankalia, H.D.**
The archaeology of Gujarat (including Kathiawar). Bombay, Natwarlal & Co., 1941.

923. **Sharan, Pramod Kant**
An introduction to Agroha excavation (Haryana). *Journal of the Bihar Puravid Parisad*, Vols. 4-5, 1980-81 : 207-209.

924. **Sharma, R.K.**
Excavation at Gilaulikhera-1982 (A brief report). *Prachya Pratibha*, Vols. 9-10, 1981-82 : 5-9.

925. **Sharma, R.K.** and **Ali, Rahman**
Archaeology of Bhopal region. Delhi, Agam Kala Prakashan, 1980.

926. **Sharma, R.S.**
Decay of Gangetic towns in Gupta and post Gupta times. *Indian History Congress Proceedings*, Session 33, 1972 : 92-104.

927. ______.
Decay of Gangetic towns in Gupta and post-Gupta times. *Journal of Indian History*, Golden Jubilee Volume, 1973 : 135-150.

928. **Sherring, M.A.**
Some account of ancient remains at Saidpur and Bhitari. *Journal of the Asiatic Society of Bengal*, Vol. 34, pt. 1, 1865 : 80-90.

929. **Shukla, B.C.**
Archaeological findings from Durvasa. *Journal of the Ganganatha Jha Kendriya Sanskrit Vidyapeetha*, Vol. 43, 1987 : 99-105.

930. **Shukla, K.S.**
Archaeology of Unnao district. Delhi, B.R. Publishing Corporation, 1986.

931. **Singh, Arun Kumar**
Archeology of Magadha region. New Delhi, Ramanand Vidya Bhawan, 1991.

932. **Singh, Ravindra N.** and **Saran, Santosh.**
A note on glass objects from Gupta levels. *Bharati*, New Series, No. 1, 1983 : 155-158.

933. **Singh, Sarva Daman** and **Singh, Sheo Bahadur**
The archaeology of Lucknow region. Lucknow, Paritosh Prakashan, 1972.

934. **Singh, Sheo Bahadur**
Archaeology of Etah district. *Panchala*, Vol. 3, 1988 : 1-11.

935. ———.
Archaeology of Panchala region. Delhi, Agam Kala Prakashan, 1979.

936. ———.
The Panchala Desa—a historical appraisal. *Kurukshetra University Research Journal*, (*Arts and Humanities*), Vol. 9, 1975 : 1-9.

937. **Singh, Udai Vir**
Excavation at Eran. *Journal of the Madhya Pradesh Itihasa Parishad*, No. 4, 1962 : 41-44.

938. ———.
Further excavations at Eran. *Journal of the Madhya Pradesh Itihasa Parishad*, No. 5, 1967 : 19-27.

939. **Sinha, B.P.** and **Roy, Sita Ram**
Vaisali excavations 1958-1962. Patna, Directorate of Archaeology and Museums, 1969.

940. **Soundara Rajan, K.V.**
Mechanics of city & village in ancient India. Delhi, Sundeep Prakashan, 1986.

941. **Srivastava, Prashant**
The site of the Buddha's descent from the Trayastrimsa heaven. *Panchala*, Vol. 7, 1994 : 95-97.

942. **Taddei, Maurizio**
India. Geneva, Nagel Publishers, 1970.

943. Temple-remains in district Panchmahals, Maharashtra. *Indian Archaeology : A Review*, 1958-59 : 70.

944. **Thakur, Upendra**
Comments and observations on the lead-paper of S.R. Goyal. In M.C. Joshi and S.K. Gupta, *ed., King Chandra and the Meharauli Pillar*. Meerut, Kusumanjali Prakashan, 1989 : 187-189.

945. **Thakur, V.K.**
The post-Kushana urban decline of India : Implications of ecology. *Indian History Congress Proceedings*, Session 53, 1992-93 : 97-105.

946. **Thakur, Vijay Kumar** and **Jha, Kalpana**
Towns in the Samarachchakaha : A study in the early medieval tradition of urbanism in India. *Journal of the Bihar Research Society*, Vols. 69-70, 1983-84 : 257-302.

947. **Tiwari, Rakesh**
Hulaskhera ka purattatvik utkhanan. *Dhyanam*, Vol. 4, 1984 : 35-43 (Hindi).

948. **Tiwari, Rakesh,** and **Srivastava, Rakesh**
Hulaskhera utkhanan 1983-84. *Bulletin of Museums & Archaeology in U.P.*, Nos. 35-36, June-December 1985 : 59-63 (Hindi).

949. **Tripathi, Krishna Kumar**
Vidisha ka sanskritik itihas. *Prachya Pratibha*, Vol. 12, 1984 : 141-151 (Hindi).

950. **Trivedi, P.K.**
Archaeology of Aguncha. *Prachya Pratibha*, Vol. 12, 1984 : 111-113.

951. **Verma, B.S.**
Archaeological excavations and sites. In Bindeshwari Prasad Sinha, ed., *Comprehensive history of Bihar*, Vol.1, pt. II. Patna, K.P. Jayaswal Research Institute, 1974 : 530-560.

952. **Wakankar, V.S.**
Runija excavation-1981. *Prachya Pratibha*, Vol. 8, 1980 : 27-31.

EPIGRAPHY

953. **Agrawal, Ashvini**
The terms *Viharasvamin* and *Viharasvamini* in the Buddhist inscriptions of the Kushana and the Gupta periods. In Ajay Mitra Shastri and others, ed., *Visvambhara : Probings in Orientology. (Prof. V.S. Pathak festschrift)*, Vol. I. New Delhi, Harman Publishing House, 1955 : 116-119.

954. **Agrawal, Jagannath**
Comments and observations on the lead-paper of S.R. Goyal. In M.C. Joshi and S.K. Gupta, ed., *King Chandra and the Meharauli Pillar*. Meerut, Kusumanjali Prakashan, 1989 : 95-104.

955. ______.
A disputed reading in the Bhitari stone pillar inscription of Skandagupta. *Vishveshvaranand Indological Journal*, Vol. 20, 1982 : 184-187.

956. ______.
On the text and tradition of a verse in the Bhitari inscription of Skandagupta. *Vishveshvaranand Indological Journal*, Vol. 25, 1987 : 155-156.

957. ______.
A passage in the Sarnath inscription of Kumaragupta and Budhagupta. *Vishveshvaranand Indological Journal*, Vol. 15, pt. 1, 1977 : 121-122.

958. ______.
Researches in Indian epigraphy and numismatics. Delhi, Sundeep Prakashan, 1986.

959. ______.
Sanghol stone inscription. *Vishveshvaranand Indological Journal*, Vol. 8, 177-178.

960. ______.
Some further observations on the Eran inscription of Samudra Gupta. *Indian History Congress Proceedings*, Session 29, Part I, 1967 : 61-67.

961. ______
Some observations on the Bihar stone pillar inscription. *Journal of Oriental Institute*, Vol. 20, No. 1, September 1970 : 44-47.

962. ______.
Some observations on the Bhitari stone pillar inscription of Skandagupta. *Vishveshvaranand Indological Journal*, Vol. 17, 1979 : 192-195.

963. ______.
Some observations on the Mehrauli iron pillar. *Annals of the Bhandarkar Oriental Research Institute*. Vol. 51, 1970 : 189-191.

964. **Agrawala, P.K.,** ed.
Imperial Gupta epigraphs. Varanasi, Books Asia, 1983.

965. ______.
Some epigraphical notes. *Bharati*, No. 15, 1971-84 : 238-242.

966. **Ahmad, Nisar**
The Bihar stone inscription of the Guptas : Some obersavations. *Indian History Congress Proceedings*, Session 52, 1992 : 1022-1025.

967. ______.
The Gadhwa inscriptions of the Guptas : Some observations. In C. Margabandhu and K.S. Ramachandran, ed.,. *Spectrum of Indian culture : Professor S.B. Deo felicitation volume*, Vol. II. Delhi, Agam Kala Prakashan, 1996 : 324-330.

968. **Aiyangar, S.K.**
Extracts from some earlier suggestions on the problem. In M.C. Joshi and S.K. Gupta, ed., *King Chandra and the Meharauli Pillar*. Meerut, Kusumanjali Prakashan, 1989 : 248.

969. **Allan, John**
Extracts from some earlier suggestions on the problem. In M.C. Joshi and S.K. Gupta, ed., *King Chandra and the Meharauli Pillar*. Meerut, Kusumanjali Prakashan, 1989 : 244.

970. **Altekar, A.S.**
Mangraon inscription of Vishnugupta's time ; The year 17. *Epigraphia Indica*, Vol. 26, 1941-42 : 241-246.

971. ______.
Patna Museum third plate of Pravarasena II. *Journal of the Bihar and Orissa Research Society*, Vol. 14, pt. 4, December 1928 : 465-475.

972. **Bajpai, K.D.**
Comments and observations on the lead paper of S.R. Goyal. In M.C. Joshi and S.K. Gupta, ed., *King Chandra and the Meharauli Pillar*. Meerut, Kusumanjali Prakashan, 1989 : 105-111.

973. ______.
Identification of Vanga and Vahlika in the Mehrauli Iron Pillar inscription. In G.T. Deshpande and others, ed., *Felicitation volume presented to Mahamahopadhyaya Dr. V.V. Mirashi*. Nagpur, Vidarbha Samshodhan Mandal, 1965 : 355-361.

974. ______.
King Chandra of the Mehrauli inscription. *Prachya Pratibha*, Vol. 13, 1985-87 : 96-100.

975. ______.
A note on `Svabhoganagara' in the Eran inscription of Skandagupta. *Bulletin of Ancient Indian History and Archaeology*, No. 1, 1967 : 69-70.

976. **Bajpai, K.D., Agarwal, K.L.** and **Bajpai, Santosh,** *ed*.
Etihasik Bharatiya abhilekha. Jaipur, Publications Scheme, 1992 (Hindi).

977. **Bajpai, S.K.**
Bagh hoard of copper plate inscriptions. *Journal of the Epigraphical Society of India*, Vol. 10, 1983 : 86-89.

978. ———.
Bagh hoard of copper plate inscriptions. *Puratan*. Vol. 1, 1984 : 20-24.

979. ———.
New epigraphical light on the history of Madhya Pradesh. *Journal of the Epigraphical Society of India*, Vol. 7, 1980 : 93-97.

980. **Bakker, Hans and Isaacson, Harunaga**
The Ramtek inscriptions II : The Vakataka inscription in the Kevala-Narasimha temple. *Bulletin of the School of Oriental and African Studies*, Vol. 56, pt. 1, 1993 : 46-74.

981. **Bandyopadhyay, Saikat**
Scribes and engravers of ancient Indian inscriptions (3rd century B.C. to 6th century A.D.). *Indian Museum Bulletin*, Vol. 14, 1979 : 74-81.

982. **Bandyopadhyay, Samaresh**
Sanchi stone inscription of Candragupta II. *Journal of Ancient Indian History*, Vol. 4, 1970-71 : 214-217.

983. **Bandyopadhyaya, Rakhala Dasa**
Two inscriptions of Kumaragupta I. *Journal & Proceedings of the Asiatic Society of Bengal*, New Series, Vol. 5, 1909 : 457-461.

984. **Banerjee, Manabendu**
Inscriptional evidences of Gupta art. *Journal of the Oriental Institute*, Vol. 32, Nos. 3-4, March-June 1983 : 293-299.

985. ———.
Inscriptional evidences of Vedicism during the rule of the early Gupta monarchs. *Anviksa*, Vol. 14, 1991-1993 : 30-35.

986. ———.
Sanskrit Inscriptions as the source of the political history of India under the rule of the Gupta kings. *Anviksa*, Vol. 9, 1986 : 1-9.

987. ———.
A study of important Gupta inscriptions Calcutta, Sanskrit Pustak Bhandar, 1976.

988. **Banerjee, Priyatosh**
The Patna Museum inscription dated in the year 17 of the reign of Visnugupta (c. 700 A.D.). *Journal of the Bihar Research Society*, Vol. 30, pt. 2, June 1944 : 199-202.

989. **Banerji, Adris**
A survey of epigraphical material found at Sarnath, *Journal of the Oriental Research, Madras*, Vol. 24, 1954-1955 : 44-51.

990. **Banerji, R.D.**
Four forged grants from Faridpur. *Journal & Proceedings of the Asiatic Society of Bengal*, New Series, Vol. 10, 1914 : 425-437.

991. ———
A note on king Chandra of the Mehrauli inscription. *Epigraphia Indica*, Vol. 14, pt. 8, October 1918 : 367-371.

992. **Basak, Radhagovinda**
Baigram copper-plate inscription of the (Gupta)-year 128. *Epigraphia Indica*, Vol. 21, 1931-32 : 78-83.

993. ———.
Dhanaidaha copper-plate inscription of the time of Kumaragupta I : The year 113. *Epigraphia Indica*, Vol. 17, pt. 8, October 1924 : 345-348.

994. ———.
Extracts from some earlier suggestions on the problem. In M.C. Joshi and S.K. Gupta, ed., *King Chandra and the Meharauli Pillar*. Meerut, Kusumanjali Prakashan, 1989 : 249.

995. ———
The five Damodarpur copper-plate inscriptions of the Gupta period. *Epigraphia Indica*, Vol. 15, 1919-20 : 113-145.

996. Base of a pillar. Bharat Kala Bhawan, Varanasi, Uttar Pradesh. *Annual Report on Indian Epigraphy*, 1952-53 : 73 (B-456).

997. **Basham, A.L.**
The Mandasor inscription of the silk-weavers. In Bardwell L. Smith, ed., *Essays on Gupta culture*, Missouri, South Asia Books, 1983 : 93-105.

998. ______.
Some observations on the theory of S.R. Goyal. In M.C. Joshi and S.K. Gupta, ed., *King Chandra and the Meharauli Pillar*. Meerut, Kusumanjali Prakashan, 1989 : 199.

999. **Basu, Saktiprasad**
Kushana Brahmi alphabet—a prototype of Gupta Brahmi. *Indian History Congress Proceedings*, Session 19, 1956 : 176-177.

1000. **Beames, John**
Copper-plate grant from Kapalesvara in Orissa. *Indian Antiquary*, Vol. 5, February 1876 : 55-60.

1001. **Bhandarkar, D.R.**
Identification of the princes and territories mentioned in the Allahabad pillar inscription of Samudragupta. *Indian Historical Quarterly*, Vol. 1, No. 2, June 1925 : 250-260.

1002. ______.
A Kushana stone-inscription and the question about the origin of the Saka era. *Journal of the Bombay Branch of the Asiatic Society*, Vol. 20, 1897-1900. : 269-302.

1003. ______.
Mathura pillar inscription of Chandragupta II : G.E. 61. *Epigraphia Indica*, Vol. 21, 1931-32 : 1-9.

1004. ______.
Meharauli pillar inscription of Chandra. *Indian Culture*, Vol. 3, No. 3, January 1937 : 511-513.

1005. **Bhandarkar, D.R., Chhabra, B.Ch. and Gai, G.S.**
The inscription of king Chandra : Text and translation. In M.C. Joshi and S.K. Gupta, ed., *King Chandra and the Meharauli Pillar*. Meerut, Kusumanjali Prakashan, 1989 : 67-68.

1006. **Bhatt, Madan Chandra**
Badrinath taamrapatra ka Chandragupta, *Kosala*, Vol. 2, 1979-1980 : 27-31 (Hindi).

1007. **Bhattacharyya, D.C.**
A newly discovered copper-plate from Tippera. *Indian Historical Quarterly*, Vol. 6, No. 1, March 1930 : 45-60.

1008. **Bhattacharyya, Suresh Chandra**
A note on an expression in the Allahabad Prasasti of Samudragupta. *Indian History Congress Proceedings*, Session 24, 1961 : 50-53.

1009. Bhattakapatra grant of Dharasena II of Valabhi dated Saka 257, a decisive test of the starting point of Gupta era. *Annual Report of the Mysore Archaeological Department for the year 1927* : 27-30.

1010. **Bhattasali, N.K.**
The Ghugrahati copper-plate inscription of Samachara-Deva. *Epigraphia Indica*, Vol. 18, 1925-26 : 74-86.

1011. **Bindeshwari Prasad**
Some fresh lights on Mehrauli iron-pillar inscription of Chandra. *Indian History Congress Proceedings*, Session 6, 1943 : 124-127.

1012. **Bireshwar Singh**
Nalanda plate of Samudragupta : A reconsideration. *Journal of the Bihar Research Society*, Vol. 47, 1961 : 330-335.

1013. **Bose, Sushil K.**
A new type of *h* in the Magadhan Gupta alphabet. *Indian Historical Quarterly*, Vol. 13, No. 4, December 1937 : 713-716.

1014. ———.
Studies in Gupta paleography. *Indian Culture*, Vol. 4, No. 2, October 1937 : 181-188.

1015. ———.
Studies in Gupta paleography. *Indian Culture*, Vol. 4, No. 3, January 1938 : 325-346.

1016. Boulder near the Kaulesvari temple. Kuluha, Hazaribagh district, Bihar. *Annual Report on Indian Epigraphy*, 1953-54 : 30 (C-113).

1017. **Buddha Prakash**
"Daiva-putra-sahi-sahanusahi" in the Allahabad pillar inscription of Samudragupta. *Indian Historical Quarterly*, Vol. 33, No. 2, June 1957 : 119-128.

1018. ———.
The reference to the "Daiva-putra-sahi-sahanusahi" in the Allahabad inscription of Samudragupta. *Indian History Congress Proceedings*, Session 19, 1956 : 144-145.

1019. **Buhler, G.**
Indian inscriptions and the antiquity of Indian artificial poetry. *Journal of Ancient Indian History*, Vol. 2, 1968-69 : 188-236.

1020. ———.
Indian paleography from about B.C. 350 to about A.D. 1300. *Indian Studies : Past & Present*, Vol. 1, 1959-60 : 15-138.

1021. **Burgess, Jas**
Chandragupta and Vikramaditya. *Indian Antiquary*, Vol. 14, 1885 : 61.

1022. **Chakraborti, H.P.**
Crafts and industries as reflected in the inscriptions of the Gupta period. *Indian History Congress Proceedings*, Session 35, 1974 : 77-80.

1023. **Chakravarti, Ranabir** and **Sinha, Gopal Chandra**
A note on the Tumain inscription of Kumaragupta I, G.E. 116. *Indian Museum Bulletin*, Vol. 20, 1985 : 46-48.

1024. **Chakravarti, S.N.**
Development of the Bengali alphabet from the fifth century A.D. to the end of the Muhammadan rule. *Journal of the Royal Asiatic Society of Bengal, Letters*, Vol. 4, 1938 : 351-391.

1025. Charter of Jivagupta, district Darbhanga, Bihar. *Indian Archaeology : A Review*, 1958-59 : 59.

1026. **Chhabra, B. Ch.**

Allahabad inscription of Samudragupta is not posthumous. *Indian Historical Quarterly*, Vol. 24, No. 2, June 1948 : 104-113.

1027. ———.

Beauties of the Bhitari inscription of Skandagupta. In G.T. Deshpande and others, ed., *Felicitation volume presented to Mahamahopadhyaya Dr. V.V. Mirashi*. Nagpur, Vidarbha Samshodhan Mandal, 1965 : 362-371.

1028. ———.

Comments and observations on the lead paper of S.R. Goyal. In M.C. Joshi and S.K. Gupta, ed., *King Chandra and the Meharauli Pillar*. Meerut, Kusumanjali Prakashan, 1989 : 92.

1029. ———.

Lakhamandal fragmentary stone inscription of the Gupta period. *Journal of United Provinces Historical Society*, Vol. 17, pt. 1, July 1944 : 80-83.

1030. ———.

More light on Ghumli plates ; Gupta Samvat 513. *Epigraphia Indica*, Vol. 28, 1949-50 : 77-79.

1031. ———.

A note on Tumain inscriptions. *Journal of Oriental Research, Madras*, Vol. 17, pt. 4, June 1948 : 205-208.

1032. ———.

Some observations on the Bhitari inscription of Skandagupta. *Journal of Indian History,* Vol. 41, pt. 2, August 1963 : 543-549.

1033. **Chhabra, B.Ch., Rao, N. Lakshminarayan and Husain, M. Ashraf**

Ten years of Indian Epigraphy. (1937-46). *Ancient India*, No. 5, 1949 : 46-61.

1034. **Cunningham, A.**

Note on the Bactro-Pali inscription from Taxila. *Journal of the Royal Asiatic Society of Bengal*, Vol. 33, 1864 : 35-38.

1035. **Daji, Bhau**

Facsimile, transcript and translation of the "Sah" or Rudra Dama inscriptionon a rock at Junagur ; also of one of Skandagupta on the northern face of the rock ; with some brief remarks on the Sah, Gupta and Valabhi dynasties. *Journal of the Bombay Branch of the Royal Asiatic Society*, Vol 7, 1861-63 : 113-131.

1036. ______

Revised inscription on the Delhi "Iron" (metal) Pillar at Kootub Minar, with remarks. *Journal of the Bombay Branch of the Royal Asiatic Society*, Vol. 10, 1871-1874 : 63-65.

1037. ______.

Revised translation of the inscription on the Bhitari Lat. *Journal of the Bombay Branch of the Royal Asiatic Society*, Vol. 10, 1871-1874 : 59-62.

1038. **Das, Kalyani**

Early inscriptions of Mathura—a study. Calcutta, Punthi Pustak, 1980.

1039. **Das Gupta, Jayanti**

Davaka. *Journal of U. P. Historical Society*, New Series, Vol. 9, pt. 2, 1961 : 107-109.

1040. **Deo, S.B.**

Comments and observations on the lead-paper of S.R. Goyal. In M.C. Joshi and S.K. Gupta, ed., *King Chandra and the Meharauli Pillar*. Meerut, Kusumanjali Prakashan, 1989 : 149.

1041. **Dikshit, K.N.**

A note on the dates of the Gupta copper-plates from Damodarpur. *Epigraphia Indica*, Vol. 17, 1923 : 193.

1042. ______.

Paharpur copper-plate grant of the (Gupta) year 159. *Epigraphia Indica*, Vol. 20, 1929-30 : 59-64.

1043. **Diskalkar, D.B.**

The date of the Eran inscription of Toramana. *Journal of the Bombay Branch of the Royal Asiatic Society*, Vol. 2, No. 2, 1926 : 180-182.

1044. ———.
A new inscription of Candragupta II of G.S. 61 found in Mathura. *Annals of the Bhandarkar Oriental Research Institute*. Vol. 18, pt. 2, January 1937 : 166-170.

1045. ———.
Who is the Kumaragupta of the Mandsor inscription of M.S. 529 ? *Journal of the Bombay Branch of the Royal Asiatic Society*, New Series, Vol. 2, No. 2, 1926 : 176-178.

1046. **Diwekar, H.R.**
The Allahabad Prasasti and the Asvamedha. *Annals of the Bhandarkar Institute*. Vol. 7, pts. 1-2, 1925-26 : 164-165.

1047. ———.
Pusyamitras in Gupta period. *Annals of the Bhandarkar Institute*. Vol. 1, pt. 2, 1919-20 : 99-103.

1048. Door-screen near the eastern entrance of the great stupa, Sanchi, Madhya Pradesh. *Annual Report on Indian Epigraphy*, 1961-62 : 60 (B-146).

1049. **Dwivedi, Harihar Niwas**
Gwalior Rajya ke abhilekh. Gwalior, Madhya Bharat Puratattva Vibhag, 1947 (Hindi).

1050. Facade of cave No. 6 and 7, Udayagiri. *Annual Report on Indian Epigraphy*, 1961-62 : 175 (c. 1717-1718).

1051. **Fleet, J.F.**
Bhadrabahu, Chandragupta, and Sravana-Belgola. *Indian Antiquary*, Vol. 21, 1892 : 156-160.

1052. ———.
Bhitari seal of Kumaragupta II. *Indian Antiquary*, Vol. 19, 1890 : 224-228.

1053. ———.
The inscription of king Chandra : Text, translation and comments. In M.C. Joshi and S.K. Gupta, ed., *King Chandra and the Meharauli Pillar*. Meerut, Kusumanjali Prakashan, 1989 : 61-64.

1054. ______.
Inscriptions of the early Gupta kings. New Delhi, Archaeological Survey of India, 1981 (Corpus Inscriptionum Indicarum, Vol. III).

1055. ______.
Mandasor inscription of Kumaragupta and Bandhuvarman. *Indian Antiquary*, Vol. 15, 1886 : 194-201.

1056. Fragments of a stone slab in the Indian Museum, Calcutta, West Bengal . *Annual Report on Indian Epigraphy*, 1974-75 : 38 (C-3932).

1057. **Gai, G.S.**
Introduction to Indian epigraphy. Mysore, Central Institute of Indian Languages, 1986.

1058. ______.
Note on the Indore plates of Pravarasena II. *Journal of the Epigraphical Society of India*, Vol. 5, 1978 : 98-102.

1059. ______.
Three inscriptions of Ramagupta. *Epigraphia Indica*, Vol. 38, 1969-70 : 46-49.

1060. ______.
Three inscriptions of Ramagupta. *Journal of the Oriental Institute*, Vol. 18, No. 3, March 1969 : 247-251.

1061. ______.
The use of *B* for *V* and vice versa in early inscriptions. *Journal of the Ganganatha Jha Research Institute*, Vol. 6, pt. 4, August 1949 : 308-309.

1062. **Ganguly, D.C.**
A note on the Bhumara stone pillar inscription of the time of the Imperial Guptas. *Indian Historical Quarterly*, Vol. 21, No. 2, June 1945 : 138-140.

1063. **Garde, M.B.**
Mandasor inscription of Malava Samvat 524. *Epigraphia Indica*, Vol. 27, 1947-48 : 12-18.

1064. ______.
A new Gupta inscription. *Indian Antiquary*, Vol. 49, 1920 : 114-115.

1065. ______.
Tumain inscription of Kuamaragupta and Ghatotkachagupta, G.E. 116. *Epigraphia Indica*, Vol. 26, 1941-42 : 115-118.

1066. **Ghosh, A.**
Kosam stone image inscription of Maharaja Bhimavarman. The year 130. *Indian Culture*, Vol. 3, No. 1, July 1936 : 177-183.

1067. ______.
Nalanda plate of Samudragupta : The year 5. *Epigraphia Indica*, Vol. 25, 1939-40 : 50-53.

1068. **Ghosh, Jogendra Chandra**
Note on the Nandapur copper-plate of the Gupta year 169. *Epigraphia Indica*, Vol. 24, 1937-38 : 126-129.

1069. **Gopal, Lallanji** and **Gopal, Krishna Kanti**
Comments and observations on the lead paper of S.R. Goyal. In M.C. Joshi and S.K. Gupta, ed., *King Chandra and the Meharauli Pillar*. Meerut, Kusumanjali Prakashan, 1989 : 124-134.

1070. **Goswami, Krishnapada**
Place-names of Bengal. *Journal of the Department of Letters*, Vol. 33 : 1-70.

1071. **Goswami, Kunja Gobinda**
Role of epigraphy in Oriental studies. *Indian Museum Bulletin*, Vol. 22, 1987 : 30-33.

1072. **Goyal, S.R.**
Bihar stone pillar inscriptions of the Imperial Guptas. *Journal of the Epigraphical Society of India*, Vol. 7, 1980 : 49-53.

1073. ______.
Guptakalina abhilekha. Meerut, Kusumanjali Prakashan, 1984 (Hindi).

1074. ———.
The inscription of king Chandra : Text and translation. In M.C. Joshi and S.K. Gupta, ed., *King Chandra and the Meharauli Pillar*. Meerut, Kusumanjali Prakashan, 1989 : 69-70.

1075. ———.
Nalanda and Gaya records of Samudragupta. *Journal of the Bihar Research Society*, Vol. 52, 1966 : 52-55.

1076. ———.
Problem of the identification of king Chandra. In M.C. Joshi and S.K. Gupta, ed., *King Chandra and the Meharauli Pillar*. Meerut, Kusumanjali Prakashan, 1989 : 75-81.

1077. ———.
Re-appraisal of the problem of the identification of king Chandra. In M.C. Joshi and S.K. Gupta, ed., *King Chandra and the Meharauli Pillar*. Meerut, Kusumanjali Prakashan, 1989 : 207-237.

1078. **Goyal, Shankar**
Comments and observations on the lead paper of S.R. Goyal. In M.C. Joshi and S.K. Gupta, ed., *King Chandra and the Meharauli Pillar*. Meerut, Kusumanjali Prakashan, 1989 : 150-156.

1079. Gupta Inscription, Besnagar (Vidisha), district Vidisha, Madhya Pradesh, *Indian Archaeology : A Review*, 1977-78 : 80.

1080. Gupta Inscription, Garhwa Fort (Sheorajpur), district Allahabad, Uttar Pradesh, *Indian Archaeology : A Review*, 1977-78 : 83.

1081. Gupta Inscription, Kedarnath, district Chamoli, Uttar Pradesh, *Indian Archaeology : A Review*, 1977-78 : 83.

1082. **Gupta, P.L.**
Bihar ke shilalekh aur tamrapat. *Parishad Patrika*, Vol. 22, No. 3, October 1982 : 49-62 (Hindi).

1083. ———.
On the dates of copper plates of Samudragupta. *Indian History Congress Proceedings*, Session 16, 1953 : 94-95.

1084. ———.
Samvatsaras in the Parivrajaka inscriptions. *Indian Historical Quarterly*, Vol. 37, Nos. 2-3, June & September 1961 : 197-202.

1085. Gupta pilgrim records, Kalinjar Fort, district Banda, Uttar Pradesh. *Indian Archaeology : A Review*, 1976-77 : 63.

1086.. Gupta record, Dharampuri, district Sehore, Madhya Pradesh. *Indian Archaeology : A Review*, 1958-59 : 60.

1087. **Gupta, S.K.**
Comments and observations on the lead-paper of S.R. Goyal. In M.C. Joshi and S.K. Gupta, ed., *King Chandra and the Meharauli Pillar*. Meerut, Kusumanjali Prakashan, 1989 : 159-164.

1088. **Gupta, Sumant**
Guptavamshiya abhilekhon ka dharmik adhyayan. New Delhi, Ajay Book Service, 1981 (Hindi).

1089. **Gupte, Y.R.**
The grant of the Vakataka queen Prabhavati-Gupta, the year 19th of Pravarasena. *Indian Antiquary*, Vol. 53, 1924 : 48.

1090. ———.
A grant of the Vakataka queen Prabhavati-Gupta, the year nineteen of Pravarasena II. *Journal of the Royal Asiatic Society of Great Britain and Ireland*, 1924 : 94-96.

1091. ———.
Ridhapur plates of the Vakataka queen Prabhavati-Gupta : the 19th year. *Journal & Proceedings of the Asiatic Society Of Bengal*, New Series, Vol. 20, 1924 : 53-62.

1092. **Hoernle, A.F. Rudolf**
A note on the date of the Bower manuscript. *Indian Antiquary*, Vol. 21, 1892 :29-45.

1093. **Hultzsch, E.**
Jaina inscription dated in the year 106 of the Gupta era. *Indian Antiquary*, Vol. 11, 1882 : 310.

1094. Impressions. Katra, Muzaffarpur district, Bihar. *Annual Report on Indian Epigraphy*, 1959-60 : 34 (A-4).

1095. **Indraji, Bhagwanlal**
The Kahaun inscription of Skandagupta. *Indian Antiquary*, Vol. 10, 1881 : 125-126.

1096. ———.
Transcript and translation of the Bhitari Lat inscription. *Journal of the Bombay Branch of the Royal Asiatic Society*, Vol. 16, 1883-85 : 349-356.

1097.. Inscription of Gupta age from Rajasthan. *Indian Archaeology : A Review*, 1953-54 : 13.

1098. Inscription of Vishnugupta near Hunterganj in district Hazaribagh, Bihar. *Indian Archaeology : A Review*, 1953-54 : 13.

1099. Inscription on a broken stone pillar, Bharat Kala Bhavan, Varanasi, Uttar Pradesh. *Annual Report on Indian Epigraphy*, 1955-56 : 53 (B-361).

1100. **Jackson, A.M.T.**
Two new Vallabhi copper-plates. *Journal of the Bombay Branch of the Royal Asiatic Society*, Vol. 20, 1897-1900 : 1-10.

1101. **Jagan Nath**
The bearing of the Haraha inscription on the epoch of the Gupta era. *Indian Culture*, Vol. 5, No. 3, January 1939 : 335-337.

1102. ———.
Epigraphic notes. *Bharatiya Vidya*, Vol. 9, 1948 : 277-283.

1103. ———.
Epigraphic notes. *Journal of United Provinces Historical Society*, Vol. 13, pt. 2, December 1940 : 97-101.

1104. ———.
The Eran inscription of Samudragupta. *Journal of Indian History*, Vol. 19, 1940 : 27-29.

1105. ——.
Notes on the Eran stone inscription of Samudragupta. *All India Oriental Conference Proceedings,* Session 17, 1953 : 314-317.

1106. ——.
Notes on the Eran stone inscription of Samudragupta. *Indian History Congress Proceedings*, Session 14, 1951 : 62-64.

1107. ——.
Notes on the Eran stone inscription of Samudragupta? *All India Oriental Conference Proceedings,* Summaries of Papers, Session 17, 1953 : 212.

1108. ——.
The Pusyamitras of the Bhitari pillar inscription. *Indian Historical Quarterly,* Vol. 22, No. 2, June 1946 : 112-117.

1109. **Jain, Balchandra**
Shankarpur plate of Budhagupta and Harivarman : Gupta year 166. *Journal of the Epigraphical Society of India*, Vol. 4, 1977 : 62-66.

1110. **Jai, Prakash**
A note on the Aphsad inscription of Adityasena. *Bharati*, No. 4, 1960-61 : 85-88.

1111. **Jamuar, Bipin Kumar**
Temples in inscriptions of Bihar. *Journal of the Bihar Puravid Parishad*, Vol. 3, 1979 : 91-103.

1112. **Jayaswal, K.P.**
A passage in Samudragupta's inscription at Allahabad and Gupta coinage. *Journal of the Bihar and Orissa Research Society*, Vol. 18, pt. 2, June 1932 : 207-211.

1113. **Joshi, Jagdish Chandra**
Extracts from some earlier suggestions on the problem. In M.C. Joshi and S.K. Gupta, ed., *King Chandra and the Meharauli Pillar*. Meerut, Kusumanjali Prakashan, 1989 : 260-262.

1114. ———.
King Candra of Meharauli iron pillar inscription and Candragupta II. *Bharatiya Vidya,* Vol. 23, 1963 : 69-75.

1115. **Joshi, M.C.**
Comments and observations on the lead-paper of S.R. Goyal. In M.C. Joshi and S.K. Gupta, ed., *King Chandra and the Meharauli Pillar.* Meerut, Kusumanjali Prakashan, 1989 : 135-140.

1116. **Joshi, M.C.** and **Gupta, S.K.,** ed.
King Chandra and the Meharauli pillar. Meerut, Kusumanjali Prakashan, 1989.

1117. **Joshi, Narendra Prakash**
Kya Meharauli lekha ka "Chandra" Samudragupta hai ? *Journal of the Ganganatha Jha Kendriya Sanskrit Vidyapeetha*, Vol. 32, 1976 : 223-238 (Hindi).

1118. **Kapoor, S.N.**
Comments and observations on the lead-paper of S.R. Goyal. In M.C. Joshi and S.K. Gupta, ed., *King Chandra and the Meharauli Pillar.* Meerut, Kusumanjali Prakashan, 1989 : 166.

1119. **Kar, Rabis C.**
King Candra of the Mehrauli iron pillar inscription. *Indian Historical Quarterly*, Vol. 26, No. 3, September 1950 : 184-192.

1120. **Kielhorn, F.**
Talagunda pillar inscription of Kakusthavarman. *Epigraphia Indica*, Vol. 8, 1905-06 : 24-36.

1121. **Konow, Sten**
Karamdanda inscription of Kumaragupta (Gupta-) Samvat 117. *Epigraphia Indica*, Vol. 10, 1909-10 : 70-72.

1122. **Krishna Deva**
Nalanda seal of Vishnugupta. *Epigraphia Indica*, Vol. 26, 1941-42 : 235-239.

1123. **Krishnan, K.G.**
Comments and observations on the lead-paper of S.R. Goyal. In M.C. Joshi and S.K. Gupta, ed., *King Chandra and the Meharauli Pillar*. Meerut, Kusumanjali Prakashan, 1989 : 112-114.

1124. **Krishnaswamy, C.S.** and **Ghosh, Amalananda**
A note on the Allahabad pillar of Asoka. *Journal of the Royal Asiatic Society of Great Britain and Ireland*, 1935 : 697-706.

1125. **Lal, A.**
Buddha in the ancient Indian epigraphs. *Journal of the Department of Pali*, Vol. 3, 1985-86 : 18-21.

1126. Lower part of a Sati pillar, Pahlechpur, Sagar district, Madhya Pradesh. *Annual Report on Indian Epigraphy*, 1951-52 : 21 (B-127).

1127. **Luders, Heinrich**
Mathura inscriptions. Gottingen, Vandenhoeck & Ruprecht, 1961.

1128. **Maheshwari Prasad**
A note on the verse II of the Aphasad inscription of Adityasena. *Bharati*, No. 5, 1961-62 : 62-65.

1129. **Majumdar, N.G.**
Nandapur copper-plate of the Gupta year 169. *Epigraphia Indica*, Vol. 23, 1935-36 : 52-56.

1130. **Majumdar, R.C.**
Bihar stone pillar inscription of Skandagupta. *Indian Culture*, Vol. 10, No. 4, April-June 1944 : 170-173.

1131. ———.
Deo-Baranark inscription of Jivitagupta. *Indian Culture*, Vol. 11, No. 3, January-March 1945 : 124-125.

1132. ———.
Extracts from some earlier suggestions on the problem. In M.C. Joshi and S.K. Gupta, ed., *King Chandra and the Meharauli Pillar*. Meerut, Kusumanjali Prakashan, 1989 : 254.

1133. ______.
The Gaya and Nalanda plates of Samudra-Gupta. *Indian Culture*, Vol. 11, No. 4, April-June 1945 : 225-230.

1134. ______.
King Candra of the Meharauli iron pillar inscription. *Journal of the Royal Asiatic Society of Bengal, Letters*, Vol. 9, 1943 : 179-183.

1135. ______.
Some observations on the theory of S.R. Goyal.. In M.C. Joshi and S.K. Gupta, ed., *King Chandra and the Meharauli Pillar*. Meerut, Kusumanjali Prakashan, 1989 : 201.

1136. **Mani, V.R.**
A note on the word 'Loka-Matrnam Mandalam' in the Deogarh rock inscription of Svamibhatta. *Indian History Congress Proceedings*, Session 41, 1980 : 923-927.

1137. **Mill, W.H.**
Restoration and translation of the inscription on the Bhitari Lat, with critical and historical remarks. *Journal of the Asiatic Society of Bengal,* Vol. 6, 1837 : 1-17.

1138. ______.
Restoration of the inscription, No. 2, on the Allahabad column. *Journal of the Asiatic Society of Bengal,* Vol. 3, 1834 : 257-270.

1139. ______.
Supplement to the historical remarks on the Allahabad inscription, No. 2. *Journal of the Royal Asiatic Society of Bengal,* Vol. 3, 1834 : 339-344.

1140. **Mirashi, V.V.**
Are the grants of Maharaja Bhulunda dated in the Gupta era. *Journal of the Epigraphical Society of India*, Vol. 2, 1975 : 42-46.

1141. ______.
Bhitari stone inscription of Skandagupta. *Journal of the Epigraphical Society of India*, Vol. 7, 1980 : 86-92.

1142. ______.
The date of the Dadhimati-Mata inscription. *Journal of the Ganganatha Research Institute*, Vol. 3, pt. 2, February 1946 : 109-116.

1143. ______.
Did Candragupta II sell his own palaces at Vidisa ? *Annals of the Bhandarkar Oriental Research Institute*, Vol. 63, 1982 : 221-223.

1144. ______.
Notes on D.R. Bhandarkar's inscriptions of the early Gupta kings. *Journal of the Epigraphical Society of India*, Vol. 9, 1982 : 48-57.

1145. ______.
Prabhavatiguptecha Riddhapur tamrapat. *Vidarbha Samshodhana Mandal Varshik*, Vol. 24, 1981 : 87-101 (Marathi).

1146. **Mishra, P.L.**
King Mahendra of Allahabad Prasasti. *Indian Historical Quarterly*, Vol. 37, No. 1, March 1961 : 23-30.

1147. **Mishra, R.S.**
Comments and observations on the lead paper of S.R. Goyal. In M.C. Joshi and S.K. Gupta, ed., *King Chandra and the Meharauli Pillar*. Meerut, Kusumanjali Prakashan, 1989 : 143-148.

1148. **Mishra, Ram Swaroop**
Inscriptions of the early Gupta kings and their successors. Supplement to Fleet's *Corpus Inscriptionum Indicarum*, Vol. III. Varanasi, Banaras Hindu University, 1971. Part I : Bibliography.

1149. **Mitra, Rjendralala**
Notes on Gupta inscriptions from Aphsar and Behar. *Journal of the Asiatic Society of Bengal*, Vol. 35, pt. 1, 1866 : 267-278.

1150. ______.
On a copper-plate inscription of the time of Skandagupta, *Journal of the Asiatic Society of Bengal*, Vol. 43, pt. 1, 1874 : 363-374.

1151. **Mookerjee, Dhirendra Nath**
The Haraha inscription and the Gupta era. *New Indian Antiquary*, Vol. 3, 1940-41 : 437-440.

1152. ———.
Mandasor inscription of Kumaragupta (I). *Indian Culture*. Vol. 5, No. 3, January 1939 : 331-332.

1153. **Mookerji, R.K.**
Extracts from some earlier suggestions on the problem. In M.C. Joshi and S.K. Gupta, ed., *King Chandra and the Meharauli Pillar*. Meerut, Kusumanjali Prakashan, 1989 : 259.

1154. **Mukherjee, B.N.**
Decipherment of `Shell script'. *Bulletin of Museums & Archaeology in U.P.*, No. 31, June 1983 : 1-46.

1155. ———.
Extracts from some earlier suggestions on the problem. In M.C. Joshi and S.K. Gupta, ed., *King Chandra and the Meharauli Pillar*. Meerut, Kusumanjali Prakashan, 1989 : 263.

1156. ———.
The Hunza Valley and the Imperial Guptas. *Journal of the Bihar Research Society*, Vols. 67-68, 1981-82 : 561.

1157. ———.
A note on a passage in the Allahabad pillar inscription of Samudragupta. *Indian History Congress Proceedings*, Session 18, 1955 : 76.

1158. ———.
A note on a passage in the Allahabad pillar inscription of Samudragupta. *Journal of the Asiatic Society, Letters and Science*. Vol. 23, No. 1, 1957 : 79-80.

1159. ———.
A note on the shell script. *Indian Museum Bulletin*, Vol. 21, 1986 : 14-18.

1160. ———.
Present state of research on the Shell script. *Journal of Ancient Indian History*, Vol. 15, 1985-86 : 24-46.

1161. ———.
A Ramtek inscription and the Imperial Guptas. *Quarterly Bulletin of the School of Historical Studies*, Vol. 1, No. 2, September 1994 : 12-13.

1162. ———.
The so-called shell script—a note on its decipherment. *Indian Museum Bulletin*, Vol. 16, 1981 : 128-135.

1163. **N.R.**
The Mathura pillar inscription of Chandragupta II, G.E. 61. *Indian Antiquary*. Vol. 61, 1932 : 117-118.

1164. **Nagaswamy, R.**
Comments and observations on the lead-paper of S.R. Goyal. In M.C. Joshi and S.K. Gupta, ed., *King Chandra and the Meharauli Pillar*. Meerut, Kusumanjali Prakashan, 1989 : 141-142.

1165. **Narain, A.K.** and **Shukla, M.S.**, ed.
Prachin Bharatiya abhilekha-samgraha. Vol. 2, Varanasi, Banaras Hindu University, [n.d.] (Hindi).

1166. **Oldenberg, H.**
On the dates of ancient Indian inscriptions and coins. *Indian Antiquary*, Vol. 10, 1881 : 213-227.

1167. Palace Museum, Dhubela, Chhatarpur district, Madhya Pradesh. *Annual Report on Indian Epigraphy*, 1959-60 : 71 (B-249).

1168. **Pande, Susmita**
Comments and observations on the lead-paper of S.R. Goyal. In M.C. Joshi and S.K. Gupta, ed., *King Chandra and the Meharauli Pillar*. Meerut, Kusumanjali Prakashan, 1989 : 167-170.

1169. **Pandey, R.B.**
The Kahaum stone pillar inscription of Samudragupta. *Indian Historical Quarterly*, Vol. 28, No. 3, September 1952 : 298-300.

1170. **Pandey, Raj Bali**
Historical and literary inscriptions. Varanasi, Chowkhamba Sanskrit Series Office, 1962.

1171. **Pandey, V.C.**
The Bhitari pillar inscription of Skandagupta : A controversy. In S. Bhaskaran Nair, ed., *Bharati-Bhanam (Light of Indology) being Dr. K.V. Sharma felicitation volume*. Hoshiarpur, V.V.B. Institute of Sanskrit and Indological Studies, 1980 : 435-438.

1172. ______.
The Bhitari pillar inscription of Skandagupta : A controversy. *Vishveshvaranand Indological Journal*, Vol. 18, 1980 : 435-438.

1173. ______.
Bhitari pillar inscription : Some new interpretations. *Kosala*, Vol. 3, 1980-81 : 155-156.

1174. ______.
Bhitari pillar inscription : Some observations. *Vishveshvaranand Indological Journal*, Vol. 16, pt. 1, 1978 : 74-78.

1175. ______.
The Bhitari pillar—some observations. In Upendra Thakur and Yugal Kishore Mishra, ed., *The heritage of India : L.N. Mishra commemoraton volume*. BodhGaya, L.N. Mishra Commemoration Volume Publication Committee, 1978 : 161-165.

1176. ______.
A note on `apratirathah'. *Vishveshvaranand Indological Journal*, Vol. 11, 1973 : 91-94.

1177. ______.
Samudragupta's asvamedha—a reappraisal. *Annals of the Bhandarkar Oriental Research Institute*, Vol. 53, 1972 : 228-232.

1178. ______.
Vangas and Vahlikas of the Mehrauli pillar inscription. *Vishveshvaranand Indological Journal*, Vol. 12, 1974 : 241-245.

1179. **Pargiter, F.E.**
The Kasia copper-plate. *Archaeological Survey of India Annual Report*, 1910-11 : 73-77.

1180. **Pathak, K.B.**
A Gupta-Vakataka copperplate grant. *Indian Antiquary*, Vol. 41, September 1912 : 214-215.

1181. **Pathak, V.S.**
Prayaga in inscriptions. *Journal of the U. P. Historical Society*, New Series, Vol. 6, pt. 2, 1958 : 31-34.

1182. **Pathak, V.S.** and **Rao, V.B.**
Comments and observations on the lead-paper of S.R. Goyal. In M.C. Joshi and S.K. Gupta, ed., *King Chandra and the Meharauli Pillar*. Meerut, Kusumanjali Prakashan, 1989 : 190-196.

1183. **Patil, D.R.**
Gupta inscriptions and the puranic tradition. *Bulletin of the Deccan College Research Institute*, Vol. 2, Nos. 1-2, 1940 : 148-165.

1184. **Paul, Pramode Lal**
The development of the Bengali script. *Indian Historical Quarterly*, Vol. 12, No. 2, June 1936 : 308-334.

1185. Pedestal of a broken sand-stone image of the Buddha. The Archaeological Museum, Mathura. *Annual Report on Indian Epigraphy*, 1965-66 : 112 (B-677).

1186. Pedestal of a Buddha image. Sarnath, Varanasi district, Uttar Pradesh. *Annual Report on Indian Epigraphy*, 1959-60 : 134 (C-593-595).

1187. Pedestal of a fourth broken image. Bharat Kala Bhavan, Varanasi, Uttar Pradesh. *Annual Report on Indian Epigraphy*, 1952-53 : 73 (B-469).

1188. Pedestal of an image in Lucknow Museum. Mankuwar, Allahabad district, Uttar Pradesh. *Annual Report on Indian Epigraphy*, 1957-58 : 81 (C-320).

1189. Pedestal of a stone image of a Jaina Tirthankara. Durjanpur, Vidisha district, Madhya Pradesh. *Annual Report on Indian Epigraphy*, 1968-69 : 29 (B-67-69).

1190. **Phogat, Silak Ram**
Sources of Haryana history : Inscriptions. *Kurukshetra University Research Journal*, (*Arts and Humanities*), Vol. 10, 1976 : 16-23.

1191. Photographs of inscription on seals in Indian Museum, Calcutta, West Bengal. *Annual Report on Indian Epigraphy*, 1976-77 : 53 (B-93).

1192. Pillar. Belwa. Varanasi district, Uttar Pradesh. *Annual Report on Indian Epigraphy*, 1959-60 : 120 (B-742).

1193. Pillar in Patna Museum, *Annual Report on Indian Epigraphy*, 1960-61 : 69 (B-195).

1194. Pillar in the Archaeological Museum, Mathura. *Annual Report on Indian Epigraphy*, 1972-73 : 81 (B-392).

1195. Pillar inside the fort, Allahabad, Uttar Pradesh. *Annual Report on Indian Epigraphy*, 1952-53 : 71 (B-437).

1196. Pillars. Deo Baranark, Shahabad district, Uttar Pradesh. *Annual Report on Indian Epigraphy*, 1960-61 : 69 (B-208).

1197. Plate deposited in the Varendra Research Society, Rajshahi. *Annual Report on Indian Epigraphy*, 1969-70 : 18 (A-10).

1198. Plates in the State Museum, Lucknow. Bhitari, Uttar Pradesh. *Annual Report on Indian Epigraphy*, 1960-61 : 45 (A-55).

1199. **Pokharna, Prem Lata**
Rajasthan ke abhilekh. *Maru Bharati*, Vol. 28, No. 3, August-October 1980 : 52-56 (Hindi).

1200. **Prinsep, James**
Note on inscription No. 1 of the Allahabad column. *Journal of the Asiatic Society of Bengal*, Vol. 3, 1834 : 114-118.

1201. **Purohit, S.K.**
Comments and observations on the lead-paper of S.R. Goyal. In M.C. Joshi and S.K. Gupta, ed., *King Chandra and the Meharauli Pillar*. Meerut, Kusumanjali Prakashan, 1989 : 165.

1202. **Raghavan, V.**
Allahabad pillar inscription verses 3 & 8. *Journal of Oriental Research, Madras*, Vol. 16, pt. 3, March 1947 : 159-162.

1203. **Raman, K.V.**
Comments and observations on the lead-paper of S.R. Goyal. In M.C. Joshi and S.K. Gupta, ed., *King Chandra and the Meharauli Pillar*. Meerut, Kusumanjali Prakashan, 1989 : 122-123.

1204. **Ramesh, K.V.** and **Subramonia Iyer, S.**
A fragmentary inscription from Vidisha. *Epigraphia Indica*, Vol. 41, 1975-76 : 186-188.

1205. **Rana, S.S.**
King Candra of Meharauli iron pillar inscription. In B.R. Saksena and others, ed., *Umesha Mishra commemoration volume*. Allahabad, Ganganatha Jha Research Institute, 1970 : 669-675.

1206. ———.
King Candra of Meharauli iron pillar inscription. *Journal of the Oriental Institute*, Vol. 18, No. 4, June 1969 : 326-330.

1207. ———.
King Candra of Meharauli iron pillar inscription. *Journal of the Ganganatha Jha Research Institute*, Vol. 26, pts. 1-3, January-July 1970 : 669-675.

1208. ———.
King Candra of Meharauli iron pillar inscription. *Vishveshvaranand Indological Journal*. Vol. 6, 1968 : 106-111.

1209. ———.
The Meharauli iron pillar inscription is not posthumous. In Mohan Chand, ed., *Ancient Indian culture & literature* (*Pt. Ganga Ram commemoration volume*). Delhi, Eastern Book Linkers, 1980 : 127-130.

1210. ———.
Some observations on the theory of S.R. Goyal. In M.C. Joshi and S.K. Gupta, *ed.*, *King Chandra and the Meharauli Pillar*. Meerut, Kusumanjali Prakashan, 1989 : 202.

1211. **Raychaudhuri, H.C.**
Extracts from some earlier suggestions on the Problem. In M.C. Joshi and S.K. Gupta, ed., *King Chandra and the Meharauli Pillar*. Meerut, Kusumanjali Prakashan, 1989 : 245-246.

1212. Red sand-stone column. Eran, Sagar district. *Annual Report on Indian Epigraphy*, 1965-66 : 127 (C-2305).

1213. Rock. Mandar Hill, Bhagalpur district, Bihar. *Annual Report on Indian Epigraphy*, 1962-63 : 79-80 (B-257-258).

1214. Rock-cut caves, Doongh, district Guadaspur, Punjab. *Indian Archaeology : A Review*, 1975-76 : 77.

1215. Rock. to the east of the town, Junagadh, Gujarat. *Annual Report on Indian Epigraphy*, 1950-51 : 45 (B-386).

1216. **Sadhu Ram**
Allahabad pillar inscription of Samudragupta. In Mohan Chand, ed., *Ancient Indian culture & literature (Pt. Ganga Ram commemoration volume)*. Delhi, Eastern Book Linkers, 1980 : 131-155.

1217. ______.
`Anka' in the Allahabad pillar inscription of Samudragupta. *Vishveshvaranand Indological Journal*. Vol. 3, pt. 1, 1965 : 105-106.

1218. ______.
Epigraphical notes. *Journal of the Ganganatha Jha Kendriya Sanskrit Vidyapeetha*, Vol. 28, pts. 1-2, January-April 1972 : 549-551.

1219. ______.
Eran stone inscription of Samudragupta. *Kurukshetra University Research Journal (Arts and Humanities)*, Vol. 1, No. 1, 1967 : 13-19.

1220. ______.
Importance of a verse in the Prayaga-Prasasti of Samudragupta. *Vishveshvaranand Indological Journal*. Vol. 17, 1979 : 203-205.

1221. ———.
Interpretation of a verse in the Junagadh inscription of Samudragupta. *Journal of the Oriental Institute*, Vol. 28, Nos. 3-4, March-June 1979 : 90-91.

1222. ———.
The Mathura pillar inscription of Chandragupta II, Gupta year 61. *Kurukshetra University Research Journal*, Vol. 2, pt. 1, 1968 : 13-19.

1223. ———.
Misinterpretation of Allahabad pillar inscription. *Journal of Ancient Indian History*, Vol. 1, 1967-68 : 65-71.

1224. ———.
A new pillar inscription from Mandasor. *Indian Historical Quarterly*, Vol. 33, No. 1, March 1977 : 62-64.

1225. ———.
A note on the Aphsad inscription of Adityasena. *Vishveshvaranand Indological Journal*, Vol. 11, 1973 : 89-90.

1226. ———.
A note on the Mathura inscription of the reign of Chandragupta II, Gupta year 61. *Journal of Indian History*, Vol. 42, pt. 2, August 1964 : 515-517.

1227. ———.
Restoration and interpretation of a passage in the Bhitari pillar inscription of Skandagupta. *Vishveshvaranand Indological Journal*, Vol. 4, pt. 1, 1966 : 72-74.

1228. **Sahai, Bhagwant**
The inscriptions of Bihar. New Delhi, Ramanand Vidya Bhawan, 1983.

1229. ———.
Interpretations of Bihar. In Bhagwant Sahai and Sachidanand Sahay, ed., *Bihar past and present*. Patna, Bihar Historical Society, 1981 : 25-37.

1230. **Sahni, D.R.**
Observations on medieval inscriptions of the Meharauli Pillar. In M.C. Joshi and S.K. Gupta, ed., *King Chandra and the Meharauli Pillar*. Meerut, Kusumanjali Prakashan, 1989 : 71-72.

1231. **Saloman, Richard**
A shell character inscription on a seal from Rajghat (Varanasi). *Journal of the Epigraphical Society of India*, Vol. 7, 1980 : 6-7.

1232. **Samaddar, J.N.**
The Gupta pillar at Bihar. *Journal of the Bihar and Orissa Research Society*, Vol. 5, pt. 4, December 1919 : 641-642.

1233. Sandstone slab. Gadhwa, Allahabad district. *Annual Report on Indian Epigraphy*, 1972-73 : 95 (C-3421).

1234. **Sankaranarayanan, S.**
Comments and observations on the lead-paper of S.R. Goyal. In M.C. Joshi and S.K. Gupta, ed., *King Chandra and the Meharauli Pillar*. Meerut, Kusumanjali Prakashan, 1989 : 171-179.

1235. **Sarma, I.K.**
Bihar stone pillar inscriptions—a revised study. *Journal of the Oriental Institute*, Vol. 17, No. 3, March 1968 : 267-274.

1236. **Sastri, Hirananda**
Nalanda and its epigraphic material. Delhi, Manager of Publications, 1942. (Memories of the Archaeological Survey of India, No. 66).

1237. **Sastri, Sakuntala Rao**
The Nalanda and Gaya plates of Samudragupta. *Indian Culture*. Vol. 10, No. 2, October-December 1943 : 77-78.

1238. **Satya Vrat**
On the text of a controversial verse in the Bhitari stone pillar inscription of Skandagupta. *Vishveshvaranand Indological Journal*, Vol. 24, 1986 : 118-121.

1239. ———.
On the text of a verse in the Bhitari stone pillar inscription of Skandagupta. *Sambodhi*, Vol. 12, 1983-1984 : 99-101.

1240. **Sen, B.C.**
Extracts from some earlier suggestions on the problem. In M.C. Joshi and S.K. Gupta, ed., *King Chandra and the Meharauli Pillar*. Meerut, Kusumanjali Prakashan, 1989 : 253.

1241. **Sengupta, Gautam**
Epigraphy and art-history : On some inscribed sculptures of Eastern India. *Journal of the Epigraphical Society of India*, Vol. 16, 1990 : 112-118.

1242. **Seth, H.C.**
Extracts from some earlier suggestions on the problem. In M.C. Joshi and S.K. Gupta, ed., *King Chandra and the Meharauli Pillar*. Meerut, Kusumanjali Prakashan, 1989 : 250-251.

1243. **Shah, U.P.**
A further note on Ramagupta inscriptions. *Journal of the Oriental Institute*, Vol. 18, No. 3, March 1969 : 254-255.

1244. **Sharma, Dasharatha**
Chandasena of the Kaumudi-mahotsava. *Journal of the Bihar and Orissa Research Society*, Vol. 21, pt. 1, March 1935 : 77.

1245. ______.
The interpretation of "A-Kumaram Manushyaih" of Skandagupta's Bhitari inscription and connected problems. *Indian History Congress Proceedings*, Session 19, 1956 : 148-150.

1246. ______.
Is Candra of the Mehrauli pillar inscription identical with Kaniska ? *Journal of the Ganganatha Jha Research Institute*, Vol. 1, pt. 2, February 1944 : 185-187.

1247. ______.
Is Chandra of the Mehrauli pillar inscription, Chandragupta of the Mauryan dynasty ? *Journal of Indian History*, Vol. 17, pt. 1, April 1938 : 34-36.

1248. ———.
`Ksitipa-charana-Pithe Sthapito Vamapadah' of Skandagupta's Bhitari Pillar inscription. *Indian History Congress Proceedings*, Session 26, pt. I, 1964 : 141.

1249. ———.
The Mandasore inscription of the silk weavers' guild. *Indian Culture*, Vol. 3, No. 2, October 1936 : 379-381.

1250. ———.
The Mehrauli iron pillar inscription. *Journal of Indian History*, Vol. 16, pt. 1, April 1937 : 13-18.

1251. ———.
The non-posthumous character of the Mehrauli iron pillar inscription. *Indian Culture*, Vol. 5, No. 2, October 1938 : 206-208.

1252. ———.
On the Eran inscription of about 350 A.D. *Journal of Indian History*, Vol. 14, pt. 1, April 1935 : 27-29.

1253. ———.
A supplementary note on the Mandasore inscription of the `silk-wears guild. *Indian Culture*, Vol. 4, 1937-1938 : 262-263.

1254. ———.
Three short notes on Samudragupta's Allahabad pillar inscription. *Indian History Congress Proceedings*, Session 17, 1954 : 83-87.

1255. ———.
A verse from Skandagupta's Junagarh inscription. *Journal of the Ganganatha Jha Research Institute*, Vol. 6, pt. 4, August 1949 : 303-305.

1256. **Sharma, G.R.**
Candra of Meharauli pillar inscription. *Indian Historical Quarterly*, Vol. 21, No. 3, September 1945 : 202-212.

1257. ———.
Extracts from some earlier suggestions on the problem. In M.C. Joshi and S.K. Gupta, ed., *King Chandra and the Meharauli Pillar*. Meerut, Kusumanjali Prakashan, 1989 : 256-258.

1258. **Sharma, K.K.**
Comments and observations on the lead-paper of S.R. Goyal. In M.C. Joshi and S.K. Gupta, ed., *King Chandra and the Meharauli Pillar*. Meerut, Kusumanjali Prakashan, 1989 : 115-116.

1259. **Sharma, T.R.**
Personal and geographical names in the Gupta inscriptions. Delhi, Concept Publishing Company, 1978.

1260. ______.
A sociological interpretation of the Mandasor inscription of Kumaragupta and Bandhuvarman, the Malava years 493 and 529. *Journal of the Epigraphical Society of India*, Vol. 6, 1979 : 32-35.

1261. ______.
Some observations on the theory of S.R. Goyal. In M.C. Joshi and S.K. Gupta, ed., *King Chandra and the Meharauli Pillar*. Meerut, Kusumanjali Prakashan, 1989 : 203-204.

1262. **Shastri, A.M.**
Comments and observations on the lead-paper of S.R. Goyal. In M.C. Joshi and S.K. Gupta, ed., *King Chandra and the Meharauli Pillar*. Meerut, Kusumanjali Prakashan, 1989 : 85-91.

1263. **Shastri, Ajay Mitra**
Sanchi inscription of Chandragupta II. *Journal of Ancient Indian History*, Vol. 5, pts. 1-2, 1971-72 : 199-203.

1264. **Shastri, H.P.**
Extracts from some earlier suggestions on the problem. In M.C. Joshi and S.K. Gupta, ed., *King Chandra and the Meharauli Pillar*. Meerut, Kusumanjali Prakashan, 1989 : 242-243.

1265. **Shastri, Haraprasad**
King Chandra of the Meharauli iron pillar inscription. *Indian Antiquary*, Vol. 42, 1913 : 217-219.

1266. **Shri Arun**
Comments and observations on the lead-paper of S.R. Goyal. In M.C. Joshi and S.K. Gupta, ed., *King Chandra and the Meharauli Pillar*. Meerut, Kusumanjali Prakashan, 1989 : 157-158.

1267. **Shukla, B.C.**
A new Gupta inscription from Kausambi. *Bulletin of Museums & Archaeology in U.P.*, Nos. 33-34, June-December 1984 : 25-28.

1268. ———.
A new Gupta inscription from Kausambi. *Puratattva*, No. 16, 1985-86 : 85-86.

1269. **Siddhanta, S.**
The Jagadishpur copper plate grant of the year 128 (A.D. 447-48). *Journal of the Varendra Research Museum*, Vol. 1, No. 1, 1972 : 23-37.

1270. **Singh, Sheo Bahadur**
Sresthin in epigraphs. *Journal of the Epigraphical Society of India*, Vol. 10, 1983 : 104-107.

1271. A single copper-plate kept in the Rani Durgavati Museum, Jabalpur, Madhya Pradesh. *Annual Report on Indian Epigraphy*, 1977-78 : 30 (A-10).

1272. **Sinha, B.P.**
Comments and observations on the lead-paper of S.R. Goyal. In M.C. Joshi and S.K. Gupta, ed., *King Chandra and the Meharauli Pillar*. Meerut, Kusumanjali Prakashan, 1989 : 93-94.

1273. ———.
Extracts from some earlier suggestions on the problem. In M.C. Joshi and S.K. Gupta, ed., *King Chandra and the Meharauli Pillar*. Meerut, Kusumanjali Prakashan, 1989 : 255.

1274. **Sircar, D.C.**
Ancient Indian inscriptions. *Journal of History*, Vol. 2, 1981 : 26-70.

1275. ______.
Copper-plate grants from Bihar : Grant of Jivagupta. *Epigraphia Indica*, Vol. 35, 1963-64 : 125-130.

1276. ______.
Date of Mankuwar Buddha image inscription of the time of Kumaragupta I. *Journal of Ancient Indian History*, Vol. 3, 1969-70 : 133-137.

1277. ______.
Digvijaya of King Chandra of the Meharauli pillar inscription. *Journal of the Royal Asiatic Society of Bengal, Letters*, Vol. 5, 1939 : 407-415.

1278. ______.
Eran pillar inscription of Samudragupta. *Journal of U.P. Historical Society*, New Series, Vol. 3, pt. 2, 1955 : 91-100.

1279. ______.
Extracts from some earlier suggestions on the problem. In M.C. Joshi and S.K. Gupta, ed., *King Chandra and the Meharauli Pillar*. Meerut, Kusumanjali Prakashan, 1989 : 252.

1280. ______.
Indian epigraphy. Delhi, Motilal Banarsidass, 1965.

1281. ______.
Inscriptions from Bihar : Kaulesvari Hill inscription of Vishnugupta. *Epigraphia Indica*, Vol. 30, pt. 3, July 1953 : 84-85.

1282. ______.
Introduction to Indian epigraphy. *Journal of Ancient Indian History*, Vol. 4, 1970-71 : 72-136.

1283. ______.
Jagadishpur plate of the Gupta year 128. *Epigraphia Indica*, Vol. 38, pt. 6, April 1970 : 247-252.

1284. ______.
Kalaikuri copper-plate inscription of the Gupta year. *Indian Historical Quarterly*, Vol. 19, No. 1, March 1943 : 12-26.

1285. ———.
Note on the Aphsad inscription of Adityasena. *Epigraphia Indica*, Vol. 37, 1967-68 : 185-188.

1286. ———.
A note on the Damodarpur grant of the time of Budhagupta and Jayadatta. *Indian Culture*, Vol. 5, 1938-39 : 432-433.

1287. ———.
A note on the Mathura inscription of Candragupta II. *Indian Historical Quarterly*, Vol. 18, No. 3, September 1942 : 271-275.

1288. ———.
A passage of the Eran pillar inscription of Samudragupta. *Indian History Congress Proceedings*, Session 17, 1954 : 72-78.

1289. ———.
Recent study of epigraphic and numismatic records. *Journal of the Bihar Research Society*, Vol. 47, 1961 : 11-20.

1290. ———.
Rudradeva and Nagadatta of the Allahabad pillar inscription. *Indian History Congress Proceedings*, Session 7, 1944 : 78-81.

1291. **Sircar, D.C., ed.**
Select inscriptions bearing on Indian history and civilization. Vol. I. Calcutta, University of Calcutta, 1965.

1292. **Sircar, D.C.**
Spuriousness of the Nalanda plate of Samudragupta. *Epigraphia Indica*, Vol. 26, 1941-42 : 135-136.

1293. ———.
Sumandala plates of the time of Prithivivigrahabhattaraka : Gupta year 250. *Epigraphia Indica*, Vol. 28, 1949-50 : 79-85.

1294. ———.
Two inscriptions of Gupta age. *Epigraphia Indica*, Vol. 33, pt. 7, July 1960 : 303-308.

1295. ———.
The Vahlikas of the Meharauli pillar inscription. In S.M. Katre and P.K. Gode, ed., *A volume of studies in Indology presented to Prof. P.V. Kane on his 61st birthday 7th May 1941*. Poona, Oriental Book Agency, 1941 : 469-471.

1296. ———.
Vidisa Jain image inscriptions of the time of Ramagupta. *Journal of Ancient Indian History*, Vol. 3, 1969-70 : 145-151.

1297. Slab. Eran, Sagar district, Madhya Pradesh. *Annual Report on Indian Epigraphy*, 1962-63 : 78 (B-244).

1298. **Smith, V.A.**
Extracts from some earlier suggestions on the problem. In M.C. Joshi and S.K. Gupta, ed., *King Chandra and the Meharauli Pillar*. Meerut, Kusumanjali Prakashan, 1989 : 241 & 247.

1299. ———.
The inscription of king Chandra : Translation and comments. In M.C. Joshi and S.K. Gupta, ed., *King Chandra and the Meharauli Pillar*. Meerut, Kusumanjali Prakashan, 1989 : 65-66.

1300. ———.
The Iron Pillar of Delhi (Mihrauli) and the emperor Candra/Chandra. *Journal of the Royal Asiatic Society of Great Britain and Ireland*, 1897 : 1-18.

1301. ———.
Samudra Gupta. *Journal of the Royal Asiatic Society of Great Britain and Ireland*, 1898 : 386-387.

1302. **Sohoni, S.V.**
Epigraphic miscellanea. *Journal of the Bihar Research Society*, Vol. 61, 1975 : 189-208.

1303. ———.
First part of Samudragupta's prasasti. *Annals of the Bhandarkar Oriental Research Institute*. Vol. 39, 1958 : 34-45.

1304. ———.
Mehrauli iron pillar inscription. *Quarterly Journal of the Mythic Society*, Vol. 75, No. 2, 1984 : 187-207.

1305. ———.
Nalanda and Gaya copper plate grants of Samudragupta. *Journal of the Bihar Research Society*, Vol. 52, 1966 : 20-28.

1306. ———.
A note on Eran inscription of Samudragupta. *Journal of the Bihar Research Society*, Vol.51, 1965 : 50-54.

1307. ———.
Notes and queries on Bhitari pillar inscription of Samudragupta. *Journal of the Bihar Research Society*, Vol. 53, 1967 : 98-112.

1308. ———.
Notes on Prayaga Prasasti of Samudragupta. *Journal of the Bihar Research Society*, Vol. 51, 1965 : 29-49.

1309. ———.
So-called Bihar stone pillar inscription of Skandagupta. *Journal of the Bihar Research Society*, Vol. 49, 1963 : 170-177.

1310. **Soundara Rajan, K.V.**
Inscriptions of the Gupta period—a study of proper names and references to the gods therein, *Journal of the Oriental Research Madras*, Vol. 19, pt. 4, June 1950 : 268-277.

1311. **Srinivasan, P.R.**
Dates of the Nalanda and Gaya plates purported to be of Samudragupta's time. *Journal of Ancient Indian History*, Vol. 10, 1976-77 : 106-109.

1312. ———.
Inscriptional evidence on early Hindu temples. *Adyar Library Bulletin*, Vol. 26, pts. 1-2, 1962 : 1-25.

1313. ——.
Mathura pillar inscription of the Gupta year 61. *Journal of Ancient Indian History*, Vol. 3, 1969-70 : 113-122.

1314. ——.
Mundesvari temple inscription. In C. Margabandhu and others, ed., *Indian archaeological heritage : Shri K.V. Soundara Rajan festschrift*, Vol. I. Delhi, Agam Kala Prakashan, 1991 : 313-316.

1315. ——.
Note on Eran stone pillar inscription of Srivikrama. *Journal of the Oriental Institute*, Vol. 20, No. 1, September 1970 : 51-55.

1316. ——.
Note on four Gupta-period inscription. *Epigraphia Indica*, Vol.39, pt. 5, January 1972 : 163-166.

1317. **Srivastava, O.P.L.**
Padmavati ka Ganapati Nag. *Dhyanam*, Vol. 4, 1984 : 67-68 (Hindi).

1318. **Srivastava, V.N.**
Buddha pedestal inscription of Kumara Gupta (G.E. 125 ?). *Bulletin of Museums & Archaeology in U.P.*, No. 1, March 1968 : 15-17.

1319. ——.
Two image inscriptions from Mathura : Inscription of the time of Kumaragupta, year 125. *Epigraphia Indica*, Vol. 37, 1967-68 : 153-154.

1320. **Stein, V.N.**
Round the Meharauli inscription. *New Indian Antiquary*, Vol. 1, 1938-39 : 188-198.

1321. Stone. Gadhwa, Allahabad district, Uttar Pradesh. *Annual Report on Indian Epigraphy*, 1978-79 : 39 (B-43).

1322. A stone linga in State Museum, Lucknow. *Annual Report on Indian Epigraphy*, 1956-57 : 109 (C-217).

1323. Stones in the Museum. Gwalior, Madhya Pradesh. *Annual Report on Indian Epigraphy*, 1967-68 : 28 (B-117-118).

1324. **Subba Rao, R.**
Cheedivalasa plates of Devendravarma. *Journal of Andhra Historical Research Society*, Vol. 2, No. 2, October 1927 : 146-164.

1325. **Suryanshi, Bhagwan Singh**
Gupta inscription and antiquities. *Journal of Indian Museums*, Vol. 12, 1956 : 59-65.

1326. Terracotta seal. Monastery site No. 1, Nalanda, Patna district, Bihar. *Annual Report on Indian Epigraphy*, 1959-60 : 124 (C-447).

1327. **Tewari, S.P.**
The Bagh (M.P.) copper plate hoard of Gupta times. *Journal of the Mythic Society*, Vol. 81, Nos. 1-2, 1990 : 1-10.

1328. ———.
Inference of the term a-Gupta-yikanam. *Journal of the Epigraphical Society of India*, Vol. 13, 1986 : 91-97.

1329. **Thakur, Upendra**
A note on the "Pusyamitras" of the Bhitari inscription. *Indian Historical Quarterly*, Vol. 37, No. 4, December 1961 : 279-286.

1330. **Thaplyal, K.K.**
Comments and observations on the lead-paper of S.R. Goyal. In M.C. Joshi and S.K. Gupta, ed., *King Chandra and the Meharauli Pillar*. Meerut, Kusumanjali Prakashan, 1989 : 117-121.

1331. **Thaplyal, K.K.** and **Srivastava, Arvind**
Mathura stone pedstal inscription of the time of Budhagupta, Gupta year 161. *Journal of the Epigraphical Society of India*, Vol. 9, 1982 : 6-11.

1332. Tracing of seal. Bhitarì, Ghazipur district, Uttar Pradesh. *Annual Report on Indian Epigraphy*, 1957-58 : 14 (A-15).

1333. **Tripathi, K.B.**
The palaeography of early Oriya inscriptions. *Oriya Historical Research Journal*, Vol. 4, Nos. 1-2, 1955 : 11-27.

1334. **Tripathi, R.P.**
Bhitari pillar inscription of Skandagupta—a note on Ganga—Dhvanih. *Indian History Congress Proceedings* Session 39, Volume II, 1978 : 1010-1014.

1335. ———.
The importance and identification of Kotakulaja of the Allahabad pillar inscription. *Journal of the Ganganatha Jha Kendriya Sanskrit Vidyapeetha*, Vol. 41, 1985 : 167-172.

1336. ———.
A note on the Bhitari pillar inscription of Skandagupta. *Journal of Indian History*, Vol. 57, pts. 2-3, August & December 1979 : 199-203.

1337. **Trivedi, H.V.**
A new Mandasor stone inscription. *Indian History Congress Proceedings* Session 17, 1954 : 94-97.

1338. ———.
A new Mandasor stone inscription. *Journal of Indian Museums*, Vol. 11, 1955 : 10-14.

1339. ———.
Remarks upon the second inscription of the Allahabad pillar. *Journal of the Asiatic Society of Bengal*, Vol. 3, 1834 : 118-123.

1340. Two Buddhist image-inscriptions, Mathura, Uttar Pradesh. *Indian Archaeology : Review*, 1965-66 : 68.

1341. Two Jain image inscriptions, Vidisha, Madhya Pradesh. *Indian Archaeology : Review*, 1968-69 : 46-47.

1342. **Upadhyaya, Vasudeva**
Bharatiya abhilekho mein tithi-ganana. *Parishad Patrika*, Vol. 6, No. 1, April 1966 : 31-34 (Hindi).

1343. ———
Gupta abhilekha. Patna, Bihar Hindi Grantha Akadami, 1974 (Hindi).

1344. Upper part of the proper left-side of a stone slab in the Indian Museum, Calcutta, West Bengal. *Annual Report on Indian Epigraphy*, 1968-69 : 59 (C-2591-2593).

1345. **Vajpeyi, Raghavendra**
A note on the term catussamudranta—prthivi in the Mandasor stone inscription of Kumaragupta I. *Annals of the Bhandarkar Oriental Research Institute*. Vol. 53, 1972 : 212-220.

1346. ———.
Skandagupta's Bhitari grant to Visnu-Sarngin and Bhitari excavations. *Indian History Congress Proceedings*, Session 44, 1983 : 70-78.

1347. ———.
The Vahlikas of the Meharauli iron pillar inscription. *Indian History Congress Proceedings* Session 38, 1977 : 783-790.

1348. **Verma, T.P.**
Comments and observations on the lead-paper of S.R. Goyal. In M.C. Joshi and S.K. Gupta, ed., *King Chandra and the Meharauli Pillar*. Meerut, Kusumanjali Prakashan, 1989 : 180-186.

1349. ———.
The Mathura pedastal inscription of the time of Budhagupta. (G.E. 161 : c. 483 A.C.). *Bharati*, New Series, No. 1, 1983 : 159-163.

1350. ———.
Meharauli abhilekh ka chandra : Samudragupta ya Chandragupta II. *Dhyanam*, Vols. 5-6, 1985-86 : 111-120 (Hindi).

1351. **Vogel, J.Ph.**
Facts and fancies about the iron pillar of old-Delhi. *Journal of Panjab Historical Research Society*, Vol. 9, pt. 1, 1923 : 71-91.

1352. **Williams, Joanna**
Some observations on the theory of S.R. Goyal. In M.C. Joshi and S.K. Gupta, ed., *King Chandra and the Meharauli Pillar*. Meerut, Kusumanjali Prakashan, 1989 : 200.

NUMISMATICS

1353. **Acharya, G.V.**
History of coinage in Gujarat. *All India Oriental Conference Proceedings*, Session 7, 1933 : 689-702.

1354. ———.
A unique half dinar of Chandragupta II. *Journal of the Numismatic Society of India*, Vol. 1, 1939 : 27.

1355. **Agarwal, J.K.**
A Chhattra type coin of Chandragupta II. *Journal of the Numismatic Society of India*, Vol. 4, pt. 1, June 1942 : 59-60.

1356. ———.
A new sub-variety of the Chhattra-type coin of Chandragupta II. *Journal of the Numismatic Society of India*, Vol. 11, pt. 1, 1949 : 32.

1357. ———.
Some new varieties of Gupta coinage. *Journal of the Numismatic Society of India*, Vol. 3, 1941 : 83-86.

1358. ———.
Some unnoticed coins. *Journal of United Provinces Historical Society*, Vol. 7, pt. 2, November 1934 : 80-83.

1359. **Agrawal, Ashvini**
King and queen-type of Skandagupta. In Devendra Handa, ed., *Numismatic Studies*, Vol. 3, New Delhi, Harman Publishing House, 1993 : 57-63.

1360. ———.
Narrative in the Gupta numismatic art. In Devendra Handa and Ashvini Agrawal, ed., *Ratna-Chandrika : Panorama of Oriental studies* (*Shri R.C. Agrawala festschrift*). New Delhi, Harman Publishing House, 1989 : 159-165.

1361. ______.
A note on the identity of Kacha of the Gupta gold coins. In C.R.P. Sinha and others, ed., *Archaeology and art (Krishna Deva felicitation volume)*, Part II. New Delhi, Ramanand Vidya Bhawan, 1990 : 476-479.

1362. ______.
A note on the identity of Kacha of the Gupta gold coins. *Journal of the Numismatic Society of India*, Vol. 50, 1988 : 79-81.

1363. **Agrawal, Jagannath**
Nalanda clay sealing of Maharajadhiraja Vainya-Gupta. *Journal of the Numismatic Society of India*, Vol. 30, 1968 : 206-207.

1364. ______.
A rare clay sealing from Sunet. *Journal of the Numismatic Society of India*, Vol. 27, pt. 1, 1965 : 98-99.

1365. **Agrawal, Madhuri**
Pracheen Bharatiya sikkon aur moharo par Brahman devi-devata aur unke pratik (prarambh se lekar Gupta kaal tak). New Delhi, Ramanand Vidya Bhawan, 1988 (Hindi).

1366. **Agrawala, P.K.**
A note on the `Karttikeya' type coin of Kumara Gupta I. *Journal of the Numismatic Society of India*, Vol. 30, 1968 : 203-206.

1367. **Agrawala, V.S.**
An explanation of the Chakravikrama type coin of Chandragupta II. *Journal of the Numismatic Society of India*, Vol. 16, pt. 1, 1954 : 97-101.

1368. ______.
Samudragupta aur Chandragupta ki mudraon ke jyodharan. *Nagari Pracharini Patrika*, Vol. 49, Samvat 2001 : 260-269 (Hindi).

1369. ______.
Samudragupta aur Chandragupta ki mudraon ke jyodharan. In P.K. Agrawala, ed., *Itihasa-darsana*, Varanasi, Prithivi Prakashan, 1978 : 127-135 (Hindi).

1370. ———.
Varanasi seals and sealings. Edited with supplementary notes by P.K. Agrawala. Varanasi, Prithivi Prakashan, 1984.

1371. **Ahmad, Nisar**
Chandragupta III. *Journal of the Numismatic Society of India*, Vol. 46, 1984 : 91-95.

1372. ———.
Chandragupta IV. In S.K. Maity and Upendra Thakur, ed., *Indological studies : Prof. D.C. Sircar commemoration volume*. New Delhi, Abhinav Publications, 1987 : 143-148.

1373. ———.
Chandragupta-Kumaradevi type of gold coins : Analysis of two views. In G.K. Kuppuram and K. Kumudamani, ed., *Researches in Indian history, archaeology, art and religion*, Vol. 1. Delhi, Sundeep Prakashan, 1990 : 325-331.

1374. ———.
Chandragupta-Kumaradevi type of gold coins : Review of two hypotheses. In C.R.P. Sinha and others, ed., *Archaeology and art (Krishna Deva felicitation volume)*. Part II. New Delhi, Ramanand Vidya Bhawan, 1990 : 465-471.

1375. ———.
The Chandragupta-Kumaradevi type of Gold Coins : Observations on two opinions. *Samskriti Sandhana*, Vol. 4, 1991 : 117-119.

1376. ———.
Chandragupta-Kumaradevi type of the Gupta coinage : Examination of arguments of Allan and Altekar on the question of its issuer. *Journal of the Numismatic Society of India*, Vol. 53, 1991 : 100-113.

1377. ———.
Chronology of the rulers known from the repousse gold coins of the Garuda type. *Journal of the Numismatic Society of India*, Vol. 33, pt. 1, 1971 : 61-66.

1378. ______.

The coins of Prakasaditya : A study. *Journal of the Numismatic Society of India*, Vol. 50, 1988 : 89-96.

1379. ______.

The coins of Purugupta. *Journal of the Numismatic Society of India*, Vol. 40, 1978 : 111-115.

1380. ______.

The coins of some later Imperial Guptas : A review. In D.C. Bhattacharyya and Devendra Handa, ed., *Praci-Prabha : Perspectives in Indology* (*Essays in honour of Professor B.N. Mukherjee*). New Delhi, Harman Publishing House, 1989 : 115-125.

1381. ______.

A hoard of the Gupta gold coins from the Rajghat excavations. *Journal of the Numismatic Society of India*, Vol. 33, pt. 2, 1971 : 120-121.

1382. ______.

On a Bayana-hoard coin of chhatra type bearing the legend Kramaditya. *Journal of the Numismatic Society of India*, Vol. 30, 1968 : 84-91.

1383. ______.

On some repousse coins. *Journal of the Numismatic Society of India*, Vol. 33, pt. 2, 1971 : 115-117.

1384. ______.

On some suvarna standard coins of Chandra. *Journal of the Numismatic Society of India*, Vol. 27, pt. 2, 1965 : 177-183.

1385. ______.

On the coins of Budhagupta. *Journal of the Bihar Research Society*, Vols. 65-66, 1979-80 : 178-188.

1386. ______.

On the coins of Budhagupta. *Journal of the Bihar Research Society*, Vols. 67-68, 1981-81 : 113-121.

1387. ______.

On the copper coins of Ramagupta. *Journal of the Numismatic Society of India*, Vol. 25, pt. 1, 1963 : 105-107.

1388. ______.
On the identification of Mahendraditya and Kramaditya of repousse gold coins. *Journal of the Numismatic Society of India*, Vol. 26, pt. 1, 1964 : 31-39.

1389. ______.
On two wrongly attributed coins. *Journal of the Numismatic Society of India*, Vol. 28, pt. 1, 1966 : 64-65.

1390. ______.
The peacock type coins of Kumaragupta I : A review. In Devendra Handa and Ashvini Agrawal, ed., *Ratna-Chandrika : Panorama of Oriental studies* (*Shri R.C. Agrawala festschrift*). New Delhi, Harman Publishing House, 1989 : 149-157.

1391. ______.
A short note on the chronological order of the genealogical seals of the Guptas. *Journal of the Numismatic Society of India*, Vol. 33, pt. 1, 1971 : 125.

1392. ______.
A silver coin of Budhagupta with the new date. *Journal of the Numismatic Society of India*, Vol. 33, pt. 1, 1971 : 122.

1393. ______.
The so-called Nalanda seal of Vainya Gupta. *Journal of the Numismatic Society of India*, Vol. 29, pt. 1, 1967 : 44-45.

1394. ______.
Text-restoration of genealogical Gupta seals. *Journal of the Numismatic Society of India*, Vol. 33, pt. 2, 1971 : 41-60.

1395. **Ahmad, Nisar** and **Verma, T.P.**
A peacock type coin of Kumaragupta I found from Jaunpur. *Bulletin of Museums & Archaeology in U.P.*, Nos. 41-42, June-December 1988 : 107-108.

1396. **Allan, John**
Catalogue of the coins of the Gupta dynasties and of Sasanka, king of Gauda. London, British Museum, 1967.

1397. ______.
The legend of Samudragupta's asvamedha coin type. *Journal & Proceedings of the Asiatic Society of Bengal*, New Series, Vol. 10, 1914, 255-256.

1398. **Altekar, A.S.**
`Apratigha' coins. *Journal of the Numismatic Society of India*, Vol. 11, pt. 1, 1949 : 64.

1399. ______.
Asvamedha coins of Samudragupta. *Bharata Itihas Samshodhaka Mandala Quarterly*,. Vol. 29, Nos. 3-4, 1948 : 1-7.

1400. ______.
The attributioon of the Chandragupta-Kumaradevi type. *Journal of the Royal Asiatic Society of Bengal, Letters*, Vol. 3, 1937, Numismatic Supplement No. 47, 1937-38 : N105-N111.

1401. ______.
Bayana hoard of the Gupta gold coins. *Journal of the Numismatic Society of India*, Vol. 8, pt. 2, 1946 : 179-184.

1402. ______.
Catalogue of the Gupta gold coins in the Bayana hoard. Bombay, Numismatic Society of India, 1954.

1403. ______.
Chandragupta II ka prayank sithit Raja Rani bhanti sikka. *Kala Nidhi*, Vol. 2, No. 1 : 6-10 (Hindi).

1404. ______.
The Chandragupta-Kumaradevi type : An examination of Mr. Sohoni's theories. *Journal of the Numismatic Society of India*, Vol. 5, pt. 2, December 1943 : 145-147.

1405. ______.
The coinage of the Gupta empire and its imitations. Varanasi, Numismatic Society of India, 1957.

1406. ______.
The date and attribution of the coins of Visnugupta. *Journal of the Numismatic Society of India*, Vol. 3, 1941 : 57-59

1407. ______.

The date and attribution of the coins of Visnugupta : A correction. *Journal of the Numismatic Society of India*, Vol. 3, 1941 : 103-104.

1408. ______.

Guptakalin mudrayen. Patna, Bihar Rashtrabhasha Parishad, 1954 (Hindi).

1409. ______.

Identity of Kachagupta. *Journal of the Numismatic Society of India*, Vol. 9, pt. 2, 1947 : 131-136.

1410. ______.

King-and-queen-on-couch type coin of Chandragupta II. *Journal of the Numismatic Society of India*, Vol. 18, pt. 1, 1956 : 51-55.

1411. ______.

Lyrist type of Samudragupta in silver. *Journal of the Numismatic Society of India*, Vol. 21, 1959 : 191-192.

1412. ______.

A new variety of the archer type of Kumaragupta I. *Journal of the Numismatic Society of India*, Vol. 12, pt. 2, 1950 : 124-125.

1413. ______.

News, notes and comments. *Journal of the Numismatic Society of India*, Vol. 10, pt. 1, 1948 : 76-82.

1414. ______.

A note on Apratigha type. *Journal of the Numismatic Society of India*, Vol. 21, pt. 1, 1959 : 71-72.

1415. ______.

Rare and unique coins from the Bayana Gupta hoard. *Journal of the Numismatic Society of India*, Vol. 10, pt. 2, 1948 : 95-118.

1416. ______.

The relative prices of metals and coins in ancient India. *Journal of the Numismatic Society of India*, Vol. 2, 1940 : 1-13.

1417. ———.
Some rare and unique coins in the Prince of Wales Museum, Bombay. *Journal of the Numismatic Society of India*, Vol. 11, pt. 1, 1949 : 44-63.

1418. ———.
Underweight Gupta gold coins. *Journal of the Numismatic Society of India*, Vol. 21, 1959 : 191.

1419. ———.
A unique type of silver coin of Skandagupta (?). *All India Oriental Conference Proceedings,* Summaries of Papers, Session 17, 1953 : 86.

1420. **Altekar, Padma**
The chattra type of Chandragupta II : A new variety. *Journal of the Numismatic Society of India*, Vol. 14, 1952 : 66.

1421. ———.
Some rare Gupta coins of Mr. Poddar's collection. *Journal of the Numismatic Society of India*, Vol. 14, 1952 : 67-70.

1422. **Anand, Kumar**
Gupta gold coins from Bhabua. In C.R.P. Sinha and others, ed., *Archaeology and art* (*Krishna Deva felicitation volume*). Part II. New Delhi, Ramanand Vidya Bhawan, 1990 : 472-475.

1423. **Awasthi, A.B.L.**
Numismatic gleanings from the puranas. *Purana*, Vol. 6, No. 2, 1964 : 347-353.

1424. **Babelon, Jean**
A consolodated list of Indian coins in the Bibliotheque Nationale, Paris. *Journal of the Numismatic Society of India*, Vol. 23, 1961 : 455.

1425. **Bajpai, K.D.**
Braj-mandal mein uplabdh Nag, Gupta tatha purvamadhya kaleen sikke. *Researcher*, Vols. 12-13, 1972-73 : 25-28 (Hindi).

1426. ______.

Coins from Eran excavations : A chronological analysis. In D.W. Macdowall and others, ed., *Indian Numismatics, history, art and culture : Essays in honour of Dr. P.L. Gupta*, Vol. I. Delhi, Agam Kala Prakashan, 1992 : 79-85.

1427. ______.

Coins from Eran excavations : A chronological analysis. In Devendra Handa, ed., *Numismatic Studies*, Vol. 2. New Delhi, Harman Publishing House, 1992 : 21-25.

1428. ______.

Coins from Eran excavations : A chronological analysis. In I.M.Chahal, ed., *Approches to the art & archaeology of Madhya Pradesh*. Bhopal, Commissioner, Archaeology & Museums, 1994 : 41-45.

1429. ______.

Coins from Eran excavations : A chronological analysis.In K.D. Bajpai, ed., *The glory that was Bundelkhand : Mahendra Kumar `Manav' felicitation volume*. Bhopal, Mahendra Kumar Manav Abhinandan Samiti, 1993 : 338-345.

1430. ______.

Fire-altar (?) on the silver and copper coins of the Guptas. *Bulletin of Ancient Indian History and Archaeology*, No. 1, 1967 : 71-72.

1431. ______.

The Gupta coin from Sanchi. *Journal of the Numismatic Society of India*, Vol. 34, pt. 2, 1972 : 258-259.

1432. ______.

Indian numismatics studies. New Delhi, Abhinav Publications, 1976.

1433. ______.

An inscribed Yaksa sealing from Kausambi. *Bulletin of Ancient Indian History and Archaeology*, No. 1, 1967 : 61-62.

1434. ______.

A new copper coin of Ramagupta. *Journal of the Numismatic Society of India*, Vol. 18, pt. 1, 1956 : 108-109.

1435. ______.
Ramagupta, a Gupta king. *Journal of the Numismatic Society of India*, Vol. 23, 1961 : 340-344.

1436. ______.
A rare Gupta coin from Sanchi. *Journal of the Numismatic Society of India*, Vol. 33, pt. 1, 1971 : 120-121.

1437. ______.
Some rare early coins from Central India and Andhra Pradesh. *Journal of the Numismatic Society of India*, Vol. 41, 1979 : 38-46.

1438. ______.
Three interesting copper coins from Vidisa. *All India Oriental Conference Proceedings,* Session 20, Vol. II, pt. 1 : 232-233.

1439. **Bajpai, S.K.**
Eran se prapta pracheen sikke tatha muhare. In K.D. Bajpai, ed., *The glory that was Bundelkhand : Mahendra Kumar `Manav' felicitation volume*. Bhopal, Mahendra Kumar Manav Abhinandan Samiti, 1993 : 330-337 (Hindi).

1440. ______.
A new silver coin of Skandagupta bearing the date 141. *Journal of the Numismatic Society of India*, Vol. 38, pt. 1, 1976 : 72-73.

1441. ______.
Pagara hoard of Gupta gold coins. *Journal of the Numismatic Society of India*, Vol. 44, 1982 : 52-55.

1442. **Bandyopadhyay, Samaresh**
Geographical names from early Indian coins. *Journal of Ancient Indian History*, Vol. 15, 1985-1986 : 284-342.

1443. ______.
Observations on Vina on Indian coins. *Indian Museum Bulletin*, Vol. 22, 1987 : 42-47.

1444. **Banerjea, J.N.**
The `King to R' Variety (?) of the 1standars' type coins of Samudragupta. *Journal of the Numismatic Society of India*, Vol. 12, pt. 2, 1950 : 116-117.

1445. ———.
Gupta gold coins in the Bayana Hoard. *Journal of the Numismatic Society of India*, Vol. 41, pt. 2, June 1955 : 210-216.

1446. **Banerji, Adris**
Aspects of historical seals and sealings. *Indian Museum Bulletin*, Vol. 5, No. 2, 1970 : 35-45.

1447. ———.
Coin devices on Bhita seals. *Indian Historical Quarterly*, Vol. 29, No. 3, September 1953 : 222-232.

1448. ———.
Gupta glyptic art. *Indian Museum Bulletin*, Vol. 4, No. 2, 1969 : 13-21.

1449. ———.
Studies on Basarh sealings. *Indian Historical Quarterly*, Vol. 31, No. 4, December 1955 : 330-338.

1450. **Banerji, Arundhati**
Religion and society as revealed by the Gupta coins. In Deveddra Handa, ed., *Indological Studies* (*Essays in memory of Shri S.P. Singhal*). Delhi, Caxton Publications, 1987 : 161-177.

1451. **Banerji, R.D.**
Coins of later Guptas. *Archaeological Survey of India Annual Report*, 1913-14 : 258-259.

1452. ———.
Notes on Indian numismatics : Samudragupta—Spearman type. *Journal of the Bihar and Orissa Research Society*, Vol. 5, pt. I, March 1919 : 82.

1453. **Basu, S.P.**
The second supplementary catalogue of coins to Vol. I. Calcutta, Indian Museum, 1977.

1454. **Bayley, E.C.**
Notes on Gupta coins. *Indian Antiquary*, Vol. 6, 1887 : 57-58.

1455. **Bhardwaj, H.C.** and **Misra, S.**
A metallurgical note on Gupta period gold coins from Rajghat (Varanasi) excavations. *Journal of the Numismatic Society of India*, Vol. 33, pt. 2, 1971 : 123-127.

1456. **Bharatha Iyer, K.**
An early Gupta seal of the Mahisasurmardini. *Artibus Asiae*, Vol. 31, 1969 : 179-184.

1457. **Bhattacharyya, A.K.**
The coin collection of the Indian Museum—its history and importance. *Indian Museum Bulletin*, Vol. 7, No. 1, 1972 : 21-42.

1458. ——.
A interesting specimen of the bust-type variety of copper coin of Chandragupta II. *Journal of the Asiatic Society*, Vol. 4, Nos. 3-4, 1962 : 161.

1459. **Bhattacharyya, P.K.**
On an imitation Gupta gold coin from Sundarban. *Journal of the Numismatic Society of India*, Vol. 43, pt. 2, 1981 : 60-62.

1460. **Bhattasali, N.K.**
Attribution of the imitation-Gupta coins. *Journal & Proceedings of the Asiatic Society of Bengal*, New Series, Vol. 21, 1925, Numismatic Supplement No. 39, 1925 : N.1-N.6.

1461. ——.
Notes on Gupta and later Gupta coinage. *Journal & Proceedings of the Asiatic Society of Bengal*, New Series, Vol. 19, 1923, Numismatic Supplement No. 37, 1923 : N54-N64.

1462. **Botham, A.W.**
Catalogue of the Provincial coin cabinet Assam. Allahabad, Eastern Book House, 1930.

1463. **Brown, C.J.**
Coins of India. Varanasi, Indological Book House, 1973.

1464. **Browne, Gerald M.**
A Gupta coins legend reconsidered. *Journal of the Numismatic Society of India*, Vol. 51, 1989 : 58-59.

1465. ______.
A new sub-variety of the Chhatra type of Chandragupta II. *Journal of the Numismatic Society of India*, Vol. 50, 1988 : 28-29.

1466. **Campbell, W.E.M.**
Gupta gold coins found in the Ballia district. *Journal & Proceedings of the Asiatic Society of Bengal*, New Series, Vol. 10, 1914 : 174-177.

1467. **Chakrabortty, Surendra Kishor**
Currency problems of ancient India. *Journal of the Department of Letters*, Vol. 30 : 1-72.

1468. ______.
Foreign denominations of ancient Indian coins. *Indian Historical Quarterly*, Vol. 15, No. 1, March 1939 : 65-74.

1469. ______.
The gold coins of ancient Bengal. *Indian Culture*, Vol. 4, No. 2, October 1937 : 222-227.

1470. **Chakravarty, D.K.**
Study on Gupta kings from anthropological view point as engraved on their coins. *Journal of the Numismatic Society of India*, Vol. 51, 1989 : 60-61.

1471. **Chakravarty, D.K.**
The Hasnan hoard of the Gupta gold coins. *Indian History Congress Proceedings*, Session 38, 1977 : 757-764.

1472. **Chandra, R.G.**
Another standard type coin of Chandragupta II. *Journal of the Numismatic Society of India*, Vol. 30, 1968 : 202-203.

1473. ______.
A new Chakravikrama of Chandragupta II. *Journal of the Numismatic Society of India*, Vol. 22, 1960 : 261-263.

1474. **Chatterjee, C.D.**
Gold coins of the standard type (class I) of Chandragupta II. *Journal of the Numismatic Society of India*, Vol. 37, 1975 : 85-99.

1475. ______.
Some unique gold and brass coins of the Imperial Guptas. *Journal of the U.P. Historical Society*, New Series, Vol. 5, pt. 2, 1957 : 43-116.

1476. ______.
Some unique gold and brass coins of the Imperial Guptas. *Bullitin of the U.P. Historical Society*, No. 2, 1957.

1477. **Chattopadhyay, Bhaskar**
Coins and icons : A study of myths and symbols in Indian numismatic art. Calcutta, Punthi Pustak, 1977.

1478. **Chattopadhyaya, B.D.**
Currency in early Bengal. *Journal of Indian History*, Vol. 55, pt. 3, December 1977 : 41-60.

1479. **Chattopadhyaya, Braja Dulal**
Political significance of the alter type coins of Skandagupta. *Journal of the Numismatic Society of India*, Vol. 27, pt. 1, 1965 : 36-40.

1480. **Chaudhary, K.**
Unique gold coin of Samudragupta. *Journal of the Numismatic Society of India*, Vol. 46, 1984 : 49-50.

1481. **Chaudhary, Radhakrishna**
Two new finds from Bihar : A Kusana coin and a Guptan seal. *Indian History Congress Proceedings*, Session 35, 1974 : 452-456.

1482. **Chhabra, B. Ch.**
Catalogue of the Gupta gold coins of the Bayana hoard in the National Museum. New Delhi, National Museum, 1986.

1483. ______.
Chandragupta I ki aditiya suvarna-mudra. *Kala Nidhi*, Vol. 1, No. 2 : 113-124 (Hindi).

1484. ______.
Coin legends of Gupta emperors and Vishnusahasranama. *Journal of the Numismatic Society of India*, Vol. 9, pt. 2, 1947 : 137-145.

1485. ———.
A unique gold coin of Chandragupta I. *Journal of the Numismatic Society of India*, Vol. 11, pt. 1, 1949 : 15-31.

1486. **Chinmulgund, P.J.**
Another Rhinoceros slayer type coin of Kumaragupta I. *Journal of the Numismatic Society of India*, Vol. 17, pt. 2, 1955 : 104-106.

1487. ———.
A new type of Gupta coin. *Journal of the Numismatic Society of India*, Vol. 9, pt. 1, 1947 : 34-35.

1488. ———.
A new variety of Karttikeya type coin of Kumaragupta. *Journal of the Numismatic Society of India*, Vol. 21, 1959 : 72-73.

1489. **Choudhary, Radha Krishna**
A critical study of the so-called Apratigha coin type of Kumaragupta I. *Journal of the Numismatic Society of India*, Vol. 26, pt. 1, 1964 : 15-26.

1490. ———.
Govindagupta of Vaisali seal & Mandasor inscription (a Gupta emperor between G.E. 93 and 96). *Journal of the Oriental Institute*, Vol. 12, No. 4, June 1963 : 370-376.

1491. ———.
A rare Guptan terracotta seal of Samudra Gupta from Naulagarh. *Indian History Congress Proceedings*, Session 26, pt. I, 1964 : 137-140.

1492. Coin. Gwalior, Madhya Pradesh. *Annual Report on Indian Epigraphy*, 1952-53 : 40 (B-137).

1493. Coin from the collection of Mr. H.P. Poddar, Calcutta, West Bengal. *Annual Report on Indian Epigraphy*, 1954-55 : 96-98 (D-15-26).

1494. A coin in the Allahabad Museum, Uttar Pradesh. *Annual Report on Indian Epigraphy*, 1957-58 : 89 (E-83).

1495. Coin in the collection of the Watson Museum, Rajkot, Gujarat. *Annual Report on Indian Epigraphy*, 1963-64 : 171 (E-82).

1496. Coins from Vangiya Sahitya Parishad, Nos. 7-12. Indian Museum, Calcutta. *Annual Report on Indian Epigraphy*, 1962-63 : 237-238 (E-221-226).

1497. Coin in the collection of Shri H.P. Poddar, Calcutta, West Bengal. *Annual Report on Indian Epigraphy*, 1960-61 : 177-180 (E-8-16).

1498. Coins, Pagara, district Dhar, Madhya Pradesh. *Indian Archaeology : A Review*, 1981-82 : 89.

1499. Coins. Valabhipur (Vala), Bhavanagar district, Bombay. *Annual Report on Indian Epigraphy*, 1959-60 : 175-176 (E-125-136).

1500. Copper coin of Samudragupta, Indore, Madhya Pradesh. *Indian Archaeology : A Review*, 1963-64 : 84.

1501. Copper coin, Sanchi, district Raisen, Madhya Pradesh. *Indian Archaeology : A Review*, 1971-72 : 68.

1502. Copper coins and signet ring, Nandur, district Raisen, Madhya Pradesh. *Indian Archaeology : A Review*, 1981-82 : 89.

1503. **Curtis, James W.**
Bhanugupta Prakasaditya : Aspects of his reign, in Light of a new suvarna variety. *Journal of the Numismatic Society of India*, Vol. 20, 1958 : 73-76.

1504. **Daji, Bhau**
Report on some Hindu coins. *Journal of the Bombay Branch of the Royal Asiatic Society*, Vol. 12, 1976 : 213-214.

1505. **Dani, Ahmad Hasan**
Chandragupta I - Kumaradevi coin type. *Journal of the Numismatic Society of India*, Vol. 20, 1958 : 4-8.

1506. **Dani, B.P.**
A dated silver coin of Kumaragupta I in Watson Museum, Rajkot. *Journal of the Numismatic Society of India*, Vol. 26, pt. 1, 1964 : 104-106.

1507. **Das, H.C.**
The tradition of coinage in Orissa. *Journal of the Numismatic Society of India*, Vol. 49, 1987 : 125-134.

1508. **Dasgupta, Kalyan Kumar**
Indian coins and coin-symbols. *Journal of Ancient Indian History*, Vol. 14, 1983-84 : 41-70.

1509. ———.
Indian coins and coin symbols. *Journal of the Numismatic Society of India*, Vol. 46, 1984 : 1-18.

1510. **Das Gupta, N.N.**
The Apratigha type of coins of Kumaragupta I. *Journal of the U. P. Historical Society.* New Series, Vol. 3, pt. 2, 1955 : 156-158.

1511. **Dayal, Prayag**
A new gold coin of Chandragupta II. *Journal & Proceedings of the Asiatic Society of Bengal*, New Series, Vol. 16, 1920 : 89.

1512. ———.
Note on a gold token of Kumaragupta I (A.D. 414-55). *Journal and Proceedings of the Asiatic Society of Bengal*, New Series, Vol. 29, 1933 : N11-N12.

1513. ———.
Two gold Gupta coins. *Journal and Proceedings of the Asiatic Society of Bengal*, New Series, Vol. 19, 1923, Numismatic Supplement No. 37, 1923 : N82-N83.

1514. **De, Gourisankar**
A Chandragupta-Kumaradevi coin from Chandraketugarh. *Journal of the Numismatic Society of India*, Vol. 43, pt. 2, 1981 : 46-48.

1515. ———.
Two gold coins from Chandraketugarh. *Journal of the Numismatic Society of India*, Vol. 41, 1979 : 28-30.

1516. **Deo, S.B.**
A sealing in honour of King Chandra (?). *Journal of the Numismatic Society of India*, Vol. 35, 1973 : 155-158.

1517. **Dhavalikar, M.K.**
On the attribution of the asvamedha type of Samudragupta. *Journal of the Numismatic Society of India*, Vol. 20, 1958 : 175-177.

1518. **Dikshit, K.N.**
An early dated silver coin of Kumaragupta. *Archaeological Survey of India Annual Report*, 1923-24 : 124.

1519. **Dikshit, M.G.**
Cunningham collection of seals in the British Museum. *Journal of the Numismatic Society of India*, Vol. 22, 1960 : 123-130.

1520. ———.
A hoard of lead coins from Karvan : North Gujarat. *Journal of the Numismatic Society of India*, Vol. 13, pt. 1, 1951 : 22-32.

1521. **Dikshit, R.K.**
Simhavahini Lakshmi. *Journal of the Numismatic Society of India*, Vol. 26, pt. 1, 1964 : 102-104.

1522. **Dilip Kumar**
An interesting seal from Vaisali. *Journal of the Bihar Puravid Parishad*, Vol. 1, 1977 : 261-268.

1523. **Diskalkar, D.B.**
Bamnala (Holkar State) find of twenty-one gold coins of the Gupta dynasty. *Journal of the Numismatic Society of India*, Vol. 5, pt. 2, December 1943 : 135-144.

1524. **Dube, J.N.**
Some silver coins of Kumaragupta I in the collection of Shri Umrao Singhji Babel, Indore. *Journal of the Numismatic Society of India*, Vol. 51, 1989 : 16-18.

1525. Early and medieval coins, Ellora, district Aurangabad, Madhya Pradesh. *Indian Archaeology : A Review*, 1959-60 : 66.

1526. Early coins, Eran, district Vidisha, Madhya Pradesh. *Indian Archaeology : A Review*, 1963-64 : 84.

1527. **Fleet, J.F.**
The coins and history of Toramana. *Indian Antiquary*, Vol. 18, August 1989 : 225-230.

1528. ———.
The legends on the silver coins of the early Guptas and others connected with them. *Indian Antiquary*, Vol. 14, 1885 : 65-68.

1529. **Ganguly, D.K.**
A study of the asvamedha coin-type of Samudragupta. *Visvabharati Quarterly*, Vol. 39, Nos. 3-4, 1973-74 : 280-287.

1530. **Ghose, Ajit**
Five rare Gupta gold coins from the Bayana hoard. *Journal of the Numismatic Society of India*, Vol. 22, 1960 : 177-183.

1531. ———.
A new variety of the lion slayer type of Chandragupta II. *Journal of the Numismatic Society of India*, Vol. 1, 1939 : 28.

1532. ———.
Notes on two Gupta coins. *Journal of the Royal Asiatic Society of Bengal, Letters*, Vol. 2, 1936 : N21-N23.

1533. ———.
The rare copper coinage of Kumaragupta I. *Journal of the Royal Asiatic Society of Bengal, Letters*, Vol. 3, Numismatic Supplement No. 47, 1937-38 : N113-N116.

1534. ———.
A unique bronze coin of Samudragupta. *Journal of the Numismatic Society of India*, Vol. 34, pt. 2, 1972 : 223-225.

1535. **Ghosh, A.**
Nalanda seals of Budhagupta and Visnugupta. *Indian Historical Quarterly*, Vol. 19, June 1943 : 119-125.

1536. **Ghosh, Ajit**
Discovery of a second gold coin of Ghatotkachagupta. *Journal of the Numismatic Society of India*, Vol. 22, 1960 : 260-261.

1537. Gold Coins, Hasnan, district Hooghly, West Bengal. *Indian Archaeology : A Review*, 1976-77 : 73.

1538. **Govind Chandra, Rai**
A new chakravikrama coin. *Journal of the Numismatic Society of India*, Vol. 21, pt. 2, 1959 : 202.

1539. ———.
Two gold coins of Chandragupta II. *Journal of the Numismatic Society of India*, Vol. 19, pt. 2, 1957 : 190-191.

1540. **Goyal, S.R.**
Attribution of the coins of Prakasaditya. *Journal of the Numismatic Society of India*, Vol. 28, pt. 1, 1966 : 17-20.

1541. ———.
The dynastic coins of ancient India. Jodhpur, Kusumanjali Prakashan, 1995.

1542. ———.
An introduction to Gupta numismatics. Jodhpur, Kusumanjali Prakashan, 1994.

1543. ———.
Observations on the Shri Vikrama coin of Samudragupta. *Journal of the Numismatic Society of India*, Vol. 27, pt. 2, 1965 : 142-145.

1544. **Gupta, Chandrashekhar**
Foreign denominations of early Indian coins. *Vishveshvaranand Indological Journal*, Vol.16, pt. 1, 1978 : 79-95.

1545. ———.
Gupta lead coins. *Numismatic Digest*, Vol. 7, 1983 : 56-59.

1546. Gupta coin, Kesaria, district Champaran, Bihar. *Indian Archaeology : A Review*, 1970-71 : 61.

1547. Gupta coin, Naravala, district West Nimar, Madhya Pradesh. *Indian Archaeology : A Review*, 1979-80 : 97.

1548. Gupta coins, Anuppur and Beldi, district Shahdol. *Indian Archaeology : A Review*, 1968-69 : 60.

1549. Gupta coins, Bairh, district Tonk, Rajasthan. *Indian Archaeology : A Review*, 1960-61 : 56.

1550. Gupta coins, Boincheegram, district Hooghly, West Bengal. *Indian Archaeology : A Review*, 1981-82 : 90.

1551. Gupta coins, Eran, district Sagar, Madhya Pradesh. *Indian Archaeology : A Review*, 1961-62 : 94.

1552. Gupta coins, Lakshmi Hatir Danga, district Murshidabad, West Bengal. *Indian Archaeology : A Review*, 1971-72 : 72.

1553. Gupta coins, Pitaiband, district Raipur, Madhya Pradesh. *Indian Archaeology : A Review*, 1959-60 : 65

1554. Gupta coins, Runija, district Ujjain, Madhya Pradesh. *Indian Archaeology : A Review*, 1979-80 : 96.

1555. Gupta coins. Ujjain, Madhya Pradesh. *Indian Archaeology : A Review*, 1968-69 : 60.

1556. Gupta coins, Vidisha, Madhya Pradesh. *Indian Archaeology : A Review*, 1970-71 : 61.

1557. **Gupta, L.C.** and **Mangalam, S.J.**
Silver coins of Srigupta. Hyderabad, Numismatic Society of Hyderabad, 1994.

1558. **Gupta, P.L.**
The attribution of the coins of Prakasaditya. *Journal of the Numismatic Society of India*, Vol. 12, pt. 1, 1950 : 34-35.

1559. ———.
Bharat Kala Bhawan sangrah ke kuch durlabh Gupta suvarna dinar. *Kala Nidhi*, Vol. 1, No. 4 : 53-59 (Hindi).

1560. ———.
Chandragupta II ki ek advitiya survana mudra. *Kala Nidhi*, Vol. 1, No. 1 : 48-51 (Hindi).

1561. ———.
Chandragupta III and his coins. *Numismatic Digest*, Vol. 16, 1992 : 66-79.

1562. ———.
Chandragupta's standard type coin—its attribution. *Journal of the Numismatic Society of India*, Vol. 11, pt. 2, 1949 : 104-107.

1563. ———.
The coin-collection of the Prince of Wales Museum, Bombay. *Journal of the Numismatic Society of India*, Vol. 23, 1961 : 497-501.

1564. ———.
The coinage of Bihar. In Bindeshwari Prasad Sinha, ed., *Comprehensive history of Bihar*, Vol. 1, pt. II. Patna, K.P. Jayaswal Research Institute, 1974 : 598-624.

1565. ———.
Coins. New Delhi, National Book Trust, 1969.

1566. ———.
The coins of Ramagupta. *Journal of the Numismatic Society of India*, Vol. 12, pt. 2, 1950 : 103-111.

1567. ———.
A copper motto seal of the Gupta period. *Journal of the Numismatic Society of India*, Vol. 24, 1962 : 181-182.

1568. ———.
Crescent on the Gupta coins. *Journal of the Numismatic Society of India*, Vol. 8, pt. 1, 1946 : 38-40.

1569. ———.
The gold coins of Kumaragupta II and III. *Journal of the Numismatic Society of India*, Vol. 12, pt. 1, 1950 : 31-33.

1570. ———.
Gupta coins in the cabinet of American Numismatic Society. *Journal of the Numismatic Society of India*, Vol. 15, pt. 1, 1953 : 85-88.

1571. ———.
Heavy weight coins of Chandragupta. *Numismatic Digest*, Vol. 5, pt. 2, December 1981 : 36-43.

1572. ———.
Kacha, a step brother of Samudragupta. *Journal of the Numismatic Society of India*, Vol. 5, pt. 1, June 1943 : 33-36.

1573. ———.
Kacha—a step brother of Samudragupta (Post script). *Journal of the Numismatic Society of India*, Vol. 5, pt. 2, December 1943 : 149-150.

1574. ———.
King-and-Queen-on-couch type coin of Chandragupta II. *Journal of the Numismatic Society of India*, Vol. 18, pt. 2, 1956 : 222.

1575. ———.
Kumarkhan hoard of Gupta gold coins. *Journal of the Numismatic Society of India*, Vol. 22, 1960 : 265-266.

1576. ———.
The metrology of the gold coins of Gupta dynasty. *Journal of the Numismatic Society of India*, Vol. 14, 1952 : 118-121.

1577. ———.
A new gold coin type of Kumaragupta I. *Numismatic Digest*, Vol. 17, 1993 : 37-39.

1578. ———.
A note on the gold coin of Budhagupta. *Journal of the Numismatic Society of India*, Vol. 15, pt. 2, 1953 : 193-194.

1579. ———.
Place of Ghatotkachagupta in the Gupta chronology. *Journal of the Numismatic Society of India*, Vol. 14, 1952 : 99-102.

1580. ———.
Place of Kachagupta in the Gupta chronology. *Journal of the Numismatic Society of India*, Vol. 12, pt. 1, 1950 : 36-37.

1581. ———.
Rai Saheb Chandrika Prasad collection of the Numismatic Society of India. *Journal of the Numismatic Society of India*, Vol. 23, 1961 : 494-496.

1582. ———.
A rare archer type coin of Chandragupta II. *Journal of the Numismatic Society of India*, Vol. 32, pt. 1, 1970 : 84.

1583. ———.
Spittoon in the Gupta period. *Annals of the Bhandarkar Oriental Research Institute*. Vol.37, 1956 : 277.

1584. ———.
A standard type coin of Samudragupta. *Journal of the Numismatic Society of India*, Vol. 8, pt. 1, 1946 : 44-45.

1585. ———.
An unexplained archer type coin of Samudragupta. *Journal of the Numismatic Society of India*, Vol. 16, pt. 1, 1954 : 102-104.

1586. ———.
A unique gold coin of Chandragupta II. *Journal of the Numismatic Society of India*, Vol. 9, pt. 2, 1947 : 146-150.

1587. **Gupta, P.L.** and **Srivastava, Sarojini**
Gupta gold coins. Varanasi, Bharat Kala Bhavan, 1981.

1588. **Hamilton, Dudley**
A new type of copper coinage of Chandragupta II. *Journal of the Numismatic Society of India*, Vol. 13, pt. 1, 1951 : 103-104.

1589. ———.
A rare variety of the Asvamedha type of Samudragupta. *Journal of the Numismatic Society of India*, Vol. 13, pt. 1, 1951 : 105-106.

1590. **Handa, Devendra**
A clay sealing from Sunet. *Vishveshvaranand Indological Journal*, Vol. 9, pt. 1, 1971 : 119-120.

1591. ——.

Coins of Vidisagupta and other Huna rulers. *Indian History Congress Proceedings*, Session 42, 1981 : 669-674.

1592. ——.

Some antiquities from Sunet. *Journal of the Numismatic Society of India*, Vol. 32, pt. 1, 1970 : 79-82.

1593. **Hirananda Shastri**

The Asvamedha coins of Samudragupta. *Journal & Proceedings of the Asiatic Society of Bengal,* New Series, Vol. 11, 1915 : 477-478.

1594. ——.

Novelties in Gupta coins. *Journal & Proceedings of the Asiatic Society of Bengal,* New Series, Vol. 13, 1917 : 153-156.

1595. **Hoernle, A.F. Rudolf**

Remarks on the above (Inscribed seal of Kumaragupta II). *Journal of the Asiatic Society of Bengal,* Vol. 58, pt. 1, 1889 : 88-105.

1596. **Islam, Kamrunnisa**

Coinage in ancient Bengal. *Journal of the Varendra Research Museum*, Vol. 1, No. 1, 1972 : 38-59.

1597. **Jagan Nath**

An interesting type of Skandagupta's coins. *Journal of the Numismatic Society of India*, Vol. 8, pt. 1, 1946 : 48-50.

1598. **Jain, Bal Chandra**

The collection of Indian coins in the Raipur Museum. *Journal of the Numismatic Society of India*, Vol. 23, 1961 : 502-506.

1599. ——.

Hitherto unknown repousse coins of Kramaditya. *Journal of the Numismatic Society of India*, Vol. 22, 1960 : 184-187.

1600. ______.
Inventory of the hoards and finds of coins and seals from Madhya Pradesh (Non-Mohammadan). *Numismatic Notes and Monographs No. 5, Journal of the Numismatic Society of India*, Vol. 19, pt. 1, 1957 : 1-24.

1601. ______.
A rare chhatra type coin of Chandragupta II. *Journal of the Numismatic Society of India*, Vol. 17, pt. 2, 1955 : 103-104.

1602. **Jain, Beena**
A study of North Indian guilds based on coins, seals and sealings. *Pragdhara*, No. 1, 1990-91 : 193-198.

1603. **Jain, Rekha**
Ancient Indian coinage : A systematic study of money economy from Janapada period to early medieval period (600 B.C. to A.D. 1200). New Delhi, D.K. Printworld, 1995.

1604. **Jai Prakash**
Observations on the battle axe coin type of Samudragupta. *Journal of the Numismatic Society of India*, Vol. 28, pt. 1, 1966 : 12-16.

1605. ______.
Observations on the Mrigaya coin type of the Guptas. *Journal of the Numismatic Society of India*, Vol. 24, 1962 : 152-163.

1606. ______.
Observations on the Ramagupta legend. *Journal of the Numismatic Society of India*, Vol. 28, pt. 2, 1966 : 157-163.

1607. ______.
Observations on the so-called Khadga-trata coin type of Kumaragupta I. *Journal of the Numismatic Society of India*, Vol. 25, pt. 1, 1963 : 29-35.

1608. ______.
On the Ramagupta of coins. *Journal of the Numismatic Society of India*, Vol. 25, pt. 2, 1963 : 165-171.

1609. **Jaiswal. O.P.**
The Apratigha-type of coin. In B.P. Sinha and others, ed., *Dr. Satkari Mookerji felicitation volume.* Varanasi, Chowkhambha Sanskrit Series Office, 1969 : 348-354.

1610. **Jaiswal, S.K.**
Can Kacha be Ghatotkacha. *Journal of the Numismatic Society of India*, Vol. 55, 1993 : 114-115.

1611. **Jayaswal, K.P.**
A seal of a Janapada. *Indian Antiquary*, Vol. 58, 1929 : 139-140.

1612. **Jayaswal, P.K.**
On the attribution of the coins of Prakasaditya. *Journal of the Numismatic Society of India*, Vol. 28, pt. 1, 1966 : 65-68.

1613. **Jayaswal, Prashant Kumar**
Pracheen Bharatiya sikkon ka etihasik vivechan. *Parishad Patrika*, Vol. 9, No. 1, April 1969 : 71-78 (Hindi).

1614. **Joshi, M.C.**
Apratigha type : A study. *Journal of the Numismatic Society of India*, Vol. 21, 1959 : 34-36.

1615. ______.
The-king-and-Lakshmi or queen type coin of Skandagupta. *Journal of the Numismatic Society of India*, Vol. 22, 1960 : 263-265.

1616. ______.
Notes on some gold coin-types of the Guptas. *Journal of the Numismatic Society of India*, Vol. 24, 1962 : 34-40.

1617. ______.
The probable background of the standard type coin of king Samudragupta. *Journal of the Numismatic Society of India*, Vol. 19, pt. 1, 1957 : 14-19.

1618. ______.
Samudragupta's standard type—a further consideration. *Journal of the Numismatic Society of India*, Vol. 21, 1959 : 70-71.

1619. **Joshi, Maheshwar P.**
Horse-rider type of Chandragupta II Vikramaditya and the Kalki incarnation. *Journal of the Numismatic Society of India*, Vol. 41, 1979 : 51-54.

1620. **Joshi, N.P.**
The Numismatic section of the Sanskrit University Museum, Varanasi. *Journal of the Numismatic Society of India*, Vol. 23, 1961 : 507-510.

1621. **Kala, S.C.**
New coins inthe Allahabad Museum Cabinet. *Journal of the Numismatic Society of India*, Vol. 24, 1962 : 139-140.

1622. **Kar, Rabis C.**
The fire-alter on Gupta coins. *Indian Historical Quarterly*, Vol. 23, No. 3, September 1947 : 251-252.

1623. ——.
The fire-alter on Gupta coins. *Journal of the Numismatic Society of India*, Vol. 12, pt. 1, 1950 : 48-49.

1624. ——.
A new gold coin of Skandagupta from N. Bengal. *Journal of the Numismatic Society of India*, Vol. 7, 1945 : 13-18.

1625. ——.
A new interpretation of the Gupta chhatra and battle-axe coin-types. *Journal of the Numismatic Society of India*, Vol. 6, 1944 : 27-33.

1626. ——.
The Vamana-attendant on Gupta coins. *Indian Historical Quarterly*, Vol. 23, No. 2, June 1947 : 113-122.

1627. **Katare, Sant Lal**
The so-called coins of Srigupta. *Prachya Pratibha*, Vol. 7, 1979 : 49-54.

1628. **Khan, Ashfaq Ahmad**
Glimpses of coin cabinet in the State Museum, Lucknow. *Bulletin of Museums & Archaeology in U.P.*, Nos. 29-30, June-December 1982 : 83-87.

1629. **Kittoe, M.**
Memo on some ancient gold coins found near Benares, in 1851, and submitted by Government of India for the inspection of the members of the Asiatic Society. *Journal of the Asiatic Society of Bengal*, Vol. 21, 1852 : 390-400.

1630. **Krishna Deva**
Coin devices on Rajghat seals. *Journal of the Numismatic Society of India*, Vol. 3, 1941 : 73-77.

1631. **Krom, N.J.**
The first Hindu coin from Java. *Journal of the Numismatic Society of India*, Vol. 30, 1968 : 200-201.

1632. **Lahiri, Bela**
Complexities in the study of early medieval coins of Northern India. *Journal of the Numismatic Society of India*, Vol. 42, 1980 : 74-94.

1633. ———.
The Gupta-type coins of early medieval period. *Journal of the Numismatic Society of India*, Vol. 44, 1982 : 155-170.

1634. **Maheshwari, K.K.**
Alleged coins of Srigupta. *Prachya Pratibha*, Vols. 9-10, 1981-82 : 43-45.

1635. ———.
Western type silver coins of Skandagupta. *Numismatic Digest*, Vol. 5, pt. 1, June 1981 : 28-30.

1636. **Maity, S.K.**
Early Indian coins and currency system. New Delhi, Munshiram Manoharlal, 1970.

1637. ———.
The gold content of Gupta coins. *Indian History Congress Proceedings*, Session 19, 1956 : 85.

1638. ———.
The gold content of Gupta coins. *Journal of the Numismatic Society of India*, Vol. 18, pt. 2, 1956 : 187-197.

1639. ———.
The gold content of Gupta coins from the Indian Museum, Calcutta. *Journal of the Numismatic Society of India*, Vol. 20, 1958 : 183-188.

1640. ______.
The gold content of the later Imperial Gupta coins. *Journal of the Numismatic Society of India*, Vol. 22, 1960 : 266-268.

1641. ______.
Metrological study of the gold coins of early India. *Journal of the Numismatic Society of India*, Vol. 23, 1961 : 259-266.

1642. ______.
Panoramic culture of early Indian coins. *Journal of the Numismatic Society of India*, Vol. 49, 1987 : 1-12.

1643. **Majumdar, R.C.**
Apratigha coins of Kumaragupta I. *Journal of the Numismatic Society of India*, Vol. 12, pt. 1, 1950 : 72-73.

1644. ______.
Hoards of coins. *Journal of the Numismatic Society of India*, Vol. 23, 1961 : 128-132.

1645. ______.
The seal of Vainya-gupta. *Indian Historical Quarterly*, Vol. 24, No. 1, March 1948 : 67-68.

1646. **Mani, B.R.**
New evidence concerning gold proto-type silver coins of the Gupta emperors. *Journal of the Numismatic Society of India*, Vol. 43, pt. 2, 1981 : 54-59.

1647. **Mankad, B.L.**
The coin-collection of the Baroda Museum. *Journal of the Numismatic Society of India*, Vol. 23, 1961 : 435-446.

1648. **Mankad, B.L.** and **Mehta, R.N.**
Some interesting coins from Karvan. *Journal of the Numismatic Society of India*, Vol. 13, pt. 2, 1951 : 219-222.

1649. **Manmohan Kumar**
Gupta coin moulds : Forgery or trade compulsion ? In Devendra Handa, ed., *Numismatic Studies*, Vol. 2. New Delhi, Harman Publishing House, 1992 : 119-122.

1650. ——.
A unique Gupta copper coin from Sanghol. *Prachya Pratibha*, Vol. 6, No. 1, January 1978 : 67-70.

1651. **Mathur, I.D.**
The coin-collection in the National Museum, New Delhi. *Journal of the Numismatic Society of India*, Vol. 23, 1961 : 491-493.

1652. **Miller, Barbara Stoler**
A dynasty of patrons : The representation of Gupta royalty in coins and literature. In Barbara Stoler Miller, ed., *The power of art : Patronage in Indian culture*. Delhi, Oxford University Press, 1992 : 54-64.

1653. **Mirashi, V.V.**
The Apratigha coins of Kumaragupta I. *Journal of the Numismatic Society of India*, Vol. 12, pt. 1, 1950 : 68-71.

1654. ——.
A note on the Khairtal hoard of the coins of Mahendraditya. *Journal of the Numismatic Society of India*, Vol. 11, pt. 2, 1949 : 108-110.

1655. Miscellaneous coins, Vidisha, district Vidisha, Madhya Pradesh. *Indian Archaeology : A Review*, 1967-68 : 63.

1656. Miscellaneous finds, Durga-Asthan, district Bhagalpur, Bihar. *Indian Archaeology : A Review*, 1959-60 : 65.

1657. **Mishra, C.N.**
A rare specimen of an archer coin-type of Narasimhagupta (Baladitya). *Indian Antiquary*, Third Series, Vol. 1, 1964 : 203-218.

1658. **Misra, B.N.**
The Nalanda clay-seal of the monastery of Sakraditya. *Prachya Pratibha*, Vol. 12, 1984 : 49-62.

1659. **Misra, Shive Nandan**
The Simhavahini on the Gupta coins. *Journal of the Numismatic Society of India*, Vol. 30, 1968 : 80-83.

1660. **Mitchell, Helen**
The collection of Indian coins in Ashmolean Museum, Oxford. *Journal of the Numismatic Society of India*, Vol. 23, 1961 : 421-423.

1661. **Mitra, Rajendralal**
Note on three ancient coins found at Mohammadpur, in the Jessore district. *Journal of the Asiatic Society of Bengal*, Vol. 21, 1852 : 401-402.

1662. **Moller, Jurgen**
Lead coins of the Gupta dynasty. *Numismatic Digest*, Vol. 5, pt. 1, June 1981 : 19-27.

1663. **Mookerji, Radha Kumud**
Some aspects of Gupta coinage. *Journal of the Numismatic Society of India*, Vol. 5, pt. 2, 1943 : 151-152.

1664. ______.
Some considerations on Gupta coinage. In D.R. Bhandarkar and others, ed., *B.C. Law volume*, Part I. Calcutta, Indian Research Institute, 1945 : 164-169.

1665. **Mukherjee, B.N.**
Art in Gupta and post-Gupta coinages of Northern India. Lucknow, State Museum, 1985.

1666. ______.
Coins and currency system in Gupta Bengal (c. A.D. 320-550). New Delhi, Harman Publishing House, 1992.

1667. ______.
An interesting gold coin. *Journal of the Asiatic Society*, Vol. 27, No. 3, 1985 : 140-141.

1668. ______.
A note on Gupta numismatic art. In Jayanta Chakrabarty and D. C. Bhattacharyya, ed., *Aspects of Indian art and culture : S.K. Saraswati commemoration volume*. Calcutta, Rddhi-India, 1983 : 135-138.

1669. ______.
A note on musical instruments on Indian coins. *Journal of the Numismatic Society of India*, Vol. 48, 1986 : 121-122.

1670. ______.
A note on the history of Indian coin-collection in the British Museum. *Journal of the Numismatic Society of India*, Vol. 23, 1961 : 456-466.

1671. ——.
Obverse legend on the coins of Vainyagupta. In *J.N. Banerjea volume*. Calcutta, Department of Ancient Indian History and Culture, 1960 : 336-338.

1672. ——.
A plea for study of art in coinage. *Journal of the Numismatic Society of India*, Vol. 43, pt. 2, 1981 : 1-37.

1673. ——.
"Rhinoceros-Slayer" type coins of Kumaragupta I. *Indian Historical Quarterly*, Vol. 31, No. 2, June 1955 : 175-181.

1674. **Mukherjee, B.N.** and **Raychaudhuri, T.N.**
The Indian gold : An introduction to the cabinet of gold coins in the Indian Museum Calcutta, Indian Museum, 1990.

1675. **Mukherjee, Bikash**
A note on the king, peacock and Garuda type coins of the Gupta rulers. *Journal of the Numismatic Society of India*, Vol. 50, 1988 : 82-83.

1676. **Mukherjee, Chhanda**
Garuda on coins and seals of the Imperial Guptas. *Journal of the Numismatic Society of India*, Vol. 46, 1984 : 96-97.

1677. ——.
Gupta coinage from Bengal and contemporary trade & commerce. *Indian Museum Bulletin*, Vol. 26, 1991 : 36-41.

1678. ——.
Gupta coins : Their social bearing. *Indian Museum Bulletin*, Vol. 20, 1985 : 78-79.

1679. ——.
Gupta numismatic art : An artistic and iconographic study. Delhi, Agam Kala Prakashan, 1991.

1680. **Mukherjee, D.**
Gaja-Laksmi motif on some sealings in the Indian Museum. *Indian Museum Bulletin*, Vol. 21, 1986 : 97-99.

1681. **Mukherji, Chhanda**
The depiction of royal personages on Gupta gold coins. *Journal of Ancient Indian History*, Vol. 12, 1978-1979 : 118-125.

1682. **Mukhopadhyay, Chhanda**
Goddess Ganga on Gupta coins. *Journal of the Numismatic Society of India*, Vol. 44, 1982 : 148-150.

1683. ——.
The representation of Visnu on Gupta coins. *Journal of Ancient Indian History*, Vol. 13, 1980-82 : 30-33.

1684. **Mukhopadhyay, Samir K.**
An interesting gold disc from Bhita. *Monthly Bulletin of the Asiatic Society*, Vol. 5, No. 10, November 1970 : 4-5.

1685. **Nagar, M. M.**
New Gupta coins in the State Museum, Lucknow. *Journal of the Numismatic Society of India*, Vol. 15, pt. 1, 1953 : 80-84.

1686. ——.
A Rhinoceros slayer type coin of Kumaragupta I. *Journal of the Numismatic Society of India*, Vol. 11, pt. 1, 1949 : 7-8.

1687. **Nagarch, B.L.**
Numismatics as a source of iconographic and architectural studies. *Journal of Indian History*, Vol. 63, 1985 : 7-17.

1688. **Nahar, P.S.**
Some rare Gupta coins. *Journal and Proceedings of the Asiatic Society of Bengal*, New Series, Vol. 29, 1933 : N13-N14.

1689. **Nanavati, J.M.**
The coin-collection in Watson Museum, Rajkot. *Journal of the Numismatic Society of India*, Vol. 23, 1961 : 511.

1690. **Narain, A.K.**
Budhagupta and his gold coins. *Journal of the Numismatic Society of India*, Vol. 12, pt. 2, 1950 : 112-115.

1691. ———.

A very rare silver plated coin of Kumaragupta I. *Journal of the Numismatic Society of India*, Vol. 13, pt. 1, 1951 : 76-77.

1692. **Nath, B.N.**

Recent numismatic discoveries in Orissa. *Journal of the Numismatic Society of India*, Vol. 13, pt. 1, 1951 : 92-94.

1693. **Pal, Pratapaditya**

The Chowrie-bearing goddess on the asvamedha type of Samudragupta's coin. *Ars Orientalis*, Vol. 18, 1988 : 197-199.

1694. **Pandey, Deena Bandhu**

Numismatic data in the Amarakosa. *Bulletin of Ancient Indian History and Archaeology*, No. 2, 1968 : 81-83.

1695. **Pandey, Indu Prakash**

Vikramah : A very rare title of Samudragupta. *Bulletin of Museums & Archaeology in U.P.*, Nos. 41-42, June-December 1988 : 93-95.

1696. **Pandey, M.S.**

The Chandragupta-Kumaradevi type of coins. In B.P.Sinha and others,ed., *Dr. Satkari Mookerji felicitation volume*. Varanasi, Chowkhamba Sanskrit Series Office, 1969 : 282-285.

1697. **Pandey, V.C.**

Candragupta-Kumaradevi type of coins and the dual character of Samudragupta's royality. *Journal of the Numismatic Society of India*, Vol. 38, pt. 1, 1976 : 58-64.

1698. **Pandeya, Indu Prakash**

Chandragupta II ki durlabh mudra. *Dhyanam*, Vol. 4, 1984 : 63-65 (Hindi).

1699. ———.

Lucknow Sanghralaya ka Gupta kalin swarna mudrakush. *Bulletin of Museums & Archaeology in U.P.*, Nos. 35-36, June-December 1985 : 75-106 (Hindi).

1700. ______.
`Vikrama' virud : Samudragupta ki durlabh mudra. *Dhyanam*, Vols. 5-6, 1985-86 : 105-106 (Hindi).

1701. **Panna Lal**
A gold coin of Kumara Gupta I. *Journal and Proceedings of the Asiatic Society of Bengal*, New Series, Vol. 21, 1925, Numismatic Supplement, No. 39, 1925 : N21-N23.

1702. **Pant, G.N.**
Representation of weapons on ancient Indian coins. *Journal of the Asiatic Society of Bombay*, New Series, Vols. 56-59, 1981-84 : 244-258.

1703. **Parmar, B.M.S.**
A note on the coin collections of Jhalawar and Kota Museums, *Researcher*, Vols. 12-13, 1972-73 : 33-38.

1704. ______.
Rajasthan ki khoj : Sikkon ke madhyam se. *Rajasthan Bharati*, Vol. 10, No. 2, 1967 : 5-8 (Hindi).

1705. ______.
Some more Gupta gold coins from Bairh (Rajasthan). *Journal of the Numismatic Society of India*, Vol. 32, pt. 2, 1970 : 203-205.

1706. **Pathak, V.S.**
Motifs on Gupta coins and Sassanian wares. *Numismatic Digest*, Vol. 10, 1986 : 81-90.

1707. ______.
Motifs on Gupta coins and Sassanian wares-II. *Numismatic Digest*, Vols. 12-13, 1988-89 : 40-62.

1708. ______.
Notes on the Gupta coinage : Chandragupta I-Kumaradevi coin-type. *Journal of the Numismatic Society of India*, Vol. 19, pt. 2, 1957 : 135-144.

1709. ______.
Religious sealings from Rajghat. *Journal of the Numismatic Society of India*, Vol. 19, pt. 2, 1957 : 168-179.

1710. **Paul, R.K.**
Terracotta sealings from Pakhna-Bihar. *Panchala*, Vol. 3, 1988 : 119-124.

1711. Photograph of a clay seal in the Indian Museum, Calcutta, West Bengal. *Annual Report on Indian Epigraphy*, 1976-77 : 45 (B-56-58).

1712. **Rajgor, Dilip**
Silver coins of Skandagupta from Kutch. *Numismatic Digest*, Vol. 14, 1990 : 25-27.

1713. Ramagupta and other coins, Vidisha, Madhya Pradesh. *Indian Archaeology : A Review*, 1960-61 : 55.

1714. **Rao, Bhatta Sankara**
Study of gold and copper coins using non-destructive techniques. *Journal of the Numismatic Society of India*, Vol. 52, 1990 : 116-123.

1715. **Rapson, E.J.**
The coins of Acyuta, a prince defeated by Samudra Gupta. *Journal of the Royal Asiatic Society of Great Britain and Ireland*, 1897 : 420-421.

1716. ———.
Indian coins. Strassburg, Verlag Von Karl J. Trubner, 1897.

1717. ———.
Sources of Indian History : Coins; Hindi translation by Ram Kumar Rai. Varanasi, Chowkhamba Vidyabhawan, 1966 (Hindi).

1718. ———.
Sources of Indian History : Coins. In G. Buhler, ed., *Encyclopedia of Indo-Aryan Research*, Vol. II, pt. 3, B : 1-56.

1719. **Raven, Ellen M.**
Candragupta III : Tracing the coins of a Gupta king. In Catherine Jarrige, ed., *South Asian Archaeology 1989*. Madison, Prehistory Press, 1992 : 441-448.

1720. ______.
Gupta gold coins with a Garuda-banner : Samudragupta-Skandagupta. 2 Vols. Groningen, Egbert Forsten, 1994.

1721. ______.
Invention and innovation : Royal Gupta gold coins. *Marg*, Vol. 45, No. 4 : 39-56.

1722. ______.
Styles in early Gupta gold coins. In Nalini Balbir and Joachimk Bautze, ed., *Festschrift : Klaus Bruhn*. Reinbek, Dr. Inge Wezler, Verlag fur Orientalistische Fachpublicationen, 1994 : 523-544.

1723. **Ray, S.C.**
Coins & culture : An archaeollogical approach. New Delhi, Angkor Publishers, 1995.

1724. ______.
Numismatic evidences of a new monarch of the Gupta period. *Journal of the Numismatic Society of India*, Vol. 32, pt. 1, 1970 : 35-39.

1725. ______.
On coins recovered from Nalanda Excavations. *Journal of the Numismatic Society of India*, Vol. 18, pt. 1, 1956 : 101-107.

1726. **Ray Chowdhury, Chittaranjan**
A new light on the identification of Kaca. *Indian Historical Quarterly*, Vol. 35, No. 4, December 1959 : 333-339.

1727. **Rode, V.P.**
The coin-collection in the Central Museum, Nagpur. *Journal of the Numismatic Society of India*, Vol. 23, 1961 : 488-490.

1728. ______.
Khairtal hoard of the coins of Mahendraditya. *Journal of the Numismatic Society of India*, Vol. 10, pt. 2, 1948 : 137-142.

1729. **Roy, Brajdeo Prasad**
Inscribed terrcaotta sealings from Vaisali. *Journal of the Numismatic Society of India*, Vol. 44, 1982 : 91-95.

1730. ———.
Significance of the crescent on the coins of Chandragupta I. (A vedic point of view). *Prajna-Bharati*, Vol. 4, 1984 : 109-112.

1731. ———.
The so-called Apratigha coin type of Kumaragupta I. *Journal of the Numismatic Society of India*, Vol. 24, 1962 : 164-167.

1732. **Roy Choudhury, Chittaranjan**
Observations on the apratigha coins of Kumara-gupta I. *Indian Historical Quarterly*, Vol. 34, No. 3-4, September & December 1958 : 270-275.

1733. **Sahay, S.N.**
Coins of Bihar. In Bhagwant Sahai and Sachidanand Sahay, ed., *Bihar Past and Present*. Patna, Bihar Historical Society, 1981 : 38-42.

1734. **Samanta, Sailendra Nath**
Some notes on the gold coins of Chandragupta II Vikramaditya in the collection of the University Museum, Burdwan (West Bengal). *Indian History Congress Proceedings*, Session 31, 1969 : 55.

1735. **Saraswati, Bandana**
Amba-Nanda-Durga. *Journal of the Asiatic Society*, Vol. 7, Nos. 1-2, 1965 : 95-98.

1736. **Saraswati, S.K.**
A gold coin of Budhagupta. *Indian Culture*, Vol. 1, No. 4, April 1935 : 691-692.

1737. ———.
Two seal matrices of the Gupta period. *Bharatiya Vidya*, Vol. 10, 1949 : 166-169.

1738. **Satya Prakash**
The coin-collection of the Jaipur Museum. *Journal of the Numismatic Society of India*, Vol. 23, 1961 : 468-470.

1739. ———.
Interesting numismatic finds at Naliasar-Sambhar. *Journal of the Numismatic Society of India*, Vol. 12, pt. 1, 1950 : 54-56.

1740. ———.
An interesting terracotta seal in the Bikaner Museum. *All India Oriental Conference Proceedings*, Session 16, Vol. 2, 1951 : 236-237.

1741. **Satya Prakash and Rajendra Singh**
Coinage in ancient India : A numismatic, archaeological and metallurgical study of ancient Indian coins. New Delhi, The Research Institute of Ancient Scientific Studies, 1968.

1742. **Sethi, R.K.**
A copper seal of the Gupta period. *Journal of the Numismatic Society of India*, Vol. 31, pt. 1, 1969 : 74-75.

1743. ———.
Maharaj Srigupta. *Prachya Pratibha*, Vol. 6, No. 2, July 1978 : 135-143 (Hindi).

1744. ———.
The problem of Maharaja Srigupta. *Journal of the Numismatic Society of India*, Vol. 43, pt. 2, 1981 : 63-69.

1745. **Sharan, Mahesh Kumar**
Tribal coins—a study. New Delhi, Abhinav Publications, 1972.

1746. **Sharma, Dashratha**
The expression Samara-sata-vitata-vijao in relation to the chronological position of Samudragupta's standard type coins. *Journal of the Numismatic Society of India*, Vol. 28, pt. 1, 1966 : 62-63.

1747. ———.
Mahadevi Prabhudama of the Vaisali seal a Gupta queen. *Indian History Congress Proceedings*, Session 19, 1956 : 146-148.

1748. **Sharma, R.S.**
Coins and problems of early Indian economic history. *Indian History Congress Proceedings*, Session 30, 1968 : 103-109.

1749. **Sharma, S.R.**
Two Gupta gold coins from Shahdol district. *Journal of the Numismatic Society of India*, Vol. 41, 1979 : 123.

1750. **Shastri, Ajay Mitra**
Coins in the Brihatsamhita of Varahamihira. *Journal of the Numismatic Society of India*, Vol. 29, pt. 2, 1967 : 40-45.

1751. ———.
Contemporary forgeries of silver coins of Kumaragupta I. In B.N. Mukherjee and others, ed., *Sri Dinesacandrika : Studies in Indology; Shri D.C. Sircar festchrift*. Delhi, Sundeep Prakashan, 1983 : 97-102.

1752. ———.
The couch type coins of Chandragupta II. *Journal of the Numismatic Society of India*, Vol. 46, 1984 : 86-90.

1753. ———.
Did Srigupta issue coins. *Prachya Pratibha*, Vols. 9-10, 1981-82 : 37-41.

1754. ———.
Impact of Western Kshatrapa coinage on early Indian Indigenous coins. *Journal of the Andhra Historical Research Society*, Vol. 38, pt. 1, 1983-1984 : 151-161.

1755. **Shrivastava, Prasant**
Observation of a Gupta sealing. In I.M. Chahal, ed., *Approaches to the art & archaeology of Madhya Pradesh*, Bhopal, Commissioner, Archaeology & Museums, 1994 : 47-48.

1756. **Shukla, K.S.**
A rare copper coin of Kumaragupta I from Newal. *Journal of the Numismatic Society of India*, Vol. 54, 1992 : 62-64.

1757. ______.
A unique gold coin of Bhanugupta and Prakasaditya. *Journal of the Numismatic Society of India*, Vol. 42, 1980 : 120-126.

1758. **Shukla, S.M.**
Some interesting sub-varieties of the Gupta coins. *Journal of the Numismatic Society of India*, Vol. 22, 1960 : 188-192.

1759: **Sindhu, Iqbal Singh**
Coin as a source of early history of Haryana from earliest times to c. 550 A.D. *Indian History Congress Proceedings*, Session 47, Volume II, 1986 : 197.

1760. **Singh, A.N.**
The Rhinoceros-slayer type of Kumaragupta I and its significance. *Journal of the Numismatic Society of India*, Vol. 45, 1983 : 150-151.

1761. **Singh, B.B.**
Chandragupta-Kumaradevi coin type—a re-appraisal. *Journal of the Numismatic Society of India*, Vol. 41, 1979 : 78-81.

1762. **Singh, Jai Prakash**
Gupta copper coin or temple medal. *Journal of the Numismatic Society of India*, Vol. 34, pt. 2, 1972 : 253-257.

1763. ______.
Is Gupta gold a gift money ? *Indologica Taurinensia*, Vol. 13, 1985-86 : 313-320.

1764. ______.
The king and peacock type of Kumaragupta I and its significance. *Journal of the Numismatic Society of India*, Vol. 39, 1977 : 124-127.

1765. ______.
The king and queen type of Skandagupta. *Journal of the Numismatic Society of India*, Vol. 31, pt. 2, 1969 : 155-159.

1766. ______.
On a Gupta period copper seal. *Journal of the Numismatic Society of India*, Vol. 34, pt. 2, 1972 : 260-262.

1767. ______.
On the hoarseman type of the Guptas. *Journal of the Numismatic Society of India*, Vol. 32, pt. 2, 1970 : 172-175.

1768. ______.
Rama on Indian coins. In Lallanji Gopal, ed., *Ayodhya : History, archaeology and tradition*. Varanasi, All India Kashiraj Trust, 1994 : 117-126.

1769. ______.
Rama on Indian coins. *Purana*, Vol. 36, No. 1, 1994 : 117-126.

1770. **Singh, O.P.**
A note on silver coin of Chandragupta I and Kumaradevi. *Journal of the Numismatic Society of India*, Vol. 44, 1982 : 48-51.

1771. ______.
Obverse devise of horseman lion slayer type of Prakasaditya's coin. *Journal of the Numismatic Society of India*, Vol. 33, pt. 1, 1971 : 122-125.

1772. ______.
Ornaments as depicted on early Indian coins. *Journal of the Numismatic Society of India*, Vol. 43, pt. 2, 1981 : 121-126.

1773. ______.
Samkarsana, Vasudeva and Sarvamangala on coins. *Bulletin of Museums & Archaeology in U.P.*, Nos. 17-18, June-December 1976 : 16-22.

1774. ______.
Social aspects of art in early Indian coinage. *Journal of the Numismatic Society of India*, Vol. 42, 1980 : 66-73.

1775. **Singh, R.B.**
Physical activities as revealed on Gupta coins. *Journal of the Numismatic Society of India*, Vol. 54, 1992 : 165-167.

1776. **Singh, Ram Shekhar**
Terracotta sealings from Naulagarh. *Journal of the Bihar Puravid Parishad*, Vols. 7-8, 1983-84 : 287-291.

1777. **Singh, Sarjug Prasad**
Early Indian coins discovered from Basadha (Bihar). *Journal of the Numismatic Society of India*, Vol. 46, 1984 : 18-21.

1778. **Singh, Shatrughna Sharan**
Early coins of North India : An iconographic study. Patna, Janaki Prakashan, 1984.

1779. **Singh, Y.B.**
A note on the Rhinoceros type of Kumaragupta I. *Journal of the Numismatic Society of India*, Vol. 43, pt. 1, 1981 : 67-70.

1780. ———.
Some recently found silver coins of the Imperial Guptas. *Journal of the Numismatic Society of India*, Vol. 41, 1979 : 47-50.

1781. **Singhal, C.R.**
A hoard og Gupta coins found in Gujarat. *Journal of the Numismatic Society of India*, Vol. 15, pt. 2, 1953 : 195-196.

1782. **Sinha, B.P.**
`Apratigha' coins. *Journal of the Numismatic Society of India*, Vol. 16, pt. 2, 1954 : 210-214.

1783. ———.
Coins in the reconstruction of the political history of ancient Bihar. In D.W. Macdowall and others, ed., *Indian numismatics, history, art and culture : Essays in honour of Dr. P.L. Gupta*, Vol. I. Delhi, Agam Kala Prakashan, 1992 : 61-62.

1784. ———.
King and queen (?) of Skandagupta. *Journal of the Numismatic Society of India*, Vol. 50, 1988 : 84-88.

1785. ———.
Remarks on `Apratigha' coins. *Indian History Congress Proceedings*, Session 17, 1954 : 104-109.

1786. **Sircar, D.C.**
Copper coins of Ramagupta. *Journal of Indian History*, Vol. 40, pt. 3, December 1962 : 533-536.

1787. ———.
Evidence of the Nalanda seals. *Indian Historical Quarterly*, Vol. 19, No. 3, September 1943 : 272-281.

1788. ———.
Modern imitation of a Gupta numismatic motif. *Journal of the Numismatic Society of India*, Vol. 29, pt. 1, 1967 : 52-54.

1789. ———.
Rhinoceros-slayer type coins of Kumaragupta I . *Journal of the Numismatic Society of India*, Vol. 28, pt. 2, 1966 : 211-213.

1790. ———.
Studies in Indian coins. Delhi, Motilal Banarsidass, 1968.

1791. **Sitholey, B.S.**
The art of Gupta coins. *Journal of the Numismatic Society of India*, Vol. 10, pt. 2, 1948 : 119-131.

1792. ———.
The origin of Samudragupta's standard type coin. *Journal of the Numismatic Society of India*, Vol. 10, pt. 1, 1948 : 64-71.

1793. ———.
Symbols on Gupta coins. *Journal of the Numismatic Society of India*, Vol. 11, pt. 2, 1949 : 111-113.

1794. **Sivaramamurti, C.**
Chakravikrama type. *Journal of the Numismatic Society of India*, Vol. 13, pt. 2, 1951 : 180-182.

1795. **Smith, V.A.**
A classified and detailed catalogue of the gold coins of the Imperial Gupta dynasty of Northern India, with an introductory essay. *Journal of the Asiatic Society of Bengal*, Vol. 53, pt. 1, 1984 : 119-206.

1796. ______.
The coinage of the early or Imperial Gupta dynasty of Northern India. *Journal of the Royal Asiatic Society of Great Britain and Ireland*, New Series, Vol. 21, 1889 : 1-158.

1797. ______.
Coins of ancient India : Catalogue of coins in Indian Museum, Calcutta, Vol. I. Delhi, Indological Book House, 1972.

1798. ______.
The coins of the Imperial Gupta dynasty. *Indian Antiquary*, Vol. 14, 1885 : 179-180.

1799. ______.
Further observations on the history and coinage of the Gupta period. *Journal of the Asiatic Society of Bengal*, Vol. 63, pt. 1, 1894 : 164-212.

1800. ______.
Inscribed seal of Kumara Gupta. *Journal of the Asiatic Society of Bengal*, Vol. 58, pt. 1, 1889 : 84-88.

1801. ______.
Observations on the Gupta coinage. *Journal of the Royal Asiatic Society of Great Britain and Ireland*, 1893 : 77-148.

1802. ______.
Pistapura, Mahendragiri, and king Achyuta. *Journal of the Royal Asiatic Society of Great Britain and Ireland*, 1897 : 643.

1803. ______.
Vaisali; seals of Gupta period. *Journal of the Royal Asiatic Society of Great Britain and Ireland*, 1905 : 152-154.

1804. **Sohoni, S.V.**
Alleged cornucopiae and fillet on Gupta coinage. *Journal of the Numismatic Society of India*, Vol. 19, pt. 2, 1957 : 162-167.

1805. ———.
Apratigha coin type of Kumaragupta I. *Journal of the Bihar Research Society*, Vol. 41, pt. 3, September 1955 : 387-395.

1806. ———.
Apratigha coin type of Kumaragupta I. *Journal of the Numismatic Society of India*, Vol. 18, pt. 1, 1956 : 56-63.

1807. ———.
Chandragupta I-Kumaradevi coin type A re-examination. *Journal of the Bihar Research Society*, Vol. 42, pts. 3-4, September-December 1956 : 407-416.

1808. ———.
Chandragupta I-Kumaradevi coin type A re-examination. *Journal of the Numismatic Society of India*, Vol. 19, pt. 2, 1957 : 145-154.

1809. ———.
Chandragupta I-Kumaradevi type. *Journal of the Numismatic Society of India*, Vol. 5, pt. 1, June 1943 : 37-42.

1810. ———.
Death's axe coin type of Samudragupta. *Journal of the Bihar Research Society*, Vol. 42, pt. 1, March 1956 : 142-151.

1811. ———.
Dewaitha hoard of Gupta gold coins, 1940. *Journal of the Numismatic Society of India*, Vol. 20, 1958 : 219-220.

1812. ———.
Eagle on Gupta coins and seals. *Journal of the Bihar Research Society*, Vol. 42, pt. 1, March 1956 : 152-156.

1813. ———.
Elephant-rider coin-type of Kumaragupta I. *Journal of the Numismatic Society of India*, Vol. 19, pt. 2, 1957 : 191-193.

1814. ______.
Jamuns or grapes. *Journal of the Numismatic Society of India*, Vol. 20, pt. 1, 1958 : 76-78.

1815. ______.
"Khadga-Trata" coins of Kumaragupta I. *Journal of the Bihar Research Society*, Vol. 41, pt. 3, September 1955 : 377-386.

1816. ______.
"Khadga-Trata" coins of Kumaragupta I. *Journal of the Numismatic Society of India*, Vol. 18, pt. 2, 1956 : 178-186.

1817. ______.
A note on Revanta coin type of Chandragupta II Vikramaditya and Kumaragupta I etc. In Devendra Handa, ed., *Numismatic Studies*, Vol. 3. New Delhi, Harman Publishing House, 1993 : 55-56.

1818. ______.
On a king-and-queen-on couch type coin of Chandragupta II. *Journal of the Numismatic Society of India*, Vol. 20, 1958 : 178-182.

1819. ______.
The repousse pieces of Mahendraditya etc. *Journal of the Numismatic Society of India*, Vol. 45, 1983 : 152-158.

1820. ______.
Samudragupta and the Kaca type coinage. *Puratan*, Vol. 1, 1984 : 7-14.

1821. ______.
So-called apratigha coin type of Kumaragupta I. *Journal of the Numismatic Society of India*, Vol. 23, 1961 : 345-356.

1822. ______.
"Standard" type of Samudragupta. *Journal of the Numismatic Society of India*, Vol. 19, pt. 2, 1957 : 186-190.

1823. ______.
Tiger hunt and water sport coin type of Samudragupta. *Journal of the Bihar Research Society*, Vol. 42, pt. 1, March 1956 : 157-163.

1824. ______.
Vina coin type of Samudragupta and Kumaragupta I. *Journal of the Bihar Research Society*, Vol. 42, pts. 3-4, September-December 1956 : 417-424.

1825. ______.
Vina coin type of Samudragupta and Kumaragupta I. *Journal of the Numismatic Society of India*, Vol. 19, pt. 2, 1957 : 155-161.

1826. **Soundara Rajan, K.V.**
Three silver plated Gupta coins from Sherdi, Junagadh district (Gujarat State). *Journal of the Numismatic Society of India*, Vol. 26, pt. 1, 1964 : 27-30.

1827. **Srivastava, A.K.**
Coin collection in the State Museum, Lucknow. *Journal of the Numismatic Society of India*, Vol. 35, 1973 : 225-232.

1828. ______.
Mathura as known through the coins. *Bulletin of Museums & Archaeology in U.P.*, Nos. 11-12, June-December 1973 : 30-36.

1829. **Srivastava, A.L.**
Coins of Prayaga Mandala. *Bulletin of Museums & Archaeology in U.P.*, Nos. 17-18, June-December 1976 : 61-66

1830. ______.
A silver coin of Chandragupta-Kumaradevi type. *Journal of the Numismatic Society of India*, Vol. 37, 1975 : 83-84.

1831. **Srivastava, O.P.**
A rare terracotta sealing from Allahabad throwing new light on the office of Kumaramatya. *Indian History Congress Proceedings*, Session 40, 1979 : 1102-1108.

1832. ______.

A rare terracotta sealing from Allahabad throwing new light on the office of Kumaramatya. *Journal of the Ganganatha Jha Kendriya Sanskrit Vidyapeetha*, Vol. 35, pts. 1-2, January-June 1979 : 101-109.

1833. **Srivastava, Prashant**

Aspects of ancient Indian numismatics. Delhi, Agam Kala Prakashan, 1996.

1834. ______.

The controversial `Apratigha' coin of Kumaragupta I. *Journal of the Numismatic Society of India*, Vol. 49, 1987 : 86-89.

1835. ______.

Joint coin types of ancient India. *Journal of the Numismatic Society of India*, Vol. 52, 1990 : i-viii, 1-26.

1836. ______.

Saka-Pahlava monetary elements in Imperial Gupta coinage. *Bulletin of Museums & Archaeology in U.P.*, Nos. 47-48, June-December 1991 : 53-58

1837. **Srivastava, Surendra Kumar**

Fire Worship as depicted on ancient Indian Coins. *Journal of the Numismatic Society of India*, Vol. 51, 1989 : 74-76.

1838. **Srivastava, V.N.**

The coin collection in the Archaeological Museum, Mathura. *Journal of the Numismatic Society of India*, Vol. 23, 1961 : 485-487.

1839. **Stapleton, H.E.**

Contributions to the history and ethnology of North-Eastern India. *Journal & Procedings of the Asiatic Society of Bengal*, New Series, Vol. 6, 1910 : 141-166.

1840. **Suhle, A.**

A list of Indian coins in the collection of the State Museum of Berlin. *Journal of the Numismatic Society of India*, Vol. 23, 1961 : 447-454.

1841. **Thakur, Upendra**
Some observations on Chandragupta I-Kumaradevi coin type. *Journal of the Numismatic Society of India*, Vol. 22, 1960 : 172-176.

1842. ______.
Source of gold for early gold coins of India. *East and West*, New Series, Vol. 30, 1980 : 99-115.

1843. ______.
Source of gold for early gold coins of India. *Journal of the Numismatic Society of India*, Vol. 39, 1977 : 89-107.

1844. ______.
A study in the copper coins of Ramagupta. *Journal of the Numismatic Society of India*, Vol. 26, pt. 2, 1964 : 162-170.

1845. ______.
A unique silver coin of Samudragupta. *East and West*, New Series, Vol. 24, Nos. 1-2, March-June 1974 : 121-125.

1846. **Thaplyal, K.K.**
Art motifs on Gupta sealing. *Roopa-Lekha*, Vol. 37 : 30-32.

1847. ______.
`Chandragupta-Kumaradevi' commemorative modals. *Puratattva*, No. 12, 1980-81 : 152-154.

1848. ______.
Elephant and lion motif : A glyptic depiction. *Rtam*, Vol. 1, No. 1, 1969 : 121-126.

1849. ______.
Imperial Gupta seals : A review. *Journal of the Numismatic Society of India*, Vol. 33, pt. 1, 1971 : 49-60.

1850. ______.
Kausambi sealing of Maharaja Tila (bhatta). *Pragdhara*, No. 1, 1990-91 : 123-125.

1851. ———.
The Nalanda seal of Vishnugupta—some problems. *Journal of the Numismatic Society of India*, Vol. 35, 1973 : 166-170.

1852. ———.
Observations on a Kausambi seal-die with an incomplete legend. *Pragdhara*, No. 2, 1991-92 : 113-115.

1853. ———.
Observations on a seal-die bearing incomplete legend. *Epigraphia Indica*, Vol. 42, 1977-78 : 158-160.

1854. ———.
Seals and sealings as a source of history and culture. *Sanskriti Darshan*, No. 4, 1991 : 48-54.

1855. ———.
Studies in ancient Indian seals. Lucknow, Akhila Bharatiya Sanskrit Parishad, 1972.

1856. **Theobald, W.**
On certain symbols or devices on the gold coins of the Guptas. *Journal of the Asiatic Society of Bengal*, Vol. 54, pt. 1, 1885 : 84-92.

1857. **Thomas, Edward**
Indo-Scythian coins, with Hindi legends. *Indian Antiquary*, Vol. 12, 1883 : 6-11.

1858. **Tripathi, R.R.**
The coin-collection in the Allahabad Museum. *Journal of the Numismatic Society of India*, Vol. 23, 1961 : 414-416.

1859. ———.
Some new and rare copper coins in the Allahabad Museum. *Journal of the Numismatic Society of India*, Vol. 24, 1962 : 20-23.

1860. ———.
Two new clay sealings in Allahabad Museum. *Journal of the Numismatic Society of India*, Vol. 30, 1968 : 218-220.

1861. **Tripathy, S.**
Ancient coins as ornaments. *Orissa Historical Research Journal*, Vol. 29, No. 1, 1983 : 62-70.

1862. ——.
Epigraphic and numismatic sources of the history of Orissa. *Orissa Historical Research Journal*, Vol. 30, Nos. 2-4, 1984 : 66-78.

1863. **Trivedi, H.V.**
The Chakravikrama coin of Chandragupta II. *Journal of the Numismatic Society of India*, Vol. 17, pt. 1, 1955 : 108-109.

1864. ——.
Numismatic studies in Madhya Bharata. *Journal of the Numismatic Society of India*, Vol. 15, pt. 1, 1953 : 94-107.

1865. ——.
Numismatic studies in Madhya Pradesh. *Journal of the Madhya Pradesh Itihasa Parishad*, No. 8, 1970 : 22-29.

1866. ——.
Some more copper coins of Ramagupta (?). *Journal of the Numismatic Society of India*, Vol. 13, pt. 2, 1951 : 128-130.

1867. **Upasak, C.S.**
Some salient features of Brahmi on Gupta coins. *Journal of the Numismatic Society of India*, Vol. 23, 1961 : 216-240.

1868. **Vanaja, R.**
The coin collection in the Government Museum, Madras. *Journal of the Numismatic Society of India*, Vol. 23, 1961 : 474-484.

1869. ——.
Gupta coinage. In Karl Khandalavala, ed., *The golden age : Gupta art—empire, province and influence*. Bombay, Marg Publications, 1991 : 109-114.

1870. ——.
Gupta coinage. *Marg*, Vol. 42, No. 3 : 37-42.

1871. ——.
Indian coinage. New Delhi, National Museum, 1983.

1872. **Vats, Madho Sarup**
A gold coin of Samudragupta of the `battle-axe type'. *Archaeological Survey of India Annual Report*, 1926-27 : 233-234.

1873. **Verma, T.P.**
Chandragupta-Kumaradevi coin type. *Journal of the Numismatic Society of India*, Vol. 33, pt. 1, 1971 : 44-48.

1874. ——.
Samudragupta : An examination of epigraphic and numismatic sources. *Journal of the Numismatic Society of India*, Vol. 53, 1991 : 114-138.

1875. ——.
A so-called lyrist type copper coin. *Journal of the Numismatic Society of India*, Vol. 26, pt. 1, 1964 : 106-109.

1876. **Vidya Prakash**
Some aspects of material life on Gupta coins. *Journal of the Numismatic Society of India*, Vol. 23, 1961 : 267-296.

1877 **Wright, H.N.**
Samudra Gupta—a new variety of the battle-axe type. *Journal of the Asiatic Society of Bengal*, Vol. 73, pt. 1, No. 1, Numismatic Supplement, 1904 : 65.

1878. **Yadav, Soberan Singh**
A rare silver coin of "Samudragupta". *Prachya Pratibha*, Vol. 12, 1984 : 83-84.

ART, ICONOGRAPHY AND SCULPTURE

1879. **Agrawala, P.K.**
Gupta-kalin kala evam vastu. Varanasi, Books Asia, 1994 (Hindi).

1880. ______.
Gupta period sculpture : Stylistic origins and chronology. *Bharati*, Vol. 20, 1993-94 : 85-95.

1881. ______.
Gupta pillars at Bhitari, Ghazipur. *Journal of the Indian Society of Oriental Art*, New Series, Vol. 6, 1974-1975 : 14-18.

1882. ______.
Srivatsa : The Babe of goddess Sri. Varanasi, Prithivi Prakashan, 1974.

1883. ______.
Studies in Indian iconography. Jaipur, Publication Scheme, 1994.

1884. **Agrawala, R.C.**
More sculptures from Amjhara, Rajasthan. *Arts Asiatiques*, Vol. 12, 1965 : 175-184.

1885. ______.
Some Saiva antiquities from Rajasthan. *Adyar Library Bulletin*, Vol. 20, pts. 1-2, 1956 : 57-83.

1886. ______.
Some unpublished sculptures in the State Museum, Lucknow. *Artibus Asiae*, Vol. 22, 1959 : 205-209.

1887. ______.

Unpublished Gupta reliefs from Sultan Ghari near Delhi. *East and West*, New Series, Vol. 18, Nos. 3-4, September-December 1968 : 315-318.

1888. **Agrawala, V.S.**

Catalogue of the Mathura Museum : Architectural pieces. *Journal of the Uttar Pradesh Historical Society*, Vols. 24-25, 1951-1952 : 1-160.

1889. ______.

Catalogue of the Mathura Museum. *Journal of the Uttar Pradesh Historical Society*, Vol. 23, 1950 : 1-147.

1890. ______.

The charming role of Gupta art. *Roopa-Lekha*, Vol. 3, No. 1, 1946 : 39-42.

1891. ______.

Gupta art. *Journal of the United Provinces Historical Society*, Vol. 18, 1945 : 101-134.

1892. ______.

Gupta art. Varanasi, Prithivi Prakashan, 1977.

1893. ______.

Gupta-yug mein Madhya Pradesh ka kalatmak chitran. *Nagri Pracharini Patrika*, Vol. 48, Samvat 2000 : 43-48 (Hindi).

1894. ______.

The heritage of Indian art. New Delhi, Publication Division, 1964.

1895. ______.

Indian sculpture—a cultural saga. *Roopa-Lekha*, Vol. 20, 1948 : i-v.

1896. ______.

Lalita kala. *Marg*, Vol. 4, No. 2 : 2-14.

1897. ______.

Masterpieces of Mathura sculpture. Varanasi, Prithivi Prakashan, 1965.

1898. ______.
Mathura-kala. Ahmedabad, Gujarat Vidyasabha, 1964 (Hindi).

1899. ______.
Mathura Museum Catalogue, pt. III : Jaina Tirthankaras and other miscellaneous figures. Varanasi, Prithivi Prakashan, 1963.

1900. ______.
Mathura Museum Catalogue, pt. IV : Architectural pieces in Mathura Museum. Varanasi, Prithivi Prakashan, 1963.

1901. ______.
A note on the new Mathura head. *Journal of the United Provinces Historical Society*, Vol. 12, pt. 2, December 1939 : 107-108.

1902. ______.
Rupa-sattra : Specimens of Gupta period sculpture in the Mathura Museum. *Marg*, Vol. 5, No. 2 : 45-50.

1903. ______.
Studies in Indian art. Varanasi, Vishwavidyalaya Prakashan, 1965.

1904. **Anand Krishna**
The Gupta style of sculpture from the city of Banaras. In Bettina Baumer, ed., *Rupa-Pratirupa : Alice Boner commemoration volume*. New Delhi, Biblia Impex, 1982 : 87-98.

1905. ______.
The Gupta style of sculpture from the city of Banaras. In Mahendra Shah, convener, *Smrti : Brijpal Das commemoration volume*. Varanasi, Brijpal Das-Rama Devi Foundation, 1995 : 77-89.

1906. **Anjani Kumar**
Art and architecture of the Gaya and Bodh Gaya. New Delhi, Ramanand Vidya Bhawan, 1992.

1907. **Asher, Frederick M.**
The art of Eastern India, 300-800. Minneapolis, The University of Minnesota Press, 1980.

1908. ———.
Gupta art in Eastern India. In Karl Khandalawala, ed., *The golden age : Gupta art—empire, province and influence*. Bombay, Marg Publications, 1991 : 73-80.

1909. ———.
Historical and political allegory in Gupta art. In Bardwell L. Smith, ed., *Essays on Gupta culture*. Missouri, South Asia Books, 1983 : 53-66.

1910. **Ashton, Leigh**, ed.
The art of India and Pakistan : A commemorative catalogue of the exhibition held at the Royal Academy of Arts, London, 1947-8. London, Faber and Faber, 1950.

1911. **Bajpai, K.D.**
Five phases of Indian art. Jodhpur, Rajasthan-Vidya Prakashan, 1991.

1912. ———.
Madhya Pradesh ki pracheen kala ke moulik tattva. *Sanskriti Darshan*, No. 2, 1990 : 1-6 (Hindi).

1913. ———.
Madhya Pradesh sculpture through the ages. *Marg*, Vol. 26, No. 3, June 1973 : 27-49.

1914. ———.
Religious background of ancient Indian art. *Prajna Bharati*, Vol. 3, pt. 1, 1983 : 43-47.

1915. ———.
Some new finds of early Gupta period from Mathura. *Indian History Congress Proceedings*, Session 10, 1947 : 98-101.

1916. ———.
Source-material for Indian art history. *Journal of the Ganganatha Jha Kendriya Sanskrit Vidyapeetha*, Vols. 38-39, 1982-1983 : 23-33.

1917. ———.
Survey of art activities in Madhya Pradesh upto 900 A.D. *Bulletin of Museums & Archaeology in U.P.*, No. 8, December 1971 : 19-23.

1918. **Bajpai, S.K.**
Guptakalin murtikala ka saundaryatamak adhyayan. Delhi, Eastern Book Linkers, 1992 (Hindi).

1919. **Bandyopadhyay, Bimal**
Metal sculptures of Eastern India. Delhi, Sundeep Prakashan, 1981.

1920. ———.
Survey of Indian metal sculpture. Delhi, Sundeep Prakashan, 1987.

1921. **Banerji, Adris**
Gupta sculptures of Benares—A study. In D.R.Bhandarkar and others, ed., *B.C. Law volume*, Part I. Calcutta, Indian Research Institute, 1945 : 504-518.

1922. **Banerji, Arundhati**
Images, attributes & motifs : Studies in early Indian art and numismatics. Delhi, Sundeep Prakashan, 1993. 2 vols.

1923. **Banerji, R.D.**
Some sculptures from Kosam. *Archaeological Survey of India Annual Report*, 1913-14 : 262-264.

1924. **Bhattacharya, S.K.**
The story of Indian art. Delhi, Atma Ram & Sons, 1966.

1925. **Bhattacharya, U.C.**
Catalogue & guide to Rajputana Museum, Ajmer, Rajasthan, pt. I : Sculptures. Jaipur, Department of Archaeology & Museums, 1961.

1926. **Bhattacharyya, D.C.**
Kalidasa in the light of Gupta art. In Karl Khandalvala, ed., *The golden age : Gupta art—empire, province and influence*. Bombay, Marg Publications, 1991 : 121-124.

1927. **Biswas, T.K.** and **Jha, Bhogendra**.
Gupta sculptures : Bharat Kala Bhavan. New Delhi, Books & Books, 1985.

1928. **Bloch, Theodor**
Supplementary catalogue of the Archaeological Collection of the Indian Museum. Calcutta, Baptist Mission Press, 1911.

1929. **Bussagli, Mario and Sivaramamurti, C.**
5000 years of the art of India. New York, Harry N. Abrams, [n.d.].

1930. Catalogue & guide to Sardar Museum, Jodhpur. Jaipur, Department of Archaeology & Museums, 1961.

1931. **Chaitanya, Krishna**
Arts of India. New Delhi, Abhinav Publications, 1987.

1932. **Chakravarti, S.N.**
A sculptured lintel of Gupta date from Sarnath. *Journal of the Royal Asiatic Society of Bengal, Letters*, Vol. 3, 1937 : 39--43.

1933. **Chanda, Rama Prasad**
The Mathura School of sculpture. *Indian Museum Bulletin*, Vol. 10, No. 1, 1975 : 35-40.

1934. ———.
Medieval Indian sculpture. *Archaeological Survey of India Annual Report*, 1929-30 : 215-221.

1935. ———.
Medieval Indian sculpture. Varanasi, Indological Book House, 1972.

1936. **Chaturvedi, H.K.**
Mathura sculptures in the National Museum. *Bulletin of Museums & Archaeology in U.P.*, No. 14, December 1974 : 23-35.

1937. **Chhabra, B. Ch.**
Patronage of arts in ancient India. *Vishveshvaranand Indological Journal*, Vol. 12, 1974 : 68-72.

1938. **Cohn, William**
Indische plastik. Berlin, Bruno Cassirer, 1923 (German).

1939. ———.
Problems of Indian art. *Rupam*, No. 3, July 1920 : 2-11.

1940. **Commaraswamy, Ananda K.**
History of Indian and Indonesian art. New York, Dover Publications, 1965.

1941. ———.
Introduction to Indian art. Delhi, Munshiram Manoharlal, 1969.

1942. ———.
La sculpture de Bodhagaya. *Ars Asiatica*, Vol. 18, 1935 : 1-72.

1943. **Craven, Roy C.**
A concise history of Indian art. New Delhi, Vikas Publishing House, 1979.

1944. **Davidson, J. Leroy**
Art of the Indian subcontinent from Los Angeles collections. Los Angeles, University of California, 1968.

1945. **Desai, Devangana**
Art under feudalism in India (c.A.D. 500-1300). *Indian Historical Review*, Vol. 1, No. 1, March 1974 : 10-17.

1946. ———.
Erotic sculpture of India : A socio-cultural study. New Delhi, Munshiram Manoharlal, 1985.

1947. ———.
Social dimensions of art in early India. *Indian History Congress Proceedings*, Session 50, 1990 : 21-56.

1948. **Dhavalikar, M.K.**
Early Indian art and the cultural pattern. *Journal of the Indian Society of Oriental Art*, New Series, Vol. 8, 1976-1977 : 69-75.

1949. ———.
Mathura art in the Baroda Museum. Baroda, Department of Museums, Gujarat, 1970.

1950. **Dikshit, S.K.**
A guide to the Central Archaeological Museum, Gwalior. Bhopal, The Department of Archaeology & Museums, 1962.

1951. **Dutta, Monoranjan**
Sculptures of Assam. Delhi, Agam Kala Prakashan, 1990.

1952. **Dwivedi, V.P.**
Indian ivories. Delhi, Agam Prakashan, 1976.

1953. ______.
Mathura art in the museums of United States of America. *Journal of Indian Museums*, Vol. 29, 1973 : 22-29.

1954. Early sculptures at Dharampur, district Lucknow, Uttar Pradesh. *Indian Archaeology : A Review*, 1964-65 : 75.

1955. Exhibition of art : Chiefly from the dominions of India & Pakistan, Royal Academy of Arts, London, 1947-48. London, Country Life, [n.d.].

1956. An exhibition of the sculpture of Greater India : A fully illustrated catalogue. New York, C.T. Loo & Co., 1942.

1957. **Frederic, Louis**
Indian temples and sculpture. London, Thames and Hudson, 1959.

1958. **Gangoly, O.C.**
A Gupta head : A fragment. *Rupam*, Nos. 42-44, 1930 : 1.

1959. **Ghosh, Niranjan**
Concept and iconography of the goddess of abundance and fortune in three religions of India. Burdwan, University of Burdwan, 1979.

1960. **Goetz, H.**
"Late Gupta" sculptures from Patan-Anhilwada : Archaeological evidence on Vanaraja and the Chapotkata dynasty. *Bulletin of the Baroda Museum and Picture Gallery*, Vol. 7, 1949-50 : 25-37.

1961. ______.
School of Gupta. In *Encyclopedia of World Art*, Vol. 7. New York, Mcgraw-Hill Book Company, 1963 : 248-264.

1962. ______.
The time-lag problem in Indian art history. *All India Oriental Conference Proceedings*, Session 15, 1949 : 304-309.

1963. **Gorakshkar, Sadashiv**
Gupta bronzes. In Karl Khandalawala, ed., *The golden age : Gupta art—empire, province and influence*. Bombay, Marg Publications, 1991 : 115-120.

1964. ———.
Gupta bronzes. *Marg*, Vol. 42, No. 3 : 43-48.

1965. ———.
Sculptural activity of the Gupta period in Western India : Mirpur Khas, Devnimori, Kanheri. In Karl Khandalawala, ed., *The golden age : Gupta art—empire, province and influence*. Bombay, Marg Publications, 1991 : 81-84.

1966. **Goswami, A.**, ed.
Indian temple sculpture. Calcutta, Rupa & Co., 1959.

1967. A guide to the galleries of the National Museum of India. New Delhi, National Museum, 1956.

1968. Gupta and Medieval sculpture, Mallar, district Bilaspur, Madhya Pradesh. *Indian Archaeology : A Review*, 1962-63 : 68.

1969. **Gupta, P.L.**
Ancient handicrafts. *Marg*, Vol. 22, No. 1, December 1966 : 13-15.

1970. ———.
Art & architecture in the Gupta period. In Bindeshwari Prasad Sinha, ed., *Comprehensive history of Bihar*, Vol. 1, pt. II. Patna, K.P. Jayaswal Research Institute, 1974 : 193-220.

1971. ———.
Patna Museum catalogue of antiquities. Patna, Patna Museum, 1965.

1972. Gupta Pillar—Capital, Vidisha, Madhya Pradesh. *Indian Archaeology : A Review*, 1970-71 : 66.

1973. Gupta sculpture, Sonpura, district Vidisha, Madhya Pradesh. *Indian Archaeology : A Review*, 1976-77 : 78.

1974. **Gupta, S.P.**, ed.
Masterpieces from the National Museum collection. New Delhi, National Museum, 1985.

1975. **Hamid, Muhammad** and others
Catalogue of the Museum of Archaeology at Sanchi, Bhopal State. Calcutta, Government Printing, 1922.

1976. **Handa, Devendra**
Sculptures from Punjab. *Panjab University Research Bulletin (Arts)*, Vol. 12, 1981 : 67-88.

1977. ______.
Some sculptures from Punjab and Haryana. *Panjab University Research Bulletin (Arts)*, Vol. 7, No. 1, 1976 : 93-98.

1978. **Harle, J.C.**
The art and architecture of the Indian subcontinent. Middlesex, Penguin Books, 1986.

1979. ______.
Gupta sculpture : Indian sculpture of the fourth to the sixth centuries A.D. Oxford, Clarendon Press, 1974.

1980. ______.
Late Kusan, early Gupta : A reverse approach. In Norman Hammond, ed., *South Asian Archaeology : Papers from the First International Conference of South Asian Archaeologists held in the University of Cambridge*. London, Gerald Duckworth & Co., 1973 : 231-240.

1981. ______.
Towards understanding Gupta sculpture. In Karl Khandalawala, ed., *The golden age : Gupta art—empire, province and influence*. Bombay, Marg Publications, 1991 : 7-14.

1982. **Harle, J.C.** and **Topsfield, Andrew.**
Indian art in the Ashmolean Museum. Oxford, Ashmolean Museum, 1987.

1983. **Hartman-Goldsmith, Joan**
Gupta sculpture at Asia House Gallery. *Oriental Art*, New Series, Vol. 24, No. 4 : 1978/79 : 478-481.

1984. **Heeramaneck, Alice N.**
Masterpieces of Indian sculpture from the former collections of Nasli M. Heeramaneck. United State of America, Alice N. Heeramaneck, 1979.

1985. **Huntington, Susan L.**
The art of ancient India : Buddhist, Hindu, Jain. New York, John Weatherhill, 1985.

1986. India : Art and architecture in ancient and medieval periods. New Delhi, Publications Division, 1981.

1987. **Jamkhedkar, A.P.**
The Vakataka area and Gupta sculpture. In Karl Khandalawala, ed., *The golden age : Gupta art—empire, province and influence*. Bombay, Marg Publications, 1991 : 85-92.

1988. **Jayakar, Pupul**
Notes on some sculptures in situ at Abaneri, Rajasthan. *Lalit Kala*, Nos. 1-2 : 139-144.

1989. **Joshi, N.P.**
Mathura ki murtikala. Mathura, Archaeological Museum, 1965 (Hindi).

1990. ———.
Mathura sculptures : A handbook to appreciate sculptures in the Archaeological Museum, Mathura. Mathura, Archaeological Museum, 1966.

1991. **Kala, S.C.**
Sculptures in the Allahabad Municipal Museum. Allahabad, Kitabistan, 1946.

1992. **Kar, Chintamoni**
Classical Indian sculpture, 300 B.C. to A.D. 500. London, Alec Tiranti, 1950.

1993. **Khandalavala, Karl**
Editorial. *Marg*, Vol. 42, No. 3 : iii-xii.

1994. **Khandalavala, Karl**, ed.
The golden age : Gupta art—empire, province and influence. Bombay, Marg Publications, 1991.

1995. **Khandalavala, Karl**
Indian sculpture and painting : An introductory study. Bombay, D.B. Taraporevala Sons & Co., [n.d.].

1996. **Khandalavala, Karl,** and **Roy, Archana**
Sculpture. *Marg*, Vol. 38, No. 3 : 9-38.

1997. **Kramrisch, St.**
Indian sculpture. Calcutta, Y.M.C.A. Publishing House, 1933.

1998. **Kramrisch, Stella**
Influence of race on early Indian art. *Rupam*, No. 18, April 1924 : 73-76.

1999. **Krishna Deva**
The golden age of the Guptas. In Asha Rani Mathur, ed., *The great tradition : Indian bronze masterpieces.* New Delhi, Festival of India, 1988 : 35-45.

2000. ———.
Gupta art at Sarnath and Varanasi. In Karl Khandalawala, ed., *The golden age : Gupta art—empire, province and influence.* Bombay, Marg Publications, 1991 : 37-44.

2001. ———.
Gupta impact on the art of Nepal. In Karl Khandalawala, ed., *The golden age : Gupta art—empire, province and influence.* Bombay, Marg Publications, 1991 : 45-54.

2002. ———.
Sattra in Indian epigraphy and art. In B.N. Mukherjee and others, ed., *Sri Dinescandrika : Studies in Indology; Sri D.C. Sircar festschrift.* Delhi, Sundeep Prakashan, 1983 : 317-322.

2003. **Krishna Kumar**
The evidence of white-wash, plaster and pigment on North Indian sculpture with special reference to Sarnath. *Artibus Asiae*, Vol. 45, 1984 : 199-206.

2004. **Lee, Sherman E.**
A history of Far Eastern art. Englewood Cliffs, Prentice-Hall, [1964].

2005. **Lerner, Martin** and **Kossak, Steven**
The lotus transcendent : Indian and Southeast Asian art from the Samuel Eilenberg collection. New York, The Metropolitan Museum of Art, 1991.

2006. **Lippe, Aschwin**
The art of India : Stone sculpture. New York, The Asia Society, 1962.

2007. **Lippe, Aschwin de**
Indian mediaeval sculpture. Amsterdam, North Holland Publishing Co. 1978.

2008. **Marshall, John**
Influence of race on early Indian art. *Journal of the Indian Society of Oriental Art*, New Series, Vols. 12-13, 1981-83 : 131-138.

2009. ———.
Influence of race on early Indian art. *Rupam*, No. 18, April 1924 : 69-73.

2010. **Mathur, Asha Rani**, ed.
The great tradition : Indian bronze masterpieces. New Delhi, Festival of India, 1988.

2011. **Mathur, N.L.**
Sculpture in India; Its history & art. New Delhi, The Author, 1972.

2012. **Mehta, Rustam J.**
Masterpices of the female form in Indian art. Bombay, D.B. Taraporevala Sons & Co., 1972.

2013. ———.
Masterpices of Indian bronzes and metal sculpture. Bombay, D.B. Taraporevala Sons & Co., 1971.

2014. ———.
Masterpices of Indian sculpture. Bombay, D.B. Taraporevala Sons & Co., 1976.

2015. **Michell, George** and others, ed.
In the image of man : The Indian perception of the Universe through 2,000 years of painting and sculpture. London, Arts Council of Great Britain, 1982.

2016. **Miller, Barbara Stoler**, ed.
Exploring India's sacred art : Selected writings of Stella Kramrisch. Philadelphia, University of Pennsylvania Press, 1983.

2017. **Mishra, V.D.**
Gupta sculptures from Kausambi (Allahabad). In Govind Chandra Pande, ed., *Indian art & culture.* Allahabad, Raka Prakashan, 1994 : 173-177.

2018. **Misra, C.B.**
Gupta image from Faizabad (Uttar Pradesh). *Prachya Pratibha*, Vol. 11, 1983 : 107.

2019. **Misra, R.N.**
Art of Madhyadesa : The case of Kausambi as a School. In Govind Chandra Pande, ed., *Indian art & culture.* Allahabad, Raka Prakashan, 1994 : 76-94.

2020. ______.
The Gupta art of Uttar Pradesh and Madhya Pradesh. In Karl Khandalawala, ed., *The golden age : Gupta art—empire, province and influence.* Bombay, Marg Publications, 1991 : 55-72.

2021. **Mital, Prabhu Dayal**
Braj ki kalaon ka itihas. Mathura, Sahitya Sansthan, 1975 (Hindi).

2022. **Mitra, Sisir Kumar,** ed.,
East Indian bronzes. Calcutta, Centre of Advanced Study in Ancient Indian History and Culture, Calcutta University, 1979.

2023. **Mookerji, Radha Kumud**
Notes on early Indian art. *Journal of the United Provinces Historical Society*, Vol. 12, pt. 1, July 1939 : 49-80.

2024. **Morley, Grace**
Indian sculpture. Varanasi, Lustre Press, 1985.

2025. **Moti Chandra**
Ancient Indian ivories. *Prince of Wales Museum Bulletin*, No. 6, 1957-1959 : 4-63.

2026. ______.
Indian art exhibition, New Delhi. *Roopa-Lekha*, Vol. 20, No. 2, 1948-49 : 139-158.

2027. ______.
Nidhisringa (Cornucopia) : A study in symbolism. *Prince of Wales Museum Bulletin*, No. 9, 1964-1966.

2028. ______.
Stone sculpture in the Prince of Wales Museum. Bombay, Prince of Wales Museum of Western India, 1974.

2029. **Mukerjee, Radhakamal**
The culture and art of India. London, George Allen & Unwin, 1959.

2030. ______.
The flowering of Indian art : The growth and spread of a civilization. Bombay, Asia Publishing House, 1964.

2031. **Mukhopadhyay, Mihir Mohan**
A fragmentary sculpture of a female from Mathura. *Indian History Congress Proceedings*, Session 28, 1966 : 23-24.

2032. ______.
Sculptures of Ganga-Yamuna Valley. New Delhi, Abhinav Publications, 1984.

2033. **Mullick, C.C.**
Nalanda sculptures : Their bearing on Indonesian sculptures. Delhi, Pratibha Prakashan, 1980.

2034. **Munshi, K.M.**
Saga of Indian sculpture. Bombay, Bharatiya Vidya Bhavan, 1957.

2035. **Nagar, M.M.**
Some newly acquired archaeological antiquities in the State Museum, Lucknow. *Journal of Indian Museums*, Vol. 9, 1953 : 53-56.

2036. **Nagarch, B.L.**
The Hindu, Buddhist and Jaina archaeological remains at Barauni Khurd, Datia district, Madhya Pradesh. *The Andhra Pradesh Journal of Archaeology*, Vol. 1, No. 2, 1979 : 71-80.

2037. **Narinder Nath and Saxena, J.P.**
Archaeological Museum Sanchi. New Delhi, Archaeological Survey of India, 1966.

2038. **Nath, R.**
Wave motif in ancient Indian art. *Journal of the Indian Society of Oriental Art*, New Series, Vol. 6, 1974-1975 : 43-51.

2039. **Newman, Richard**
The stone sculpture of India : A study of the materials used by Indian sculptors from ca. 2nd century B.C. to the 16th century. Cambridge, Harvard University Art Museums, 1984.

2040. **Pal, J.N.**
Some masterpices of Kausambi School of art of Gupta period. In Govind Chandra Pande, ed., *Indian art & culture.* Allahabad, Raka Prakashan, 1994 : 102-104.

2041. **Pal, Pratapaditya**
The ideal images : The Gupta sculptural tradition and its influence. New York, The Asia Society, 1978.

2042. ______.
Indian sculpture. *Arts of Asia*, Vol. 15, No. 6, November-December 1985 : 68-79.

2043. ______.
Indian sculpture : A catalogue of the Los Angeles Country Museum of Art collection, Vol. I : circa 500 B.C.-A.D. 700. Los Angeles, Los Angeles Country Museum of Art, 1986.

2044. ______.
Notes on two sculptures of the Gupta period. *Archives of Asian Art*, Vol. 24, 1970-1971 : 76-79.

2045. ______.
The sensuous immortals : A selection of sculptures from the Pan-Asian collection. Los Angeles, Los Angeles County Museum of Art, [n.d.].

2046. **Pandeya, Om Prakash**
Sarnath ka sanskritik vaibhav. *Prajna Bharati*, Vol. 6, 1992 : 109-113 (Hindi).

2047. **Pawan, Veena**
Bharatiya murtikala ka itihas. Delhi, Eastern Book Linkers, 1991 (Hindi).

2048. **Pramod Chandra**
The sculpture and architecture of Northern India. In Basil Gray, ed., *The Arts of India*. Oxford, Phaidon Press, 1981 : 30-52.

2049. ______.
Some remarks on Bihar sculpture from the fourth to the ninth century. In Pratapaditya Pal, ed., *Aspects of Indian art : Papers presented in a symposium at the Los Angeles Country Museum of Art*, October, 1970. Lieden, E.J. Brill, 1972 : 59-64.

2050. ______.
Stone sculpture in the Allahabad Museum. Poona, American Institute of Indian Studies, [1970].

2051. **Prasad, Prakash Charan**
Dancing figures in the Patna Museum. *Journal of the Bihar Research Society*, Vol. 53, 1967 : 130-136.

2052. **Randhawa M.S.**
The cult of trees and tree-worship in Buddhist-Hindu sculpture. New Delhi, All India Fine Arts & Crafts Society, 1964.

2053. ______.
The cult of trees and tree-worship in Buddhist-Hindu sculpture. *Roopa-Lekha*, Vol. 33 : 1-42.

2054. **Randhawa M.S.** and **Randhawa, Doris Schreier**
The background of Indian art : Economy, climate, social life and literature. *Roopa-Lekha*, Vol. 59, 1987 : 17-26.

2055. ______.
Indian sculpture : The scene, themes and legends. Bombay, Vakils, Feffer & Simons, 1985.

2056. **Rao, M.**
Gupta sculptures at Sanci. In C.R.P. Sinha and others, ed., *Archaeology and art (Krishna Deva felicitation volume)*, Part I, New Delhi, Ramanand Vidya Bhawan, 1990 : 285-294.

2057. Rare sculptures : Selections from some Indian Museums exhibited in Japan. New Delhi, National Museum, 1984.

2058. **Rastogi, Shailendra Kumar**
Ahicchatra ka murti shilpa. *Panchala*, Vol. 2, 1986 : 128-132.

2059. **Reddy, Guntaka Vijaya Bhaskara**
Erotic element in Central Indian rock-art. *Indian History Congress Proceedings*, Session 47, volume I, 1986 : 138-140.

2060. **Rowland, Benjamin**
The art and architecture of India : Buddhist, Hindu, Jain. Middlesex, Penguin Books, 1956.

2061. **Sahai, Bhagwant**
The bronzes of Bihar. *Prajna-Bharati*, Vol. 2, 1982 : 4-24.

2062. ______.
Iconography of minor Hindu and Buddhist deities. New Delhi, Abhinav Publications, 1975.

2063. **Sahay, S.N.**
Art and monuments of Bihar. In Bhagwant Sahai and Sachidanand Sahay, ed., *Bihar past and present*. Patna, Bihar Historical Society, 1981 : 16-24.

2064. **Sahni, Daya Ram**
Catalogue of the Museum of Archaeology at Sarnath. Calcutta, Government Printing, 1914.

2065. **Saraswati, S.K.**
Early sculptures of Bengal. Calcutta, Sambodhi Publications, 1962.

2066. ______.
Early sculptures of Bengal. *Journal of the Department of Letters*, Vol. 30 : 1-85.

2067. ______.
A survey of Indian sculpture. New Delhi, Munshiram Manoharlal, 1975.

2068. **Satya Prakash**
Rajasthan's contributions to Indian Culture—At a glance. *Researcher*, Vol. 1 : 37-47.

2069. **Schastok, Sara L.**
The Samalaji sculptures and 6th century art in Western India. Leiden, E. J. Brill, 1985.

2070. Sculptures from the Bharatpur Museum, Bharatpur. Jaipur, Department of Archaeology & Museums, [n.d.].

2071. Sculptures, Newal, district Unnao, Uttar Pradesh. *Indian Archaeology : A Review*, 1962-63 : 71.

2072. **Shah, U.P.**
Sculptures from Samalaji and Roda (North Gujarat) in the Baroda Museum. *Bulletin Museum and Picture Gallery, Baroda*, Vol. 13, 1960.

2073. ———.
Western Indian sculpture and the so-called Gupta influence. In Pratapaditya Pal, ed., *Aspects of Indian art : Papers presented in a symposium at the Los Angeles County Museum of Art*, October, 1970. Lieden, E.J. Brill, 1972 : 44-48.

2074. **Shah, U.P.** and **Mehta, R.N.**
A few early sculptures from Gujarat. *Journal of the Oriental Institute,* Vol. 1, No. 2, December 1951 : 160-164.

2075. **Shamsul Alam, A.K.M.**
Sculptural art of Bangladesh: Pre-Muslim period. Dhaka, Department of Archaeology and Museums, 1985.

2076. **Shanti Singh**
Nachna ki kalakritiyon mein vadhyakala ka ankan. *Prachya Pratibha,* Vol. 15, 1990-91 : 87-92 (Hindi).

2077. **Shanti Swarup**
5000 years of arts and crafts in India and Pakistan. Bombay, D.B. Taraporevala Sons & Co., 1968.

2078. **Sharma, B.N.**
Some unpublished sculptures from Rajasthan. *Researcher*, Vols. 5-6, 1964-65 : 33-35.

2079. **Sharma, R.C.**
Buddhist and Brahmanical Gupta sculptures from Mathura. *Marg*, Vol. 42, No. 3 : 15-24.

2080. ______.
Buddhist and Brahmanical Gupta sculptures from Mathura. In Karl Khandalawala, ed., *The golden age : Gupta art—empire, province and influence*. Bombay, Marg Publications, 1991 : 15-24.

2081. ______.
Gupta sculpture from Mathura. *Bulletin of Museums & Archaeology in U.P.*, Nos. 27-28, June-December 1981 : 89-109.

2082. ______.
Mathura Museum and art. Mathura, Covernment Museum, 1976.

2083. ______.
The sculptural art of Uttar Pradesh. In Devendra Handa, ed., *Indological studies* (*Essays in memory of Shri S.P. Singhal*). Delhi, Caxton Publications, 1987 : 105-109.

2084. ______.
The splendour of Mathura art and Museum. New Delhi, D.K. Print World, 1994.

2085. **Shukla, S.P.**
Art heritage of Haryana. *Sanskriti Darshan*, No. 3, 1990 : 7-12.

2086. **Singh, Arvind Kumar**
Pracheen Bharatiya murtikala evam chitrakala. Bhopal, Madhya Pradesh Hindi Granth Akademi, 1994 (Hindi).

2087. **Singh, Shanti Devi**
Gupta kalin kala mein chhatra. In C.R.P. Sinha and others, ed., *Archaeology and art* (*Krishna Deva felicitation volume*), Part I. New Delhi, Ramanand Vidya Bhawan, 1990 : 282-284 (Hindi).

2088. **Singh, Vindheswari Prasad**
Bharatiya kala ko Bihar ki den. Patna, Bihar-Rashtrabhasa Parishad, 1958 (Hindi).

2089. **Sinha, B.P.**
Recent enrichment art-treasure in Bihar. *Sanskriti Sangam*, Vol. 2, 1987 : 61-74.

2090. **Sinha, C.R.P.**
Early sculptures of Bihar. Patna, Indological Book Corporation, 1980.

2091. ______.
Some important sculptural acquisitions of the Patna Museum. *Journal of the Bihar Research Society*, Vol. 53, 1967 : 155-160.

2092. **Sinha, Vinod Chandra**
Puratatva Sangrhalaya, Gurukul Kangri Visvavidyalaya, Haridwar. *Bulletin of Museums & Archaeology in U.P.*, Nos. 19-20, June-December 1977 : 38-42 (Hindi).

2093. **Sivaramamurti C.**
An album of Indian sculpture. New Delhi, National Book Trust, 1975.

2094. ______.
The art of India. New York, Harry N. Abrams, 1977.

2095. ______.
Geographical and chronological factors in Indian iconography. *Ancient India*, No. 6, 1950 : 21-63.

2096. ______.
Indian sculpture. Bombay, Allied Publishers, 1961.

2097. ______.
Invitation to Indian art. New Delhi, Arnold-Heinemann Publishers, 1985.

2098. ______.
Masterpieces of Indian sculpture in the National Museum, New Delhi, National Museum, 1971.

2099. **Smith, Bardwell L.**
Religion and art in the Gupta age : A bibliographic essay. In Bardwell L. Smith, ed., *Essays on Gupta culture*, Missouri, South Asia Books, 1983 : 311-344.

2100. **Smith, V.A.**
A history of fine art in India & Ceylon. Bombay, D.B. Taraporevala Sons & Co., [n.d.].

2101. **Spink, Walter M.**
The great cave at Elephanta : A study of sources. In Bardwell L. Smith, ed., *Essays on Gupta culture*, Missouri, South Asia Books, 1983 : 235-282.

2102. **Srinivasan, P.R.**
Evolution of some iconographic concepts. *Archaeological Society of South Indian Transactions* for the year 1959-60 : 28-42.

2103. **Srivastava, A.K.** and **Shukla, Sri Ranjan**
Masterpieces in the Mathura Museum. *Bulletin of Museums & Archaeology in U.P.*, Nos. 19-20, June-December 1977 : 75-81.

2104. **Srivastava, A.L.**
Bharatiya kala. Allahabad, Kitab Mahal, 1988 (Hindi).

2105. ______.
Silpa-Sri : Studies in Indian art and culture. Delhi, Sundeep Prakashan, 1990.

2106. **Srivastava, Alakhdeva Prasad**
Nalanda ki sthapatya evam murtikala. New Delhi, Ramanand Vidya Bhawan, 1994 (Hindi).

2107. **Srivastava, B.B.**
Prachin Bharatiya pratima-vigyan evam moorti-kala. Varanasi, Vishvavidyalaya Prakashan, 1990 (Hindi).

2108. **Srivastava, Kamal Shankar**
The art of Magadha (from the sixth century B.C. to Pala-Sena period). Varanasi, Sangeeta Prakashan, 1995.

2109. **Srivastava, V.N.**
Gupta sculpture at Mathura, circa 300 to 650 A.D. *Marg*, Vol. 15, No. 2, March 1962 : 50-58.

2110. **Srivastava, V.N.** and **Misra, Shivodhar**
Inventory of Mathura Museum sculptures since 1939 uptodate. *Bulletin of Museums & Archaeology in U.P.*, Nos. 11-12, June-December 1973 : 42-122.

2111. **Srivastava, V.S.**
Catalogue & guide to Ganga Golden Jubilee Museum, Bikaner. Jaipur, Department of Archaeology & Museums, 1961.

2112. ———.
Rajasthan ka murti tatha sathapatya shilpa. *Sanskriti Darshan*, No. 4, 1991 : 37-47 (Hindi).

2113. Stone sculpture, Sarnath, district Varanasi, Uttar Pradesh. *Indian Archaeology : A Review*, 1964-65 : 77.

2114. **Subrahmanyam, Savitri**
Dinna : The Mathura-Gupta artist. In Karl Khandalawala, ed., *The golden age : Gupta art—empire, province and influence*. Bombay, Marg Publications, 1991 : 125-128.

2115. **Sudhi, Padma**
Gupta art : A study from aesthetic and canonical norms. New Delhi, Galaxy Publications, 1993.

2116. **Sundaram, K.**
Monumental art and architecture of India. Bombay, D.B. Taraporevala Sons & Co., 1974.

2117. **Taddei, Maurizo**
India. London, Barrie & Jenkins, 1970.

2118. **Thakore, S.R.**
Catalogue of sculptures in the Archaeological Museum, Gwalior. Lashkar, Modern Printing Press, [n.d.].

2119. **Thapar, D.R.**
Icons in bronze : An introduction to Indian metal images. Bombay, Asia Publishing House, 1961.

2120. **Tomory, Edith**
A history of fine arts in India and the West. Bombay, Orient Longman, 1982.

2121. ———.
Introduction to the history of fine arts in India and the West. Bombay, Orient Longmans, 1968.

2122. **Tripathi, R.R.**
Allahabad Sanghralaya mein mahatvapurna pradarsh sankshipta itihas. *Bulletin of Museums & Archaeology in U.P.*, Nos. 19-20, June-December 1977 : 5-12 (Hindi).

2123. **Trivedi, C.B.**
Two Gupta sculptures from Madhya Pradesh. *Andhra Pradesh Journal of Archaeology*, Vol. 2, No. 1, 1984 : 73-75.

2124. **Trivedi, S.D.**
Masterpieces in the State Museum, Lucknow. Lucknow, The State Museum, 1989.

2125. ———.
Masterpieces of Mathura Museum. *Journal of Indian Museums*, Vol. 29, 1973 : 30-32.

2126. **Upadhyaya, B.S.**
Bharatiya kala aur sanskriti ki bhumika. Delhi, Ranjit Printers and Publishers, 1965 (Hindi).

2127. **Upadhyaya, Padma**
Female images in the museums of Uttar Pradesh and their social background. Varanasi, Chaukhamba Orientalia, 1978.

2128. **Upadhyaya, Vasudeva**
Bharatiya sanskriti aur Bihar. *Parishad Patrika*, Vol. 22, No. 4, January 1983 : 31-39 (Hindi).

2129. **Vijay Kumar**
Puratattva va Rajasthan : Murtiyan. *Maru Bharati*, Vol. 16, No. 1, April 1968 : 66-68 (Hindi).

2130. **Vogel, J. Ph.**
La sculpture de Mathura. *Ars Asiatica*, Vol. 15, 1930 : 1-131.

2131. **Wakanker, V.S.**
An important image from Mandsuar. *All India Oriental Conference Proceedings*, Summaries of Papers, Session 17, 1953 : 89.

2132. **Wales, H.G. Quaritch**
Culture change in Greater India. *Journal of the Royal Asiatic Society of Great Britain and Ireland*, 1948 : 2-32.

2133. **Weiner, Sheila L.**
From Gupta to Pala sculpture. *Artibus Asiae*, Vol. 25, 1962 : 167-192.

2134. **Wellesz, Emmy**
A new museum of Eastern art in Oxford. *Artibus Asiae*, Vol. 13, 1950 : 99-101.

2135. **Williams, Joanna**
The art of Gupta India : Empire and province. New Delhi, Heritage Publishers, 1983.

2136. ———.
A recut Asokan Capital and the Gupta attitude towards the past. *Artibus Asiae*, Vol. 35, 1973 : 225-240.

2137. ———.
The sculpture of Mandasor. *Archives of Asian Art*, Vol. 26, 1972-73 : 50-66.

2138. ———.
Vakataka art and the Gupta mainstream. In Bardwell L. Smith, ed., *Essays on Gupta Culture*. Missouri, South Asia Books, 1983 : 215-233.

2139. **Yamamoto, Chikyo**
Introduction to Buddhist art. New Delhi, International Academy of Indian Culture, 1990.

2140. **Zimmer, Heinrich**
The art of Indian Asia : Its mythology and transformations. New York, Bollingen Foundation, 1964. 2 vols.

HINDU

2141. **Agrawala, P.K.**
The earliest known depiction of Ravana-Sirahkrnttana in Indian sculpture. In Lallanji Gopal, ed., *Ayodhya : History, archaeology and tradition*. Varanasi, All India Kashiraj Trust, 1994 : 253-258.

2142. ______.
The earliest known depiction of Ravana-Sirahkrnttana in Indian sculpture. *Purana*, Vol. 36, No. 2, July 1994 : 253-258.

2143. ______.
Iconoplastic beginnings of multi-headed and multi-armed images at Mathura. *Journal of the Indian Society of Oriental Art*, New Series, Vol. 15, 1985-86 : 21-28.

2144. ______.
A literary motif inGupta sculpture. *Journal of the Indian Society of Oriental Art*, New Series, Vols. 12-13, 1981-83 : 82-84.

2145. ______.
A note on so-called Surya statue from Pawaya. *Bulletin of Ancient Indian History and Archaeology*, No. 2, 1968 : 67-69.

2146. ______.
Ravana-Sirahkrnttana in Indian sculpture. *Puratan*, Vol. 8, 1991 : 12-14.

2147. ______.
Skanda-Karttikeya [A study in the origin and development]. Varanasi, Banaras Hindu University, 1967.

2148. ______.
The twin of sankha and padma on Gupta doorframe. *Journal of the Indian Society of Oriental Art*, New Series, 10, 1978-1979 : 69-73.

2149. ______.
Vahana-Purusa in early medieval art. *Journal of the Indian Society of Oriental Art*, New Series, Vols. 18-19, 1989-91 : 1-13.

2150. **Agrawala, R.C.**
Agni in early Indian art. *Journal of Indian History*, Vol. 43, pt. 1, April 1965 : 151-157.

2151. ______.
Ancient sculptures and terracottas from Rajasthan. *Researcher*, Vol. 1, : 16-21.

2152. ______.
Animal-faced sculptures from Rajasthan. *Bharatiya Vidya*, Vols. 20-21, 1960-61 : 303-309.

2153. ______.
Antiquity of Srivatsa mark of Visnu in Indian art. *Journal of the Bihar Research Society*, Vol. 56, 1970 : 47-49.

2154. ______.
Cakra purusa in early Indian art. *Bharatiya Vidya*, Vol. 24, 1964 : 41-45.

2155. ______.
Carved pillar of Gupta year 61. *Journal of the Oriental Institute*, Vol. 19, No. 4, June 1970 : 355-356.

2156. ______.
Dancing Siva in Gupta art. *Orissa Historical Research Journal*, Vol. 13, No. 1, 1965 : 36-37.

2157. ______.
Early Vaisnava icons from Rajasthan. In Ratan Parimoo, ed., *Vaisnavism in Indian arts and culture*. New Delhi, Books & Books, 1987 : 328-334.

2158. ______.
Krsna and Balarama in Rajasthan sculptures and epigraphs. *Indian Historical Quarterly*, Vol. 30, No. 4, December 1954 : 339-353.

2159. ______.
Krsna lila scenes in early Rajasthani sculptures. *Bulletin of Museums & Archaeology in U.P.*, Nos. 21-24, June 1978-December 1979 : 27-31.

2160. ______.
Mahishamardini in early Rajasthani art. *Researcher*, Vols. 5-6, 1964-65 : 11-15.

2161. ______.
Malaw Nagar ki pracheen prastar kala. *Maru Bharati*, Vol. 12, No. 2, July 1994 : 24-26 (Hindi).

2162. ______.
Matrka reliefs in early Indian art. *East and West*, New Series, Vol. 21, Nos. 1-2, March-June 1971 : 79-89.

2163. ——.
Nrsimha-Varaha-Vishnu images and some allied problems. *Lalit Kala*, No. 16 : 11-21.

2164. ——.
Rajasthan ki advitiya prastar pratimayen. *Shodh Patrika*, Vol. 17, No. 3, 1966 : 17-22 (Hindi).

2165. ——.
Rajasthan ki pracheen murti-kala mein Ramayana digdarshana. *Shodh Patrika*, Vol. 6, No. 1, 1954 : 1-12 (Hindi).

2166. ——.
Rajasthan ki pracheen murti-kala mein Shivalinga. *Maru Bharati*, Vol. 19, No. 4, January 1972 : 41-43 (Hindi).

2167. ——.
Rajasthan mein Visnu-puja pracheen murti-kala tatha shilalekho ke aadhar par. *Rajasthan Bharati*, Vol. 4, No. 4, 1955 : 3-39 (Hindi).

2168. ——.
Rajasthan's contribution to ancient Indian sculptures. *Researcher*, Vols. 3-4, 1963-64 : 31-37.

2169. ——.
Skanda in early Rajasthani sculptures. *Researcher*, Vols. 12-13, 1972-73 : 15-19.

2170. ——.
Skanda-Karttikeya in sculptures from Rajasthan. *Lalit Kala*, Nos. 3-4 : 109-111.

2171. ——.
Some unpublished sculptures from Western Rajasthan. *Journal of the Gujarat Research Society*, Vol. 19, No. 4, October 1957 : 40-44.

2172. ——.
Some Vishnu sculptures in the Sardar Museum (Jodhpur). *Journal of Indian Museums*, Vol. 9, 1953 : 104-105.

2173. ——.
Two unpublished antiquities from the Sardar Museum, Jodhpur. *Lalit Kala*, Nos. 1-2 : 75-76.

2174. ______.
Unpublished sculptures and terracottas in the National Museum, New Delhi, and some allied problems. *East and West*, New Series, Vol. 17, Nos. 3-4, September-December 1967 : 276-286.

2175. ______.
Uttar Bharat ki murtikala mein Ramkatha. *Rajasthan Bharati*, Vol. 11, No. 1 : 51-54 (Hindi).

2176. ______.
Vasudhara plaque in National Museum, New Delhi, *Bulletin of Ancient Indian History and Archaeology*, No. 2, 1968 : 71-72.

2177. **Agrawala, V.S.**
Brahmanical images in Mathura. *Journal of the Indian Society of Oriental Art*, Vol. 5, 1937 : 122-130.

2178. ______.
A catalogue of the Brahmanical images in Mathura art. Lucknow, U.P. Historical Society, 1951.

2179. ______.
A catalogue of the Brahma, Vishnu and Siva in Mathura art. *Journal of the United Provinces Historical Society*, Vol. 22, 1949 : 102-210.

2180. ______.
Further acquisitions to the Mathura Museum. *Journal of the United Provinces Historical Society*, Vol. 10, pt. 1, July 1937 : 88-90.

2181. ______.
A note on a Gupta Shiva Linga at Mathura. *Journal of the U. P. Historical Society*, Vol. 8, pt. I, July 1935 : 83-85.

2182. ______.
A survey of Gupta art and some new Gupta sculptures. *Bharati*, No. 4, 1960-61 : 16-30.

2183. ______.
A survey of Gupta art and some sculptures from Nachna Kuthara and Khoh. *Lalit Kala*, No. 9 : 16-26.

2184. ——.
Yajna-Varaha-an interpretation. *Purana*, Vol. 5, No. 2, 1963 : 199-236.

2185. **Akhouri, Gayatri**
Saivism in ancient Bihar. Patna, Pataliputra Prakashan, 1988.

2186. **Anand, Mulk Raj**
Bhitargaon : Art and architecture of Humanism. *Marg*, Vol. 22, March 1969 : 2-23.

2187. ——.
Of kamakala : Some notes on the philosophical basis of Hindu erotic sculpture. *Marg*, Vol. 10, No. 3, June 1957 : 45-64.

2188. **Awasthi, A.B.L.**
Some observations on the Anantasayi-Narayana at Deogarh. *Bulletin of Museums & Archaeology in U.P.*, No. 7, June 1971 : 50-53.

2189. **Bajpai, K.D.**
Bharatiya parampara mein Sri-Laksmi. *Bulletin of Ancient Indian History and Archaeology*, No. 2, 1968 : 139-140 (Hindi).

2190. ——.
Bundelkhand ka Guptakalin kala kendra : Nachna. In K.D. Bajpai, ed., *The Glory that was Bundelkhand : Mahendra Kumar 'Manav' felicitation volume*. Bhopal, Mahendra Kumar Manav Abhinandan Samiti, 1993 : 543-545.

2191. ——.
The Saiva art of Madhya Pradesh with reference to Kalidasa and Banabhatta. *Puratan*, Vol. 8, 1991 : 7-9.

2192. ——.
Some interesting Gana figures from Panna. *Lalit Kala*, No. 10, October 1961 : 21-24.

2193. ——.
Sri Rama in ancient literature and art. In B.P. Sinha, ed., *Sri Rama in art, archaeology and literature*. Patna, The Bihar Puravid Parishad, 1989 : 80-86.

2194. **Banerjea, J.N.**
An Abhicarika Visnu image. *Journal of the Indian Society of Oriental Art.*, Vol. 8, 1940 : 159-161.

2195. ———.
Hindu iconography : Vhuhas and Vibhavas of Visnu. *Journal of the Indian Society of Oriental Art.*, Vol. 14, 1946 : 1-74.

2196. ———.
Hindu iconography : Visnu. *Journal of the Indian Society of Oriental Art.*, Vol. 13, 1945 : 55-129.

2197. ———.
Surya, Adityas and the Navagrahas. *Journal of the Indian Society of Oriental Art.*, Vol. 16, 1948 : 47-100.

2198. ———.
The representation of Surya in Brahmanical art. *Indian Antiquary*, Vol. 54, 1925 : 161-171.

2199. **Banerjee, P.**
Ekapada Gajasamharamurti from Central Asia. *Bulletin National Museum*, No. 3 : 11-15.

2200. **Banerji, Adris**
Some sculptures from Rajghat, Benares. *Journal of the Ganganatha Jha Research Institute*, Vol. 3, pt. 1, November 1945 : 1-9.

2201. **Banerji, Arundhati**
Iconography of two-armed Ganesa. *Roopa-Lekha*, Vol. 55, 1984 : 21-40.

2202. **Barrett, Douglas**
A terracotta plaque of Mahisasurmardini. *Oriental Art*, New Series, Vol. 21, No. 1, 1975 : 64-67.

2203. **Basu, S.P.**
The concept of Brahma (Its origin and development). Delhi, Sundeep Prakashan, 1986.

2204. **Berkson, Carmel**
Some new finds at Ramgarh Hill, Vidisha district. *Artibus Asiae*, Vol. 40, 1978 : 215-232.

2205. **Bhattacharya, U.C.**
Two masterpieces of Rajasthani sculpture. *Journal of the U.P. Historical Society*, New Series, Vol. 8, pt. 2, 1960 : 83-84.

2206. **Bolon, Carol Radcliffe**
Forms of the goddess Lajja Gauri in Indian art. Pennsylvania, The Pennsylvania State University Press, 1992.

2207. Brahmanical sculptures, Bahuriband, district Jabalpur, Madhya Pradesh. *Indian Archaeology : A Review*, 1962-63 : 68.

2208. Brahmanical sculptures, Tumain, district Guna, Madhya Pradesh. *Indian Archaeology : A Review*, 1972-73 : 59.

2209. **Chakravarti, Mahadev**
The concept of Rudra-Siva through the ages. Delhi, Motilal Banarsidass, 1986.

2210. **Chakravarti, Mathura Mohan**
Sculptural assets of the Gupta period in Gaya. In B.N. Mukherjee and others, ed., *Sri Dinescandrika : Studies in Indology; Sri D.C. Sircar festschrift*. Delhi, Sundeep Prakashan, 1983 : 311-316.

2211. **Chanda, Rama Prasad**
The Brahmanic sculpture of the Gupta period. *Indian Museum Bulletin*, Vol. 14, 1979 : 134-138.

2212. **Chatterjee, Asim Kumar**
The cult of Skanda-Karttikeya in ancient India. Calcutta, Punthi Pustak, 1970.

2213. **Chatterjee, Bhaswati**
Early iconographic development of Vishnu on coins. *Journal of the Numismatic Society of India*, Vol. 53, 1991 : 180-183.

2214. **Chhabra, B. Ch.**
Garuda of Vishnu. *Journal of the Indian History*, Vol. 43, pt. 2, August 1965 : 387-390.

2215. **Coomaraswamy, Ananda**
Some Indian sculptures in American museums. *Rupam*, No. 18, April 1924 : 65-68.

2216. **Craven, Roy C.**
A unique Vaikunta-style Visnu (Narasimha-Varaha) sculpture from the Mathura area. *Oriental Art*, New Series, Vol. 38, No. 3, 1992 : 145-153.

2217. **Darian, Steven**
The Ganges in Indian art. *East and West*, New Series, Vol. 23, Nos. 3-4, September-December 1973 : 307-325.

2218. **Das Gupta, C.C.**
Some notes on the iconography of Lakshmi. *Bharatiya Vidya*, Vol. 15, No. 3, 1956 : 61-71.

2219. **Desai, Kalpana S.**
Iconography of Visnu. New Delhi, Abhinav Publications, 1973.

2220. ———.
Vaikuntha caturmurti. *Journal of the Indian Society of Oriental Art.*, New Series, Vol. 2, 1967-1968 : 22-33.

2221. **Desai, Kalpana**
Varaha. *Journal of the Asiatic Society of Bombay*, New Series, Vols. 43-44, 1968-69 : 106-118.

2222. **Deshpande, M.N.**
Early sculptures from Pushkar. *Bulletin National Museum*, No. 3 : 8-10.

2223. **Dhaky, M.A.**
Late Gupta sculptures from Patan Anhilwad-Reviewed. *Bulletin Museum & Picture, Gallery, Baroda*, Vol. 19, 1965-66 : 17-28.

2224. **Diskalkar, D.B.**
Some Brahmanical sculptures in the Mathura Museum. *Journal of the United Provinces Historical Society*, Vol. 5, pt. 1, January 1932 : 18-57.

2225. **Dwivedi, Shiva Kant**
Temple sculptures of India. Delhi, Agam Kala Prakashan, 1991.

2226. **Dye III, Joseph M.**
Hindu sculpture of Northern India. In Pratapaditya Pal, ed., *Asian art : Selections from the Norton Simon Museum*. Pasadena, Norton Simon Museum, 1988 : 20-33.

2227. Early sculpture, district Sagar, Madhya Pradesh. *Indian Archaeology : A Review*, 1960-61 : 62.

2228. **Gail, Adalbert J.**
On the symbolism of three-and four-faced Visnu images : A reconsideration of evidence. *Artibus Asiae*, Vol. 44, 1983 : 297-307.

2229. **Gangoly, O.C.**
The mithuna in Indian art. *Rupam*, Nos. 22-23, April-July 1925 : 54-61.

2230. ______.
Two images of Visnu. *Rupam*, Nos. 35-36, 1928 : 38-39.

2231. **Ganguly, D.C.**
A new Gupta sculpture. *Indian Historical Quarterly*, Vol. 9, No. 2, June 1933 : 588-590.

2232. **Gaston, Anne-Marie**
Siva in dance, myth and iconography. Delhi, Oxford University Press, 1982.

2233. **Ghosh, D.P.**
Symbolism of the kirttimukha-makara motif in Indian art. *Lalit Kala*, No. 27 : 29-32.

2234. **Giri, Kamal**
A new Surya image of the Gupta period. *Journal of the Indian Society of Oriental Art*, New Series, Vol. 11, 1980 : 76-79.

2235. **Glynn, Catherine**
Some reflections on the origin of the type of Ganga image. *Journal of the Indian Society of Oriental Art*, New Series, Vol. 5, 1972-1973 : 16-27.

2236. **Goetz, H.**
Gupta sculptures from Northern Gujarat. *Journal of the Gujarat Research Society*, Vol. 14, No. 1, January 1952 : 1-5.

2237. ———.
Late Gupta sculpture in Afghanistan : The "Scorretti Marble" and cognatt sculptures. *Arts Asiatiques*, Vol. 4, 1957 : 13-19.

2238. **Govind Chandra, Rai**
Pracheen Bharat mein Lakshmi-pratima. Varanasi, Hindi Pracharak Pustakalaya, 1964 (Hindi).

2239. Gupta images, Sulaimanpur, district Ghazipur, Uttar Pradesh. *Indian Archaeology : A Review*, 1963-64 : 91.

2240. Gupta sculptures, Bhitari, district Ghazipur, Uttar Pradesh. *Indian Archaeology : A Review*, 1977-78 : 83.

2241. Gupta sculptures, Durjanpur, district Vidisha, Madhya Pradesh. *Indian Archaeology : A Review*, 1968-69 : 67.

2242. Gupta sculptures, Vidisha, Madhya Pradesh. *Indian Archaeology : A Review*, 1962-63 : 69.

2243. **Gupta, Shakti M.**
Karttikeya : The son of Shiva. Bombay, Somaiya Publications, 1988.

2244. **Handa, Devendra**
Gupta reliefs from Haryana. *Bulletin of Museums & Archaeology in U.P*, Nos. 35-36, June-December 1985 : 15-22.

2245. ———.
Late Gupta relics from Kapala-Mocana. *Panjab University Research Bulletin (Arts)*, Vol. 22, No. 2, 1991 : 147-150.

2246. ———.
Some interesting sculptures from Pehowa. *Panjab University Research Bulletin (Arts)*, Vol. 16, No. 1, 1985 : 127-135.

2247. ______.
Vaikuntha images from Haryana. *Journal of the Indian Society of Oriental Art*, New Series, Vol. 14, 1984-85 : 54-58.

2248. ______.
Vaishnava icons from Haryana. *Panjab University Research Bulletin (Arts)*, Vol. 16, No. 2, 1985 : 125-157.

2249. **Harle, J.C.**
Mathura sculpture in the Ashmolean Museum. *Bulletin of Museums & Archaeology in U.P*, Nos. 15-16, June-December 1975 : 15-17.

2250. ______.
Towards understanding Gupta sculpture. *Marg*, Vol. 42, No. 3 : 7-14.

2251. **Harper, Katherine Anne**
Seven Hindu goddess of spiritual transformation : The iconography of the Saptamatrikas. Lewiston, The Edwin Mellen Press, 1989.

2252. **Hazra, R.C.**
Is the Devi-Bhagavata the source of the Deogarh relief of Nara-Narayana ? *Indian Historical Quarterly*, Vol. 29, No. 4, December 1953 : 387-392.

2253. **Jamkhedkar, Arvind**
Devgarhchya Narainshilpa-patatil audhpurusanche. *Vidarbha Samshodhana Mandal Varshik*, Vol. 18, 1975 : 85-89 (Marathi).

2254. **Jayaswal, Kusum Kumari**
Uttar Bharat ki pracheen Hindu devi-murtiyan. Delhi, Atmaram and Sons, 1992 (Hindi).

2255. **Jha, V.D.**
Remarkable Brahmanical icons in Sagar district. *Puratan*, Vol. 1, Nos. 2-3, 1984 : 26-33.

2256. **Joshi, Arjun**
Ganapati images in early Orissan temples. *Orissa Historical Research Journal*, Vol. 8, No. 2, 1959 : 139-146.

2257. **Joshi, M.C.**
Two interesting Sun images from Nachna. *Journal of Indian History*, Vol. 48, pt. 1, April 1970 : 81-87.

2258. **Joshi, M. P.**
A newly discovered early image of Visnu. *East and West*, New Series, Vol. 30, 1980 : 97-98.

2259. **Joshi, N. P.**
Catalogue of the Brahmanical sculptures in the State Museum, Lucknow, pt. I, Lucknow, The State Museum, 1972.

2260. ______.
Early Brahmanical sculptures in Bharat Kala Bhavan. In Anand Krishna and Chandramani Singh, ed., *Chhavi : Golden Jubilee Volume*. Varanasi, Bharat Kala Bhavan, 1971 : 178-182.

2261. ______.
Hayagriva in Brahmanical iconography. *Journal of the Indian Society of Oriental Art*, New Series, Vol. 5, 1972-1973 : 36-42.

2262. ______.
Iconography of Balarama. New Delhi, Abhinav Publications, 1979.

2263. ______.
Kartikeya's Sakti as ayudha devi. *Vishveshvaranand Indological Journal*, Vol. 8, 1970 : 214-216.

2264. ______.
Krsna in art-whether two-armed or multi-armed. *Bulletin of Museums & Archaeology in U.P*, Nos. 21-24, June 1978-December 1979 : 19-25.

2265. ______.
A note on trisula-purusha. *Journal of the U.P. Historical Society*, New Series, Vol. 8, pt. 2, 1960 : 79-81.

2266. ______.
On the iconography of Balarama in the north India. *Bulletin of Museums & Archaeology in U.P*, No. 10 December 1972 : 15-25.

2267. ______.
Some early Gupta Saptamatrka panels. *Bharati*, No. 16, 1985-87 : 145-148.

2268. ______.
Uttar Bharat ki sthanak Siva-Parvati pratimayen. *Sanskriti Darshan*, No. 3, 1990 : 27-36 (Hindi).

2269. **Kala, Jayantika**
Epic scenes in Indian plastic art. New Delhi, Abhinav Publications, 1988.

2270. ______.
Govardhanadhari images in Indian plastic art. *Prachya Pratibha*. Vol. 5, No. 2, July 1977 : 25-34.

2271. **Kramrisch, Stella**
Manifestations of Shiva. Philadelphia, Philadelphia Museum of Art, 1981.

2272. **Krishan, Y.**
The origins of Ganesa. *Artibus Asiae*, Vol. 43, 1981-1982 : 285-301.

2273. **Krishna Deva**
Gupta Ramayana panels from Nachna. In Anand Krishna and Kamal Giri, ed., *Chhavi-2 : Rai Krishnadasa felicitation Volume*. Varanasi, Bharat Kala Bhavan, 1981 : 10-14.

2274. ______.
Scupltural representations of some Ramayana episodes-regional varities. In B.P. Sinha, ed., *Sri Rama in art, archaeology and literature*. Patna, The Bihar Puravid Parishad, 1989 : 65-69.

2275. ______.
Siva-Parvati playing dice. *Journal of the Indian Society of Oriental Art*, New Series, Vols. 16-17, 1987-89 : 44-49.

2276. **Krishna Kumar**
Some Brahmanical sculptures in the Archaeological Museum, Sarnath. *Bharati*, Nos. 12-14, 1968-1971 : 137-151.

2277. **Krishna, Nanditha**
The art and iconography of Vishnu-Narayana. Bombay, D.B. Taraporevala Sons & Co., 1980.

2278. **Lalit Kumar**
A new Visnu pillar from Banaras. *Bulletin of Museums & Archaeology in U.P*, Nos. 29-30, June-December 1982 : 45-48.

2279. **Lall, S.S.**
Images of incarnatory forms of Visnu in Bihar. *All India Oriental Conference Proceedings*, Session 32, 1985 : 383-390.

2280. Late Gupta sculptures, district Vidisha, Madhya Pradesh. *Indian Archaeology : A Review*, 1963-64 : 89.

2281. **Leoshko, Janice**
The Vajrasana Buddha. *Marg*, Vol. 40, No. 1 : 29-44.

2282. **Maitra, Akshay Kumar**
The river-goddess Ganga. *Rupam*, No. 6, April 1921 : 2-10.

2283. **Malaiya, Sudha**
Nateśa sculptures in the early art of Central India. *Puratattva*, No. 16, 1985-86 : 47-54.

2284. **Mani, V.R.**
Sons of Siva : A study in the religious cults of Ganesa and Karttikeya. Delhi, Sharada Prakashan, 1990.

2285. **Mankodi, K.L.**
Ganga Tripathaga. *Samskriti Darshan*, No. 1, 1989 : 24-28.

2286. **Maxwell, T.S.**
The Deogarh Visvarupa : A structural analysis. *Art and Archaeology Research Papers*, No. 8, 1975 : 8-23.

2287. ———.
The evidence for a Visvarupa iconographic tradition in Western India, 6th-9th centuries A.D. *Artibus Asiae*, Vol. 44, 1983 : 213-234.

2288. ______.
Visvarupa. Delhi, Oxford University Press, 1988.

2289. Medieval temple and sculpture, district Panna, Madhya Pradesh. *Indian Archaeology : A Review*, 1960-61 : 61.

2290. **Meister, Michael W.**, ed.
Discourses on Siva : Proceedings of a symposium on the nature of religious imagery. Bombay, Vakils, Feffer & Simons, 1984.

2291. **Meister, Michael W.**
Regional variations in Matrka conventions. *Artibus Asiae*, Vol. 47, 1986 : 233-262.

2292. **Mishra, Vijayakanta**
Mahishamardini. New Delhi, Rajesh Publications, 1984.

2293. **Mitra, Debala**
Varaha-cave of Udayagiri—an iconographic study. *Journal of the Asiatic Society*, Vol. 5, 1963 : 99-103.

2294. **Mitterwallner, Gritli Von**
The Kusana type of the goddess Mahisasuramardini as compared to the Gupta and mediaeval types. In *German scholars on India : Contributions to Indian studies*, Vol. II. Bombay, Nachiketa Publications, 1976 : 196-213.

2295. **Nagar, M.M.**
Karttikeya ki ek nav prapta pratima. *Journal of the U.P. Historical Society*, New Series, Vol. 5, pt. 2, 1957 : 117-120 (Hindi).

2296. ______.
A new type of Vishnu image from Aligarh. *Indian History Congress Proceedings*, Session 6, 1943 : 89-90.

2297. ______.
A new type of Vishnu image from Aligarh. *Journal of the United Provinces Historical Society*, Vol. 18, 1945 : 98-100.

2298. **Nagar, S.L.**

Hanuman in art, culture, thought and literature. New Delhi, Intellectual Publishing House, 1995.

2299. ———.

Surya and Sun cult (In Indian art, culture, literature and thought). New Delhi, Aryan Books International, 1995.

2300. ———.

Varaha in Indian art, culture, and literature. New Delhi, Aryan Books International, 1993.

2301. **Nagarch, B.L.**

Art and architecture in the works of Kalidasa. *Prachya Pratibha*, Vol. 13, 1985-87 : 24-47.

2302. **Narain, H.K.**

Two rare Surya images from village Tripatti in district Deoria (U.P.). *Journal of the Bihar Puravid Parishad*, Vol. 3, 1979 : 104-106.

2303 **Nath, R.**

Bhu-Varaha sculptures. *Annals of the Bhandarkar Oriental Research Institute*, Vols. 58-59, 1977-1978 : 799-811.

2304. **Pandey, Durga Prasad**

Surya : Iconographical study of the Indian Sun god. Delhi, Parimal Publications, 1989.

2305. **Pandey, Lalta Prasad**

Sun-worship in ancient India. Delhi, Motilal Banarsidass, 1971.

2306. **Pandey, Prabha Shankar**

Prateek-vidhan mein Lakshmi-pratima. *Prachya Pratibha*, Vol. 11, 1983 : 155-157 (Hindi).

2307. **Pandeya, Om Prakash**

Sarnath ki kala mein Ram-akhyan. In B.P. Sinha, ed., *Sri Rama in art, archaeology and literature*. Patna, The Bihar Puravid Parishad, 1989 : 158-160 (Hindi).

2308. **Pandeya, Shyam Kumar**

Dakshin Koshala ka kala vaibhav. *Prachya Pratibha*, Vol. 5, No. 2, July 1977 : 125-141 (Hindi).

2309. **Pandeya, Sudhakar**
The origin and antiquity of the images of Ganga and Yamuna : A new approach. *Journal of the Ganganatha Jha Kendriya Sanskrit Vidyapeetha*, Vol. 41, 1985 : 151-161.

2310. **Parekh, V.S.**
The depictions of Sivalingas from Gujarat. *Journal of the Oriental Institute*, Vol. 33, Nos. 3-4, March-June 1984 : 325-329.

2311. **Parimoo, Ratan**
Vishnu's weapons and their representation in Indian art. *Kalakshetra Quarterly*, Vol. 7, No. 4 : 15-38.

2312. ——.
Weapons of gods as embodiments of their power. *Orissa Historical Research Journal*, Vol. 31, No. 1, 1985 : 72-92.

2313. **Pathak, Naresh Kumar**
Kendriya Sangrahalaya, Gujari Mahal, Gwalior mein sanrakshita Lakulisha-pratimayen. *Maru-Bharati*, Vol. 34, No. 3, October 1986 : 47-48 (Hindi).

2314. **Rahman, Mukhlesur**
Siva Nataraja. *Journal of the Varendra Research Museum*, Vol. 6, 1980-81 : 73-100.

2315. **Ramachandran, T.N.**
Fresh light on the Deogarh relief of Nara-Narayana. *Indian Historical Quarterly*, Vol. 27, No. 3, September 1951 : 191-196.

2316. ——.
The Kiratarjuniyam or "Arjuna's penance" in Indian art. *Journal of the Indian Society of Oriental Art*, Vol. 18, 1950-51 : 1-110.

2317. **Rangarajan, Haripriya**
Spread of Vaisnavism in Gujarat upto 1600 A.D. (A study with special reference to the iconic forms of Visnu). Bombay, Somaiya Publications, 1990.

2318. **Rao, Manjushree**
Gupta shilpa mein Ramayani drashya. In B.P. Sinha, ed., *Sri Rama in art, archaeology and literature*. Patna, The Bihar Puravid Parishad, 1989 : 140-152 (Hindi).

2319. Rock-cut Gupta sculpture, Shankargarh Hill, district Satna, Madhya Pradesh. *Indian Archaeology : A Review* 1967-68 : 67.

2320. **Roy, U.N.**
Salabhanjika in art, philosophy and literature. Allahabad, Lokbharati Publications, 1979.

2321. **Sahai, Bhagwant**
Agni in North Indian art. *Journal of the Bihar Research Society*, Vol. 53, 1967 : 143-154.

2322. ———.
Ardhanarisvara in North Indian art. *Journal of the Bihar Research Society*, Vol. 60, 1974 : 14-27.

2323. **Sahai, Sachchidanand**
A rare sculpture of Revanta from Sultanganj. *Journal of the Bihar Research Society*, Vol. 47, 1961 : 211-213.

2324. ———.
Some Brahmanical rock-sculptures from Sultanganj. *Journal of the Bihar Research Society*, Vol. 49, 1963 : 137-146.

2325. **Sanghamitra**
Sristi karta Brahma-ek pratima shastriya adhyayana *Sanskriti Sandhana*, Vol. 4, 1991 : 36-45 (Hindi).

2326. **Sankaranarayana N.**
Dwarfs in Indian art. *Vishveshvaranand Indological Journal*, Vol. 16, pt. 1, 1978 : 96-98.

2327. **Sarma, I.K.**
The development of early Saiva art and architecture. Delhi, Sundeep Prakashan, 1982.

2328. **Sastri, T.V.G.**
Dwarf in the Indian Sculpture. *Arts Asiatiques*, Vol. 6, 1959 : 33-58.

2329. **Schastok, Sara**
A sixth-century Kubera image from Mandasor. In Anand Krishna and Kamal Giri, ed., *Chhavi-2 : Rai Krishnadasa felicitation Volume*. Varanasi, Bharat Kala Bhavan, 1981 : 105-108.

2330. Sculptural remains in district Jhansi, Uttar Pradesh. *Indian Archaeology : A Review*, 1958-59 : 75.

2331. Sculptures, district Mirzapur, Uttar Pradesh. *Indian Archaeology : A Review*, 1977-78 : 84.

2332. **Shah, U.P.**
Ancient sculptures from Gujarat and Saurashtra. *Journal of Indian Museums*, Vol. 8, 1952 : 49-57.

2333. ———.
Gupta sculptures from Idar State (Gujarat). *Journal of Indian Museums*, Vol. 9, 1953 : 90-103.

2334. **Sharma, B.N.**
Ardhanarishvara-Shiva. *Roopa-Lekha*, Vol. 50, 1978-79 : 36-45.

2335. ———.
The enduring charm of Gupta sculptures. *Roopa-Lekha*, Vol. 52, 1981 : 28-38.

2336. ———.
Iconography of Revanta. New Delhi, Abhinav Publications, 1975.

2337. ———.
Iconography of Vainayaki. New Delhi, Abhinav Publications, 1979.

2338. ———.
An image of Haragauri from Mathura. *Journal of Indian Museums*, Vol. 29, 1973 : 40-42.

2339. ———.
Murtikala mein Srikrishna. *Parishad Patrika*, Vol. 14, No. 3, October 1974 : 61-68 (Hindi).

2340. ———.
A rare image of Gajalaksmi from Mathura in the National Museum, New Delhi. *Bulletin of Ancient Indian History and Archaeology*, No. 2, 1968 : 73-75.

2341. ______.
Ravana lifting mount Kailasa in Indian art. *East and West*, New Series, Vol. 23, Nos. 3-4, September-December 1973 : 327-338.

2342. ______.
Revanta in literature and art. *Purana*, Vol. 13, No. 2, 1971 : 133-159.

2343. ______.
Revanta in literature, art and epigraphs. *East and West*, New Series, Vol. 23, Nos. 1-2, March-June 1973 : 155-168.

2344. ______.
Some Saiva sculptures in the National Museum, New Delhi. *National Museum Bulletin*, Nos. 4-6 : 28-38.

2345. ______.
Visnu-Trivikrama in literature, art and epigraphs. *East and West*, New Series, Vol. 18, Nos. 3-4, September-December 1968 : 323-334.

2346. **Sharma, Braj Bhanu**
Ek ati vishista Gupta-kaleen Nag-pratima. *Maru-Bharati*, Vol. 36, No. 1, 1988 : 4-6 (Hindi).

2347. **Sharma, Madhuri**
Madhya Pradesh ki vilakshan pratimayen. *Puratan*, Vol. 8, 1991 : 74-78 (Hindi).

2348. **Shastri, Ajay Mitra**
Rama : His divinity in literature, numismatics and epigraphy. *Purana*, Vol. 36, No. 1, January 1994 : 184-194.

2349. **Shetti, B.V.**
Gupta-Vakataka parallels in Chalukyan art. In Karl Khandalawala, ed., *The golden age : Gupta art—empire, province and influence*. Bombay, Marg Publications, 1991 : 103-108.

2350. **Shukla, S.P.**
Durga relief from Bhitargaon. *Bulletin of Museums & Archaeology in U.P*, No. 10 December 1972 : 13-14.

2351. ———.
Relics of ancient art from Pehowa. *Panjab University Research Bulletin (Arts)*, Vol. 11, 1980 : 69-86.

2352. **Singh, Amrendra Kumar**
Pracheen Bharatiya dharma evam kala mein Yaksa, Kinnar aur Dikpala. Allahabad, Parimal Prakashan, 1990 (Hindi).

2353. **Singh, O.P.**
Iconography of Gaja-Lakshmi. Varanasi, Bharati Prakashan, 1983.

2354. **Singh, Sheo Bahadur**
Brahmanical icons in Northern India. New Delhi, Sagar Publications, 1977.

2355. ———.
Rama and his early images. In Lallanji Gopal, ed., Ayodhya : *History, archaeology and tradition*. Varanasi, All India Kashiraj Trust, 1994 : 247-252.

2356. ———.
Rama and his early images. *Purana*, Vol. 36, No. 2, July 1994 : 247-252.

2357. ———.
Rama and his early images. *Pragdhara : Journal of the U.P. State Archaeological Organisation*, No. 5, 1994-95 : 161-164.

2358. **Singh, Sri Bhagwan**
Gupta kalin Hindu dev-pratimayen. New Delhi, Ramanand Vidya Bhawan, 1982 (Hindi).

2359. **Sinha, Ajoy Kumar**
An iconographical study of Visnu images in the Bhagalpur Museum (Bihar). *Journal of the Bihar Research Society*, Vols. 67-68, 1981-82 : 59-66.

2360. **Sinha, B.P.**, ed.
Sri Rama in art, archaeology and literature. Patna, The Bihar Puravid Parishad, 1989.

2361. **Sinha, Binod Chandra**
Serpent worship in ancient India. New Delhi, Books Today, 1979.

2362. **Sinha, C.R.P.**
Nataraja in the art of Bihar. *Journal of the Bihar Puravid Parishad*, Vol. 3, 1979 : 149-152.

2363. ______.
Ramayana scenes in Bihar sculptures. In B.P. Sinha, ed., *Sri Rama in art, archaeology and literature*. Patna, The Bihar Puravid Parishad, 1989 : 114-116.

2364. ______.
Varaha-Visnu in art and epigraph of Bihar. *Journal of the Bihar Research Society*, Vol. 56, 1970 : 54-60.

2365. **Sinha, Kanchan**
Karttikeya in Indian art and literature. Delhi, Sundeep Prakashan, 1979.

2366. **Sinha, Pushpa**
Bihar ki kala mein Revanta. *Journal of the Bihar Puravid Parishad*, Vols. 7-8, 1983-84 : 281-286 (Hindi).

2367. **Sivaramamurti, C.**
Ganga. New Delhi, Orient Longman, 1976.

2368. ______.
Iconographic gleanings from epigraphy. *Arts Asiatiques*, Vol. 4, 1957 : 35-70.

2369. ______.
An interesting Gupta chaturmukha of Surya. *Bulletin National Museum*, No. 3 : 1-7.

2370. ______.
Nataraja in art, thought and literature. New Delhi, National Museum, 1974.

2371. ______.
Sri Lakshmi in Indian art and thought. New Delhi, Kanak Publications, 1982.

2372. **Sohoni, S.V.**
Varaha avatara panel at Udayagiri, Vidisa. *Journal of the Bihar Research Society*, Vol. 57, 1971 : 49-56.

2373. Some Indian images in the worcester Art Museum. *Marg*, Vol. 6, No. 3, June 1953 : 12-18.

2374. **Srinivasan, Doris**
Early Krsna icons : The case at Mathura. *Bulletin of Museums & Archaeology in U.P*, Nos. 21-24, June 1978-December 1979 : 1-17.

2375. ______.
Early Krsna icons : The case at Mathura. In Joanna G. Williams, ed., *Kaladarsana : American studies in the art of India*. New Delhi, Oxford & IBH Publishing Co., 1981 : 127-136.

2376. ______.
A unique Mathura eight-armed Visnu of the 4th century A.D. *Oriental Art*, New Series, Vol. 34, No. 4, 1988-89 : 276-281.

2377. **Srivastava, A.K.**
Rajakiya Sanghralaya Mathura mein Krsna kathanak kalakritiya-ek surveykshan. *Bulletin of Museums & Archaeology in U.P*, Nos. 21-24, June 1978- December 1979 : 127-237.

2378. **Srivastava, A.L.**
Bharatiya sahitya aur kala mein Rajya-Lakshmi. *Maru Bharati*, Vol. 30, No. 2, July 1982 : 44-54 (Hindi).

2379. ______.
Simhavahini Gaja-Lkksmi : A unique icon in Indian sculptural art. *East and West*, Vol. 42, Nos. 2-4, 1992 : 485-488.

2380. **Srivastava, M.C.P.**
Mother goddess in Indian art, archaeology & literature. Delhi, Agam Kala Prakashan, 1979.

2381. **Srivastava, V.C.**
Sun-worship in ancient India. Allahabad, Indological Publications, 1972.

2382. **Srivastava, V.S.**
Rajasthani murtikala mein Krsnalila abhipraya. *Rajasthan Bharati*, Vol. 11, No. 2, 63-76 (Hindi).

2383. **Stadtner, Donald M.**
A Gupta frieze from Kandava. In Anand Krishna and Kamal Giri, ed., *Chhavi-2 : Rai Krishnadasa felicitation Volume*. Varanasi, Bharat Kala Bhavan, 1981 : 187-188.

2384. **Tandon, O.P.** and **Biswas, T.K.**
Ganga in Indian art : Bharat Kala Bhavan collection. Varanasi, Bharat Kala Bhavan, 1986.

2385. Temples and sculptures in district Sagar, Madhya Pradesh. *Indian Archaeology : A Review*, 1959-60 : 70.

2386. **Tewari, S.P.**
Hindu iconography. New Delhi, Agam Kala Prakashan, 1979.

2387. **Thakur, Upendra**
Karttikeya in literature, art and coins. *East and West*. Vol. 24, Nos. 3-4, September-December 1974 : 297-310.

2388. ———.
On Karttikeya. Varanasi, Chaukhamba Orientalia, 1981.

2389. **Tiwari, R.P.**
Gupta kalin murtikala mein Krishna-katha ka swaroop. In Krishna Deva and others, ed., *History and art : Essays on history, art, culture and archaeology presented to Prof. K.D. Bajpai in honour of his fifty years Indological studies*. Delhi, Ramanand Vidya Bhawan, 1989 : 108-110 (Hindi).

2390. **Tripathi, Krishna Kumar**
Eran ki Gupta kaleen murtikala. *Puratan*, Vol. 1, 1984 : 62-64 (Hindi).

2391. ———.
Madhya Pradesh ki pracheen shilpkala mein Balaram. *Prachya Pratibha*, Vol. 11, 1983 : 127-133 (Hindi).

2392. **Tripathi, R.R.**
Karttikeya images in Allahabad Museum. *Indian Museum Bulletin*, Vol. 5, No. 2, 1970 : 62-65.

2393. **Trivedi, C.B.**
Newly discovered Gupta sculptures from Madhya Pradesh. *Puratattva*, No. 11, 1979-80 : 150-151.

2394. ———.
Rock cut sculptures at Sindursi, district Jabalpur, Madhya Pradesh. *Prachya Pratibha*, Vol. 4, No. 1, January 1976 : 42-46.

2395. **Trivedi, R.D.**
Iconography of Parvati. Delhi, Agam Kala Prakashan, 1981.

2396. **Trivedi, S.D.**
An early Visnu sculpture from Almora. *Bulletin of Museums & Archaeology in U.P*, Nos. 47-48, June-December 1991 : 41-43.

2397. ———.
Ganesa ki prarambhik pratimayen. *Bulletin of Museums & Archaeology in U.P*, Nos. 47-48, June-December 1991 : 79-84 (Hindi).

2398. **Upadhyaya, B.S.**
Sculptures in the Provincial Museum, Lucknow. *Journal of the Indian Society of Oriental Art*, Vol. 10, 1942 : 175-190.

2399. **Van Kooij, K.R.**
Gods and attendants in the relief of Visnu Anantasayana at Deogarh. In Janine Schotsmans and Maurizio Taddei, ed., *South Asian Archaeology 1983*, Vol. 2. Naples, Instituto Universitario Orientale, 1985 : 679-701.

2400. **Varma, Mahavir Prasad**
Shadanan Karttikeya ki teen aprakashit pratimayen. *Maru Bharati*, Vol. 30, No. 2, July 1982 : 34-36 (Hindi).

2401. **Vashishtha, Neelima**
Mayura vahana Sarasvati : An example of religious tolerance during the post Gupta period. *Jijnasa : A Journal of the History of Ideas and Culture*, Vol. 1, Nos. 1-2, January-April 1974 : 88-102.

2402. **Vatsyayan, Kapila**
Goddesses and women in Indian myth and art. *Kalakshetra Quarterly*, Vol. 4, No. 3 : 3-14.

2403. **Viennot, O.**
The Mahisasuramardini from Siddhi-ki-gupha at Deogarh. *Journal of the Indian Society of Oriental Art*, New Series, Vol. 4, 1971-1972 : 66-77.

2404. **Vogel, J. Ph.**
Naga worship in ancient Mathura. *Archaeological Survey of India Annual Report*, 1908-09 : 159-163.

2405. **Vyas, Narain**
Raisen Zile (M.P.) ki mahatvapurna pracheen pratimayen. *Prachya Pratibha*, Vol. 14, 1988-90 : 75-78 (Hindi).

2406. **Williams, Joanna**
New Naga images from the Sanci area. *Oriental Art*, New Series, Vol. 22, No. 2, 1976 : 174-179.

BUDDHIST

2407. **Agrawal, Madhuri**
Lakshmi kya Baudhdevi thi ? *Parishad Patrika*, Vol. 16, No. 3, October 1976 : 25-35 (Hindi).

2408. **Amarendra Nath**
A portable stupa in the Magadha style. *Lalit Kala*, No. 26 : 15-17.

2409. **Anand, Mulk Raj**
Origin of the Buddha image. *Marg*, Vol. 15, No. 2, March 1962 : 8-14.

2410. **Asher, Frederick M.**
Bodhgaya images of the year 64 : A reconsideration. *Journal of the Bihar Research Society*, Vol. 58, 1972 : 151-157.

2411. **Banerji, Adris**
Buddha-charitra in the Banaras School. *Journal of Indian Museums*, Vol. 10, 1954 : 1-20.

2412. **Banerji, Dilip Kumar**
Influence of Buddhism on Indian and Indo-Asian art. *Prajna Bharati*, Vol. 1, 1981 : 252-274.

2413. Buddha images from votive stupa, Sarnath, district Varanasi. *Indian Archaeology : A Review*, 1963-64 : 92.

2414. Catalogue, 2500th Buddha Jayanti celebration 1956 : Exhibition of Buddhist art. New Delhi, Lalit Kala Akadami, 1956.

2415. Catalogue of exhibition of Buddhist art. Calcutta, Indian Museum, 1956.

2416. **Codrington, K. de B.**
Mathura of the gods. *Marg*, Vol. 9, No. 2, March 1956 : 41-49.

2417. **Dani, Ahmad Hasan**
Buddhist sculpture in East Pakistan. Karachi, Department of Archaeology in Pakistan, 1959.

2418. Exhibition of Buddhist art and antiquities. Rangoon, Ministry of Union Culture, 1955.

2419. **Fabri, C.L.**
Mathura of the gods. *Marg*, Vol. 7, No. 2, March 1954 : 8-22.

2420. **Fisher, Robert E.**
Buddhist art and architecture. London, Thames and Hudson, 1993.

2421. **Gangoly, O.C.**
The Earth goddess in Buddhist art. *Indian Historical Quarterly*, Vol. 19, No. 1, March 1943 : 1-11.

2422. **Ghose, Ajit**
An image of Arya Avalokitesvara of the time of Vainyagupta. *Journal of the Indian Society of Oriental Art*, Vol. 13, 1945 : 49-54.

2423. **Griswold, A.B.**
Prolegomena to the study of the Buddha's dress in Chinese sculpture with particular reference to the Rietberg Museum's collection. *Artibus Asiae*, Vol. 26, 1963 : 85-131.

2424. Gupta sculptures, Pawaya, district Gwalior, Madhya Pradesh. *Indian Archaeology : A Review*, 1973-74 : 51.

2425. **Hallade, Madeleine**
The Gandhara style and the evolution of Buddhist art. London, Thames and Hudson, 1968.

2426. **Hutington, John C.**
Sowing the seeds of the lotus : A journey to the great pilgrimage sites of Buddhism, part II. *Orientations*, Vol. 17, No. 2, 1982 : 28-43.

2427. **Irwin, John**
Some unknown Gupta sculptures from Sultanganj. *Artibus Asiae*, Vol. 17, 1954 : 34-38.

2428. **Jamkhedkar, A.P.**
Buddhist bronzes from Ramatek. *Lalit Kala*, No. 22 : 13-19.

2429. **Karetzky, Patricia Eichenbaum**
The act of pilgrimage and Guptan steles with scenes from the life of the Buddha. *Oriental Art*, New Series, Vol. 33, No. 3, 1987 : 268-274.

2430. **Khandalavala, Karl**
Commentary on Taranatha's chapter on Buddhist art. *Marg*, Vol. 4, No. 1 : 61-63.

2431. **Krishan, Y.**
The emergence of the Buddha image, Gandhara versus Mathura. *Oriental Art*, New Series, Vol. 34, No. 4, 1988/89 : 255-275.

2432. **Krishna Deva**
Buddhist art of India and Nepal. Varanasi, Central Institute of Higher Tibetan Studies, 1987.

2433. **Krishna Kumar**
Some Gupta Cauri-bearers. *Journal of the Indian Society of Oriental Art*, New Series, Vol. 6, 1974-1975 : 9-13.

2434. **Lalit Kumar**
Sarnath Buddha—origin and development of its style. *Pragdhara*, No. 2, 1991-92 : 107-112.

2435. **La Plante, John D.**
A pre-Pala sculpture and its significance for the international Bodhisattva style in Asia. *Artibus Asiae*, Vol. 26, 1963 : 247-284.

2436. **Lee, Sherman E.**
An early Javanese bronze, the Gupta international style and clay technique. *Artibus Asiae*, Vol. 19, 1956 : 271-278.

2437. **Leoshko, Janice**
Buddhist art of Northern India. In Pratapaditya Pal, ed., *Asian art : Selections from the Norton Simon Museum*. Pasadena, Norton Simon Museum, 1988 : 6-19.

2438. **Mani, B.R.**
Hariti pratima lekh. *Dhyanam*, Vols. 5-6, 1985-86 : 125-126 (Hindi).

2439. **Mani, B.R.** and **Dube, S.K.**
Gupta vamsha ke pratham shasak Sri Gupta ka Sarnath se prapta Hariti-pratima Abhilekh. *Dhyanam*, Vols. 5-6, 1985-86 : 39-43. (Hindi).

2440. **Rao, M.**
Art of Gupta sculptures at Sanchi. *Prachya Pratibha*, Vol. 13, 1985-87 : 57-69.

2441. **Rosenfield, John M.**
On the dated carvings of Sarnath : Gupta period. *Artibus Asiae*, Vol. 26, 1963 : 10-26.

2442. **Rowland, Benjamin**
The golden age of Buddhist art : Gupta period. *Marg*, Vol. 9, No. 2, March 1956 : 72-85.

2443. **Rowland, Jr., Benjamin**
The evolution of the Buddha image. New York, The Asia Society, 1976.

2444. **Sahu, Nabin Kumar**
Buddhist art in Orissa. *Marg*, Vol. 8, No. 4, September 1955 : 16-22.

2445. **Sarkar, Haribhishnu**
Begining of sculptural art under the Guptas : An inscribed image from Baraipur, near Sarnath. In Gouriswar Bhattacharya, ed., *Deyadharma : Studies in memory of Dr. D.C. Sircar*. Delhi, Sri Satguru Publications, 1986 : 231-233.

2446. **Savitri Devi, D.**
A Buddhist stele from Saheth-Maheth. *Journal of the Bihar Puravid Parishad*, Vol. 6, 1982 : 161-163.

2447. **Sen, Arun**
A bronze Buddha from the Birmingham Museum. *Rupam*, No. 21, January 1925 : 1.

2448. **Sengupta, Anusua**
Buddhist art of Bengal. Delhi, Rahul Publishing House, 1993.

2449. **Sharma, B.N.**
Bauddha murtikala ka Vikas. *Parishad Patrika*, Vol. 11, No. 1, April 1971 : 49-53 (Hindi).

2450. **Sharma, R. C.**
Buddha as appears in Mathura art. *Journal of Indian Museums*, Vol. 29, 1973 : 18-21.

2451. ——.
Buddhist art of Mathura. Delhi, Agam Kala Prakashan, 1984.

2452. ——.
New art treasures from Mathura. *National Museum Bulletin*, Nos. 4-6 : 39-43.

2453. **Sinha, Usha**
Buddhist iconography in Uttar Pradesh, A.D. 300 to 1200. Varanasi, Sanjay Book Centre, 1995.

2454. **Snellgrove, David L.**, ed.
The image of Buddha. London, Serindia Publications, 1978.

2455. **St. K.**
Colossal copper statue of Buddha. *Calcutta Review*, Third Series, Vol. 9, 1923 : 88.

2456. **Subrahmanyam, Savitri**
Dinna: The Mathura-Gupta artist. *Marg*, Vol. 42, No. 3 : 53-56.

2457. **Thaplyal, K.K. and Sharma, R.C.**
Mathura Buddhist image inscription of Sanghavarman. *Bulletin of Museum & Archaeology in U.P.*, Nos. 35-36, June-December 1985 : 1-5.

2458. **Verma, Shailendra Kumar**
Art and Iconography of the Buddha images. Delhi, Eastern Book Linkers, 1996.

2459. **Vogel, J. Ph.**
Buddhist art in India, Ceylon and Java. New Delhi, Oriental Books Reprint Corporation, 1977.

2460. ______.
De Buddhistische kunst van voor-Indie. Amsterdam, H-J. Paris, 1932 (Dutch).

2461. **Williams, Joanna**
A Mathura Gupta Buddha reconsidered. *Lalit Kala*, No. 17 : 28-32.

2462. ______.
Sarnath Gupta steles of the Buddha's life. *Ars Orientalis*, Vol. 10, 1975 : 171-192.

JAINA

2463. **Agrawala, R.C.**
Newly discovered sculptures from Vidisa. *Journal of the Oriental Institute*, Vol. 18, No. 3, March 1969 : 252-253.

2464. **Arya, Maya Rani**
Gwalior Sangrahalaya ki Jaina pratimayen. *Arhat Vacana*, Vol. 5, No. 1, January 1993 : 39-40 (Hindi).

2465. **Bajpai, K.D.**
Development of Jaina art in Madhya Pradesh. *Journal of Indian History*, Vol. 55, pt. 3, December 1977 : 81-84.

2466. ——.
Jaina art of Madhya Pradesh. *Puratan*, Vol. 1, Nos. 2-3, 1984 : 16-21.

2467. **Bajpai, V.K.** and **Srivastava, M.C.**
Jaina art and architecture of Madhya Pradesh. *Prachya Pratibha*, Vol. 8, 1980 : 37-49.

2468. **Ghosh, A.**, ed.
Jaina art and architecture. New Delhi, Bharatiya Jnanpith, 1974-1975. 3 vols.

2469. **Nahata, Agar Chand**
Gupta kalin ek bhvya Parsvanath murti. *Titthayar*, Vol. 6, No. 1, 1982 : 17-19 (Hindi).

2470. **Namdev, Shiv Kumar**
Bharatiya puratattva tatha kala mein Bhagwan Mahavir. *Shraman*, Vol. 26, Nos. 1-2, Novembar-December 1974 : 38-46 (Hindi).

2471. ——.
Vidisha se prapta Jaina pratimayen aur Ramgupta ki etihasikta. *Shraman*, Vol. 25, No. 6, April 1974 : 18-23 (Hindi).

2472. **Nautiyal, K.P.**
A few notable Jaina icons in Gwalior Museum. *Prachya Pratibha*, Vol. 4, No. 1, January 1976 : 47-54.

2473. **Nigam, M.L.**
Impact of Jainism on Mathura art. *Journal of the U.P. Historical Society*, New Series, Vol. 9, pt. 1, 1961 : 7-12.

2474. **Pandeya, Om Prakash**
Sarnath ki Jaina pratimayen. *Jaina Siddhanta Bhaskar*, Vol. 39, No. 1, June 1986 : 18-20 (Hindi).

2475. ——.
Sarnath ki Jaina pratimayen. *Vaishali Institute Research Bulletin*, No. 6, 1988 : 46-49 (Hindi).

2476. **Parmar, B.M.S.**
Jaina pratimayen : Bharatpur Sangrahalaya. *Rajasthan Bharati*, Vol. 10, No. 3, 1967 : 15-17 (Hindi).

2477. **Shah, U.P.**
Age of differentiation of Digambara and Svetambara images and the earliest known Svetambara bronzes. *Bulletin of the Prince of Wales Museum of Western India*, No. 1, 1950-1951 : 30-40.

2478. ——.
Beginnings of Jaina iconography. *Bulletin of Museums & Archaeology in U.P.*, No. 9, June 1972 : 1-14.

2479. ——.
Studies in Jaina art. Banaras, Jaina Cultural Research Society, 1955.

2480. **Sharma, B.N.**
Jaina-pratimayon ke vikas mein Narhad ki murtiyan. *Maru Bharati*, Vol. 9, No. 4, January 1962 : 14-20. (Hindi).

2481. **Sharma, R.C.**
Jaina sculptures of the Gupta age in the State Museum, Lucknow. In *Shri Mahavira Jaina Vidyalaya golden jubilee volume*, Part I. Bombay, Shri Mahavira Jaina Vidyalaya, 1968 : 143-155.

2482. ——.
Rshabhanath aur unki murti parampara. *Jaina Antiquary*, Vol. 46, Nos. 1-2, 1993 : 8-14 (Hindi).

2483. **Singh, Harihar**
Origin and development of Tirthankara images. *Shraman*, Vol. 29, No. 3, January 1978 : 22-30.

2484. ——.
Tirthankar-pratimayon ka udbhav aur vikas. *Shraman*, Vol. 25, Nos. 1-2, Novembar-December 1973 : 43-52 (Hindi).

2485. **Sinha, Chitta Ranjan Prasad**
Gupta kalin Parsvanath ki ek durlabh murti. *Parishad Patrika*, Vol. 13, No. 4, January 1974 : 29-32 (Hindi).

2486. **Tiwari, M.N.P.**
Jaina art of the Gupta period. In Karl Khandalavala, ed., *The golden age : Gupta art-empire, province and influence*. Bombay, Marg Publications, 1991 : 25-36.

2487. ——.
Jaina art of the Gupta period. *Marg*, Vol. 42, No. 3 : 25-36.

2488. ——.
Jaina images in the Sonbhandar cave at Rajgir. *Prachya Pratibha*, Vol. 11, 1983 : 23-27.

2489. ——.
An unpublished Jina image in the Bharat Kala Bhavan, Varanasi, *Vishveshvaranand Indological Journal*, Vol. 13, 1975 : 373-375.

2490. **Upadhayay, Basudeva**
Mahavira icon and Indian archaeology. *Journal of the Bihar Research Society*, Vol.58, 1972 : 145-150.

2491. **Williams, Joanna**
Two new Gupta Jina images. *Oriental Art*, New Series, Vol. 18, No. 4, 1972 : 378-380.

BIRDS AND ANIMALS

2492. **Bharatha Iyer, K.**
Animals in Indian sculpture. Bombay, D.B. Taraporevala Sons, 1977.

2493. **Biswas, T.K.**
Horse in early Indian art. New Delhi, Munshiram Manoharlal Publishers, 1987.

2494. **Ghosh, Devaprasad**
The Makara in Indian art. *Calcutta Review*, Third Series, Vol. 37, 1930 : 101-111.

2495. **Gorakshkar, Sadashiv**
Animals in Indian art. Bombay, Prince of Wales Museum of Western India, 1979.

2496. **Gupte, Y.R.**
The development of Makara or crocodile in architecture from the 4th or the 5th century A.D. to the modern times or the 12th or the 13th century A.D. *Annals of the Bhandarkar Oriental Research Institute*, Vol. 37, 1956 : 276.

2497. **Krishna Lal**
Peacock in Indian art. *Journal of the Oriental Institute*, Vol. 23, Nos. 1-2, September-December 1973 : 1-11.

2498. **Misra, Sudhakar Nath**
The lion-motif in Gupta pillars and sculptures. *Prachya Pratibha*, Vol. 11, 1983 : 43-48.

2499. **Ratnakar, Jagannath Das**
Discovery of a new historical stone horse. *Indian Historical Quarterly*, Vol. 3, No. 4, December 1927 : 719-728.

2500. **Sen, Asis**
Animal motifs in ancient Indian art. Calcutta, Firma K.L. Mukhopadhyay, 1972.

2501. **Sivaramurti, C.**
Birds and animals in Indian sculpture. New Delhi, National Museum, 1974.

2502. **Srivastava, Kamal Shankar**
The elephant in early Indian art. Varanasi, Sangeeta Prakashan, 1989.

2503. **Vogel, Jean Philippe**
The goose in Indian literature and art. Lieden, E.J. Brill, 1962.

TERRACOTTAS

2504. **Agrawala, R.C.**

Bhitargaon se prapta ek mahatvapurna phalak. *Bulletin of Museums & Archaeology in U.P.*, Nos. 45-46, June-December 1990 : 7-8 (Hindi).

2505. ______.

Two interesting Saiva terracottas in the Bikaner Museum. *Artibus Asiae*, Vol. 19, 1956 : 61-65.

2506. **Agrawala, V.S.**

Mathura terracottas. *Journal of the United Provinces Historical Society*, Vol. 9, pt. 2, July 1936 : 6-38.

2507. ______.

Mathura terracottas. Varanasi, Prithivi Prakashan, 1984.

2508. ______.

A palace scene on a terracotta panel from Mathura. *Journal of the Indian Society of Oriental art*, Vol. 10, 1942 : 69-73.

2509. ______.

Rajghat terracottas. *Journal of the Indian Society of Oriental art*, Vol. 9, 1941 : 7-11.

2510. ______.

The religious significance of the Gupta terracottas from Rang Mahal. *Lalit Kala*, No. 8 : 63-68.

2511. ______.

Some terracottas in the Baroda Museum. *Bulletin Museum and Picture Gallery, Baroda*, Vol. 12, 1955-56 : 1-10.

2512. ______.

A unique terracotta plaque from Rajghat. *Bulletin of the Prince of Wales Museum of Western India*, No. 2, 1951-1952 : 82-85.

2513. **Anand, Mulk Raj**
Beauties born in the mud of the potter's yard. *Marg*, Vol. 23, No. 1, December 1969 : 3-12.

2514. **Banerjee, P.**
A Gupta terracotta plaque and its identification. *Journal of the Indian Society of Oriental art*, New Series, Vols. 16-17, 1987-89 : 33-35.

2515. **Banerji, Arundhati**
Terracotta art expression in Indian Sub-continent. *Roopa-Lakha*, Vol. 56, 1984 : 18-36.

2516. **Bhadouria, G.S.**
Excellent femining beauty in the terracottas. *Bulletin of Museums & Archaeology in U.P.*, Nos. 45-46, June-December 1990 : 55-59.

2517. **Biswas, S.S.**
Terracotta art of Bengal. Delhi, Agam Kala Prakashan, 1981.

2518. **Biswas, T.K.**
Six large terracottas. In Devendra Handa and Ashvini Agrawala, ed., *Ratna-Chandrika : Panorama of Oriental studies (Shri R.C. Agrawala festchrift)*. New Delhi, Harman Publishing House, 1989 : 175-179.

2519. **Dasgupta, C.C.**
Origin and evolution of Indian clay sculpture. Calcutta, 1961.

2520. ———.
Some unpublished ancient Indian terracottas preserved in the British Museum. *Artibus Asiae*, Vol. 13, 1950 : 254-269.

2521. **Deo, S.B.**
Terracotta figurines and toys from Maheshwar excavation. *Journal of the Asiatic Society of Bombay*, New Series, Vols. 31-32, 1956-57 : 38-44.

2522. **Desai, Devangana**
Social background of ancient Indian terracottas (cir. 600 B.C.-A.D. 600). In Debiprasad Chattopadhyay, ed., *History and Society : Essays in honour of Professor Niharranjan Ray*. Calcutta, K.P. Bagchi & Co., 1978 : 143-168.

2523. ______.
The social milieu of ancient Indian terracottas, 600 B.C.-600 A.D. In Amy G. Poster, ed., *From Indian earth : 4,000 years of terracotta art*. New York, The Brooklyn Museum, 1986 : 29-42.

2524. ______.
Terracottas and urban culture of ancient India (circa 600 B.C. to A.D. 600). *National Museum Bulletin*, Nos. 4-6 : 59-65.

2525. **Dhavalikar, M.K.**
Masterpieces of Indian terracottas. Bombay, D.B. Taraporevala Sons & Co., 1977.

2526. **Dwivedi, Umesh Chandra**
Some important Gupta terracotta plaque depicting Ramkatha. In B.P.Sinha, ed., *Sri Rama in art, archaeology and literature*. Patna, The Bihar Puravid Parishad, 1989 : 153-157.

2527. **Goetz, H.** and **Bajpai, K.D.**
Early terracottas : Sunga, Kushan, Gupta, Suratgarh, Rangmahal, Bharatpur, Bairat, Rairh. *Marg*, Vol. 12, No. 2, March 1959 : 24-27.

2528. **Gupta, Meenu**
Terracotta art of Ahicchatra. *Panchala*, Vol. 2, 1986 : 28-46.

2529. **Gupta, P.L.**
Gangetic Valley terracotta art. Varanasi, Prithivi Prakashan, 1972.

2530. **Handa, Devendra**
A Gupta terracotta of Ganga from Haryana *Journal of the Ganganatha Jha Kendriya Sanskrit Vidyapeetha*, Vol. 40, 1984 : 165-168.

2531. ______.
Some unpublished terracottas from Haryana. *Prachya Pratibha*, Vol. 12, 1984 : 27-32.

2532. **Husain, Shahanara**
A terracotta head from Mahasthan. *Journal of Ancient Indian History*, Vol. 7, 1973-74 : 179-184.

2533. **Jayaswal, Vidula** and **Kalyan Krishna**
An ethno-archaeological view of Indian terracottas. Delhi, Agam Kala Prakashan, 1986.

2534. **Kala, Jayantika**
Ramayana in terracottas : A study. *Journal of the Ganganatha Jha Kendriya Sanskrit Vidyapeetha*, Vols. 38-39, 1982-1983 : 229-238.

2535. **Kala, S.C.**
Heritage of Madhya Pradesh, part 1, terracottas. *Marg*, Vol. 2, 1987 : 75-81.

2536. ———.
Krsna subjects in Indian terracotta art. *Bulletin of Museums & Archaeology in U.P.*, Nos. 21-24, June1978-December 1979 : 33-35.

2537. ———.
Terracotta figurines from Kausambi : Mainly in the collection of the Municipal Museum, Allahabad. Allahabad, Municipal Museum, 1950.

2538. ———.
Terracottas in the Allahabad Museum. New Delhi, Abhinav Publications, 1980.

2539. ———.
Trracottas of North India in the collection of State Museum Lucknow. Delhi, Agam Kala Prakashan, 1993.

2540. **Khandalavala, Karl** and **Roy, Archana**
Terracottas. *Marg*, Vol. 38, No. 8 : 39--52.

2541. **Khare, M.D.**
Pottery and terracotta in ancient Madhya Pradesh. *Journal of the Madhya Pradesh Itihasa Parishad*, No. 8, 1970 : 53-66.

2542. **Mandal, Prasanta Kumar**
Interpretation of terracottas from Tamralipta. Tamralipta, Tamralipta Museum and Research Centre, 1987.

2543. **Manmohan, Kumar**
Terracotta finds from Sugh. *Roopa-Lekha*, Vol. 55, 1984 : 90-91.

2544. **Misra, Vibha**
Pracheen mranmurtiyon ke Siva. *Puratan*, Vol. 6, 1989 : 191-197 (Hindi).

2545. **Mohinder Singh**
Terracotta art in Haryana. *Indian History Congress Proceedings*, Session 47, Volume II, 1986 : 166-174.

2546. ______.
Terracottas from Rohtak (Khokhrakot mound). *Panjab University Research Bulletin (Arts)*, Vol. 18, No. 1, 1987 : 145-149. -

2547. **Moti Chandra**
A study in the terracottas from Mirpurkhas. *Prince of Wales Museum Bulletin*, No. 7, 1959-1962 : 1-22.

2548. ______.
Terracotta heads from Akhnur. *Prince of Wales Museum Bulletin*, No. 12, 1973 : 54-57.

2549. **Mukherjee, Samir Kumar**
Early terracotta figurines from West Bengal : A study based on staratigraphic evidence from excavations. In Asok Datta, ed., *Studies in archaeology : Papers presented in memory of P.C. Dasgupta*. New Delhi, Books & Books, 1991 : 217-230.

2550. **Mukhopadhyay, Samir K.**
Early terracotta figurines from lower Bengal. *Monthly Bulletin of the Asiatic Society*, Vol. 6, No. 5, May 1971 :6-7.

2551. ______.
Terracottas from Bhita. *Artibus Asiae*, Vol. 34, 1972 : 71-94.

2552. **Nagar, M.M.**
Some newly acquired antiquities in the Mathura Museum. *Journal of the United Provinces Historical Society*, Vol. 12, pt. 2, December 1939 : 49-51.

2553. **Pandey, Suniti**
Salient features of terracotta art. *Prajna-Bharati*, Vol. 5, 1988 : 5-8.

2554. **Poster, Amy G.**
From Indian earth : 4,000 years of terracotta art. New York, The Brooklyn Museum, 1986.

2555. ———.
Indian terracotta art : An over view. In Amy G. Poster, *From Indian earth : 4,000 years of terracotta art*, New York, The Brooklyn Museum, 1986 : 17-28.

2556. **Prakash, P.**
A Dampati plaque from Bhitari and the Chandra Gupta-Kumardevi-type. In C.R.P. Sinha and others, ed., *Archaeology and art* (*Krishna Deva felicitation volume*), Part I. New Delhi, Ramanand Vidya Bhawan, 1990 : 295-296.

2557. ———.
Terracotta animal figurines in the Ganga-Yamuna valley (600 B.C. to 600 A.D.). Delhi, Agam Kala Prakashan, 1985.

2558. ———.
Three terracotta heads from Bansgaon. *Bharati*, New Series, No. 1, 1983 : 153-154.

2559. **Ramachandran, T.N.**
An interesting terracotta plaque from Ahicchatra (U.P.). *Indian Historical Quarterly*. Vol. 27, No. 4, December 1951 : 304-311.

2560. **Sahay, S.N.**
Terracottas of Bihar. In Bindeshwari Prasad Sinha, ed., *Comprehensive History of Bihar*, Vol. I, pt. II. Patna, K.P. Jayaswal Research Institute, 1974 : 625-651.

2561. **Sahay, Sachidanand**
Chronology of Indian terracottas. *Journal of the Bihar Research Society*, Vol. 61, 1975 : 72-78.

2562. **Sankalia, H.D.**
Early terracottas : Nagari. *Marg*, Vol. 12, No. 2, March 1959 : 24-27.

2563. **Sankalia, H.D.** and **Dhavalikar, M.K.**
The terracotta art of India. *Marg*, Vol. 23, No. 1, December 1969 : 33-54.

2564. **Saran, Satish Chandra**
Terracotta plaque of Kinnara-Mithuna from Lakha Dhora (Rajasthan). *Journal of the Bihar Puravid Parishad*, Vols. 4-5, 1980-81 : 166-168.

2565. **Satya Prakash**
Bikaner ke sangrahalaya mein pradarshit mranmaya-kala. *Rajasthan Bharati*, Vol. 4, Nos. 2-3, 1954 : 11-14 (Hindi).

2566. **Shah, U.P.**
Terracotta from former Bikaner state. *Lalit Kala*, No. 8 : 55-62.

2567. **Sharma, B.N.**
Gupta terracottas. *Kalakshetra Quarterly*, Vol. 3, No.1 : 7-16.

2568. **Sharma, B.N.** and **Khullar, G.D.**
Some terracotta figurines in the National Museum, New Delhi. *Journal of Indian History*, Vol. 52, pts. 2-3, August & December 1974 : 265-268.

2569. **Sharma, R.C.**
Terracotta art and its relevance in the cultural history of India. *Visva-Bharati Quarterly*. New Series, Vol. 3, Nos. 3-4, November 1992-April 1993 : 172-186.

2570. ——.
Terracottas as source of history and art. *Pragdhara*, No. 1, 1990-91 : 119-121.

2571. **Sharma, Shyam Bihari**
Kannauj ki mranmurtiyan. *Panchala*, Vol. 1, No. 1, 1986 : 39-41 (Hindi).

2572. **Sharotri, G.K.** and **Narain, Lala Aditya**
A note on some terracottas in the National Museum-an evaluation of technique. *National Museum Bulletin*, Nos. 4-6 : 72-75.

2573. **Shukla, K.S.**
Newal terracottas depicting Ramayana scenes. *Bulletin of Museums & Archaeology in U.P.*, Nos. 33-34, June-December 1984 : 29-32.

2574. ______.
Newal terracottas depicting Ramayana scenes. *Prachya Pratibha*, Vol. 11, 1983 : 15-17.

2575. **Shukla, Vidya Sagar**
Terracotta female archer from Ahicchatra. *Journal of the Ganganatha Jha Kendriya Sanskrit Vidyapeetha*, Vol. 43, 1987 : 143-145.

2576. **Singh, Jai Prakash**
The weaver and Visnu on a terracotta plaque. *Panchala*, Vol. 5 1992 : 204-207.

2577. **Singh, Ram Chandra**
Rajghat ki mranmurtiyan. Lucknow, U.P. Rajya Puratattva Vibhag, 1978 (Hindi)

2578. **Singh, Sarjug Prasad**
Two inscribed terracotta balls from Bhelavar. *Journal of the Epigraphical Society of India*, Vol. 4, 1977 : 82-84.

2579. **Singh, Udai Vir**
Some interesting terracottas from Haryana. In A.M. Shastri and others, ed., *Vajapeya : Essays on evolution of Indian art & culture; Prof. K.D. Bajpai felicitation volume*, Vol. II. Delhi, Agam Kala Prakashan, 1987 : 191-194.

2580. **Sinha, C.R.P.**
Belwa terracottas. *Prajna Bharati*, Vol. 3, pt. 2, 1983 : 201-204.

2581. **Srivastava, S.K.**
Identification of a terracotta plaque from Mathura. *Bharati*, No. 8, pt. 1, 1964-65 : 92-94.

2582. ______.
Technique and art of Gupta terracottas. In Anand Krishna and Chandramani Singh, ed., *Chhavi : Golden Jubilee Volume*. Varanasi, Bharat Kala Bhavan, 1971 : 374-381.

2583. ______.
A terracotta panel from Sravasti. *Prajna*. Vol. 9, pt. 2, 1964 : 274-278.

2584. **Sternbach, Ludwik**
Archaic and ancient Indian terracottas : Collection of Dr. Eugeniusz Banarinski. Bombay, 1941.

2585. Terracotta figurines in Patna Museum, Patna. Patna, Patna Museum, [1961].

2586. Terracottas in Barehat, district Bhind, Madhya Pradesh. *Indian Archaeology : A Review*, 1959-60 : 69.

2587. **Thaplyal, K.K.**
Four terracottas from Newal. *Journal of the U.P. Historical Society*, New Series, Vol. 10, pt. 2, 1962 : 127-133.

2588. ______.
Three terracotta seal impressions from Sankisa. *Journal of the U.P. Historical Society*, New Series, Vol. 9, pt. 2, 1961 : 91-95.

2589. **Verma, Nisha**
The terracottas of Bihar. New Delhi, Ramanand Vidya Bhawan, 1986.

2590. **Yadav, R.P.**
Panchal Sangrahalaya ki vishista mranmurti evam Durga pratimayen. *Puratan*, Vol. 8, 1991 : 70-73 (Hindi).

2591. **Yoganand**
Valmiki ke shloko se ankit istikaphalak. *Bulletin of Museums & Archaeology in U.P.*, Nos. 5-6, June-December 1970 : 5-7 (Hindi).

PAINTING

2592. **Anand, Mulk Raj**

Rhytham of dance and music in the Bagh caves. *Marg*, Vol. 25, No. 3, June 1972 : 2-6.

2593. **Bajpai, K.D.**

The Malva school of painting. *Journal of the Bihar Puravid Parishad*, Vols. 4-5, 1980-81 : 217-220.

2594. **Fabri, Charles**

Frescos of Ajanta : An essay. *Marg*, Vol. 9, No. 1, December 1955 : 61-76.

2595. **Farooqi, Anis**

A review of the nomenclature of Western India School. *Journal of Indian History*, Vol. 53, pt. 2, August 1975 : 223-231.

2596. **Garola, Vachaspati**

Bharatiya chitrakala. Delhi, Chowkhamba Sanskrit Pratisthan, 1990 (Hindi).

2597. **Goetz, H.**

The golden age of Buddhist art: Painting—Ajanta. *Marg*, Vol. 9, No. 2, March 1956 : 86-92.

2598. ______.

The neglected aspects of Ajanta art. *Marg*, Vol. 2, No. 4 : 36-64.

2599. **Khandalavala, Karl**

Bagh and Ajanta. In Karl Khandalavala, ed., *The golden age : Gupta art—empire, province and influence*. Bombay, Marg Publications, 1991 : 93-102.

2600. ______.

The development of style in Indian painting. Delhi, Macmillan India, 1974.

2601. **Marshall, John** and others
The Bagh caves in the Gwalior State. London, The India Society, 1927.

2602. **Moti Chandra**
Studies in early Indian painting. Bombay, Asia Publishing House, 1974.

2603. **Rawson, Philip S.**
Indian painting. Paris, Pierre Tisne, 1961.

2604. **Upadhya, Om D.**
The art of Ajanta and Sopocani : A comparative study. Delhi, Motilal Banarsidass Publishers, 1994.

ARCHITECTURE

2605. **Anand, Mulk Raj**
Reflection on the house, the stupa, the temple, the mosque, the mausoleum and the town plan from the earliest times till today. *Marg*, Vol. 17, No. 1, December 1963 : 8-40.

2606. **Bajpai, K.D.**
Rock-shelters : Literary and epigraphical evidence. *All India Oriental Conference Proceedings*, Session 31, 1982 : 417-424.

2607. **Brown, Percy**
Indian achitecture (Buddhist and Hindu periods). Bombay, D.B. Taraporevala Sons & Co., 1965.

2608. **Chatterjee, Sris Chandra**
Magadha : Architecture and Culture. Calcutta, University of Calcutta, 1942.

2609. **Coomaraswamy, Ananda K.**
Essays in early Indian architecture. New Delhi, Indira Gandhi National Centre for the Arts, 1992.

2610. **Fabri, Charles**
An introduction to Indian architecture. Bombay, Asia Publishing House, 1963.

2611. **Gangoly, O.C.**
Indian architecture. Bombay, Kutub Publications, 1954.

2612. **Grover, Satish**
The architecture of India : Buddhist and Hindu. Sahibabad, Vikas Publishing House, 1980.

2613. Gupta architectural pieces, Sulantanpur, district Mirzapur, Uttar Pradesh. *Indian Archaeology : A Review*, 1981-82 : 103.

2614. **Havell, E.B.**
The ancient and medieval architecture of India : A study of Indo-Aryan civilisation. New Delhi, S. Chand & Co., 1972.

2615. **Khare, Awadh Bihari**
Ayodhya ki sthapatya kala ek adhyayana. *Panchala*, Vol. 7, 1994 : 59-64 (Hindi).

2616. **Krishna Deva**
A comparative study of the regional styles of architecture in North India. *Indian Museum Bulletin*, Vol. 6, No. 1, 1971 : 19-27.

2617. ______.
Contribution of Bihar to early Indian achitecture. *Prajna Bharati*, Vol. 3, pt. 1, 1983 : 29-42.

2618. ______.
Varieties of North Indian style : Magadha style, phase I, c. A.D. 500-700 : Later Guptas and minor dynasties. In Michael W. Meister and others, ed., *Encyclopaedia of Indian temple architecture : North India; Foundations of North Indian style*, c. 250 B.C.-A.D. 1100, Vol. II, pt. I. Delhi, American Institute of Indian Studies, 1988 : 101-114.

2619. **Majumdar, R.C.**
The Chinese temple of Sri-Gupta. *Indian History Congress Proceedings*, Session 15, 1952 : 45-46.

2620. **Mirashi, V.V.**
The age of the Bagh caves. *Indian Historical Quarterly*, Vol. 21, No. 2, June 1945 : 79-85.

2621. **Mishra, Vineeta**
Early architecture of Bihar (From earliest time to the Gupta period). New Delhi, Ramanand Vidya Bhawan, 1992.

2622. **Nagar, S.L.**
Indian monoliths. New Delhi, Intellectual Publishing House, 1992.

2623. **Singh, Sushil Kumar**
Architectural remains of Northern India (550 A.D. to 650 A.D.). *Vishveshvaranand Indological Journal*, Vol. 24, 1986 : 131-137.

2624. **Tadgell, Christopher**
The history of architecture in India from the dawn of civilisation to the end of the Raj. New Delhi, Viking, 1990.

2625. **Upadhyaya, Vasudeva**
Pracheen Bharatiya stupa, guha evam mandir. Patna, Bihar Hindi Grantha Akademi, 1972 (Hindi).

HINDU

2626. **Agrawala, P.K.**
Deogarh Visnu temple : The glory of Bundelkhand. In K.D. Bajpai, ed., *The glory that was Bundelkhand : Mahendra Kumar `Manav' felicitation volume*. Bhopal, Mahendra Kumar Manav Abhinandan Samiti, 1993 : 539-542.

2627. ______.
Gupta temple architecture. *Prajna*, Vol. 13, pt. 1, 1967 : 51-65.

2628. ______.
Gupta temple architecture. Varanasi, Prithivi Prakashan, 1981.

2629. ______.
Gupta temples : Some observations on their chronology. In P.C. Parikh and others. ed., *Dr. H.G. Shastri felicitation volume* (*Essaya on Sanskrit literature, Indian history, culture & archaeology*). Ahmedabad, Dr. H.G. Shastri Felicitation Volume Commitee, 1994 : 29-34.

2630. ______.
The temple-sikhara as mentioned in the Gupta period records. In Biswanarayan Shastri and Pratap Ch. Choudhury, ed., *Abhinandana-Bharati : Professor Krishna Kanta Handiqui felicitation volume*. Gauhati, Kamarupa Anusandhana Samiti, 1982 : 133-138.

2631. **Agrawala, V.S.**
Evolution of the Hindu temple and other essays. Varanasi, Prithivi Prakashan, 1965.

2632. ______.
The Gupta temple at Devagarh. In K. Bharatha Iyer, ed., *Art and thought : Issued in honour of Dr. Ananda K. Coomaraswamy on the occasion of his 70th birthday*. London, Luzac & Co., 1947 : 51-54.

2633. ______.
A new Gupta temple at Darra in Malwa. *Journal of the Uttar Pradesh Historical Society*, Vol. 23, 1950 : 196-197.

2634. **Amar Singh**
Development of the brick temples in Uttar Pradesh. *Bulletin of Museums & Archaeology in U.P.*, Nos. 45-46, June-December 1990 : 47-54.

2635. **Anand, Mulk Raj**
The temple of Bhitargaon. *Sanskriti Sangam*, Vol. 2, 1987 : 45-54.

2636. Architectural survey of temples. *Indian Archaeology : A Review*, 1956-57 : 69.

2637. Architectural survey of temples. *Indian Archaeology : A Review*, 1965-66 : 104.

2638. **Asher, Frederick M.**
The Gupta temple of Tigowa. *Sambodhi*, Vol. 6, Nos. 1-2, 1977 : 1-6.

2639. **Bajpai, K.D.**
Bundelkhand ki sanskritik dharohar : Nachna. *Samskriti Sandhana*, Vol. 3, 1990 : 31-33 (Hindi).

2640. **Banerjee, Manabendu**
Matsya Purana chapters on Indian architecture and sculpture. *Purana*, Vol. 21, No. 1, 1979 : 64-71.

2641. **Banerjee, N.R.**
New light on the Gupta temples at Deogarh, *Journal of the Asiatic Society*, Vol. 5, 1963 : 37-49.

2642. **Banerji, R.D.**
The temple of Siva at Bhumara. Calcutta, Government Printing, 1924 (Memoirs of the Archaeological Survey of India, No. 16).

2643. **Bernier, Ronald M.**
Tradition and invention in Himachal Pradesh temple arts. *Artibus Asiae*, Vol. 44, 1983 : 65-91.

2644. Brick temple and terracotta images, Indhar, district Shivpuri, Madhya Pradesh. *Indian Archaeology : A Review*, 1976-77 : 77.

2645. Brick temple Bhitargaon, district Kanpur, Uttar Pradesh. *Indian Archaeology : A Review*, 1957-58 : 85.

2646. **Chakravarty, D.K.**
On the survival of some typical Gupta decorative motifs on the temples of Purulia district, West Bengal. *Journal of Indian History*, Vol. 53, pt. 2, August 1975 : 233-241.

2647. **Chandol, G.K.**
Dithvara ka Gupta kaleen inton ka mandir. *Puratan*, Vol. 1, 1984 : 55-57 (Hindi).

2648. **Dayalan, D.**
Monolithic temples of Madhya Pradesh. Delhi, Bharatiya Kala Prakashan, 1995.

2649. **Dehejia, Vidya**
Brick temples : origins and development. In Amy G. Poster, *From Indian earth : 4,000 years of terracotta art*. New York, The Brooklyn Museum, 1986 : 43-56.

2650. ______.
Early stone temples of Orissa. New Delhi, Vikas Publishing House, 1979.

2651. **Desai, Madhuri**
The Gupta temple at Deogarh. Bombay, Bhulabhai Memorial Institute, 1958.

2652. **Deshpande, M.N.**
Cultural heritage of Madhya Pradesh. *Journal of the Madhya Pradesh Itihasa Parishad*, No. 11, 1980 : 1-9.

2653. **Donaldson, Thomas**
Doorframes on the earliest Orissan temples. *Artibus Asiae*, Vol. 38, Nos. 2-3, 1976 : 189-218.

2654. **Gangoly, O.C.**
A Gupta pillar at the Museum in Benares. *Oriental Art*, Vol. 3, No. 2, 1950 : 58-60.

2655. **Goetz, H.**
Imperial Rome and the genesis of classic Indian art. *East and West*, New Series, Vol. 10, No. 3, September 1959 : 153-183.

2656. ———.
Imperial Rome and the genesis of classic Indian art. *East and West*, New Series, Vol. 10, No. 4, December 1959 : 261-268.

2657. ———.
The last masterpiece of Gupta art. *Art and Letters-India, Pakistan, Ceylon*, Vol. 29, 1955 : 47-59.

2658. Gupta temple, Deogarh, district Lalitpur, Uttar Pradesh. *Indian Archaeology : A Review*, 1975-76 : 107.

2659. Gupta temple, Marhia, Deori Kalan, district Jabalpur, Madhya Pradesh. *Indian Archaeology : A Review*, 1968-69 : 65.

2660. Gupta temple, Nachna-Kuthara, district Panna, Madhya Pradesh. *Indian Archaeology : A Review*, 1958-59 : 93.

2661. Gupta temple, Piparia, district Satna, Madhya Pradesh. *Indian Archaeology : A Review*, 1967-68 : 67.

2662. **Joshi, M.C.**
The Siva temple at Nibiyakhera (Distt. Kanpur) and the chronology of the brick temples in the neighbourhood. *Bharati*, No. 8, pt. 1, 1964-65 : 66-75.

2663. **Kanwal, Ramlal**

Pracheen Malwa mein mandir vastukala. Delhi, Swati Publications, 1984 (Hindi).

2664. **Khare, M.D.**

Early temples, with special reference to a Gupta temple at Marhia district Jabalpur (Madhya Pradesh). *Journal of* the Madhya Pradesh Itihas Parishad, No. 9, 1973-74 : 13-19.

2665. **Krishna Deva**

Beginnings of North Indian style : Uttarapatha, c. A.D. 360-575 : Guptas and their feudatories. In Michael W. Meister and others., ed., *Encyclopaedia of Indian temple architecture : North India ; Foundations of North Indian style*, c. 250B.C.-A.D. 1100, Vol. II, pt. 1, Delhi, American Institute of Indian Studies, 1988 : 18-57.

2666. ______.

Temples of India. 2 vols. New Delhi, Aryan Books International, 1995.

2667. ______.

Temples of North India. New Delhi, National Book Trust, 1985.

2668. **Mate, M.S.**

Dvara-sakha : A study in evolution. *East and West*, New Series, Vol. 24, Nos. 1-2, March-June 1974 : 127-135.

2669. ______.

Symbolism of the Dvara-sakha. *East and West*, New Series, Vol. 28, 1978 : 249-252.

2670. **Meister, Michael W.**

Darra and the early Gupta tradition. In Anand Krishna and Kamal Giri, ed., *Chhavi-2 : Rai Krishnadasa felicitation Volume*, Varanasi, Bharat Kala Bhavan, 1981 : 192-205.

2671. ______.

A note on the superstructure of the Marhia temple. *Artibus Asiae*, Vol. 36, 1974 : 81-88.

2672. **Michell, George**
The Hindu temple : An introduction to its meaning and forms. Bombay, B.I. Publications, 1977.

2673. **Mishra, S.N.**
Gupta art and architecture (with special reference to Madhya Pradesh). Delhi, Agam Kala Prakashan, 1992.

2674. ______.
Gupta temple architecture in Madhya Pradesh. *Prachya Pratibha*, Vol. 13, 1985-87 : 83-87.

2675. **Mitra, Debala**
Sankar-Madha at Kunda, district Jabalpur. *Journal of the Asiatic Society*, Vol. 7, Nos. 1-2, 1965 : 79-81.

2676. **Nagar, Sheela**
Temple architecture in Haryana. *Vishveshvaranand Indological Journal*, Vol. 22, 1984 : 253-257.

2677. **Nagarch, B.L.**
Gupta temple and other medieval sculptures at Bhatani district Vidisha (M.P.). In R.D. Choudhury and Shri Bhagwan Singh, ed., *Aspects of history and culture (Anand Chandra Agarwala commemoration volume)*. New Delhi, Ramanand Vidya Bhawan, 1991 : 268-274.

2678. ______.
Later Gupta temples at Chhapara, district Vidisha (M.P.). *Panchala*, Vol. 6, 1993 : 115-116.

2679. ______.
Ruins of Gupta temple and other sculptures from Indhar. In C.R.P. Sinha and others, ed., *Archaeology and art (Krishna Deva felicitation volume)*, Part I. New Delhi, Ramanand Vidya Bhawan, 1990 : 297-300.

2680. **Nath, R.**
Bhitargaon : The technique of architecture. *Marg*, Vol. 22, No. 2, March 1969 : 24-35.

2681. **Pramod Chandra**
A Vamana temple at Marhia and some reflections on Gupta architecture. *Artibus Asiae*, Vol. 32, Nos. 2-3, 1970 : 125-145.

2682. Rock-cut caves and inscription, Doonge, district Gurdaspur, Punjab. *Indian Archaeology : A Review*, 1981-82 : 98.

2683. Rock-cut temple, Colgong, district Bhagalpur, Bihar. *Indian Archaeology : A Review*, 1978-79 : 126.

2684. **Saraswati, S.K.**
Temple architecture in the Gupta age. *Journal of the Indian Society of Oriental Art*, Vol. 8, 1940 : 146-158.

2685. **Sarkar, Gurudas**
Notes on the history of shikhara temples. *Rupam*, No. 10, April 1922 : 43-56.

2686. **Shrimali, Govind Lal**
Kirat koop ke sthapatya-shilpa par Guptakaleen prabhav. *Maru-Bharati*, Vol. 32, No. 1, April 1984 : 21-24 (Hindi).

2687. **Singh, R.C.**
Bhitargaon brick temple. *Bulletin of Museums & Archaeology in U.P.*, No. 1, March 1968 : 9-14.

2688. ———.
Bhitargaon brick temple. *Bulletin of Museums & Archaeology in U.P.*, No. 2, 1968 : 30-35.

2689. ———.
Bhitargaon brick temple. *Bulletin of Museums & Archaeology in U.P.*, No. 8, December 1971 : 30-36.

2690. **Sinha, K.C.** and **Ghosh, Amalananda**
An old temple at Mankuar. *Journal of the United Provinces Historical Society*, Vol. 9, pt. 2, July 1936 : 97-99.

2691. **Soundara Rajan, K.V.**
Bhitargaon temple—architectural and chronological considerations. In Om Prakash Awasthi, ed., *Anuvak*. Fatehpur, Akshay Sahitya Kala Kendra, [n.d.] : 49-55.

2692. ———.
Brahmanical early structural architecture—some aspects. *Archaeological Society of South India Transactions* for the period 1960-62 : 158-165.

2693. ———.
Glimpses of Indian culture—architecture, art and religion. Delhi, Sundeep Prakashan, 1981.

2694. **Spink, Walter M.**
A temple with four Uchchakalpa (?) doorways at Nachna Kuthara. In Ananda Krishna and Chandramani Singh, ed., *Chhavi : Golden Jubilee volume*. Varanasi, Bharat Kala Bhavan, 1971 : 161-172.

2695. **Srivastava, V.S.**
Ancient temples of Mewar. *Researcher*, Vol. 2 : 39-53.

2696. ———.
Rajasthan ke arambhik Vaisnava mandir. *Shodh Patrika*, Vol. 17, Nos. 1-2, 1966 : 39-53 (Hindi).

2697. **Tahsildar Singh**
Bhavisya Purana and Brhatsamhita on temple architecture : A collative study. *Purana*, Vol. 23, No. 1, 1981 : 62-72.

2698. A temple in Deogarh : Glimpses of early Gupta temple architecture. *Roopa-Lekha*, Vol. 23, 1952 : 58-61.

2699. **Upadhyaya, B.S.**
The temple architecture of India. In Prabhakar Machwe and Jaikishandas Sadani, ed., *Bharatiya Samskriti*, Vol. 2. Calcutta, Bharatiya Samskriti Samsad, 1983 : 29-37.

2700. **Vats, Madho Sarup**
The Gupta temple at Deogarh. Delhi, Manager of Publications, 1952 (Memoirs of the Archaeological Survey of India, No. 70).

2701. **Vats, M.S.**
Gupta temple at Deogarh. *Journal of the United Provinces Historical Society*, Vol. 18, 1945 : 224-227.

2702. **Verma, T.P.**
The temples of Banaras. *Bharati*, No. 15, 1971-84 : 194-205.

2703. **Vogel, J. Ph.**
The temple of Bhitargaon. *Archaeological Survey of India Annual Report*, 1908-09 : 5-21.

2704. **Williams, Joanna**
Char-Choma and the late Gupta period in Malwa. In Anand Krishna and Kamal Giri, ed., *Chhavi-2 : Rai Krishnadasa felicitation Volume*, Varanasi, Bharat Kala Bhavan, 1981 : 47-53.

2705. ———.
Dentils and the question of wooden origin for the Gupta temple. In Joanna G. Williams, ed., *Kaladarsana : American Studies in the art of India.* New Delhi, Oxford & IBH Publishing Co., 1981 : 159-163.

2706. **Zaheer, Mohammad**
The temple of Bhitargaon. Delhi, Agam Kala Prakashan, 1981.

BUDDHIST

2707. **Anderson, John**
Bagh caves : Historical and descriptive analysis. *Marg*, 25, No. 3, June 1972 : 17-56.

2708. **Bhattacharyya, Tarapada**
The Bodh Gaya temple. Calcutta, Firma K.L. Mukhopadhyay, 1966.

2709. **Dutt, Sukumar**
Buddhist monks and monasteries of India : Their history and their contribution to Indian culture. London, George Allen and Unwin, 1962.

2710. **Huntington, Susan L.**
The Buddhist stupa at Gyaraspur. In Anand Krishna and Kamal Giri, ed., *Chhavi-2 : Rai Krishnadasa felicitation Volume*, Varanasi, Bharat Kala Bhavan, 1981 : 54-58.

2711. **Krishna Kumar**
A circular Caitya-grha at Sarnath. *Journal of the Indian Society of Oriental Art*, New Series, Vol. 11, 1980 : 63-70.

2712. ______.
Date and significance of a stupa-shrine at Sarnath. *Journal of the Indian Society of Oriental Art*, New Series, Vol. 15, 1985-86 : 8-15.

2713. ______.
On the identification of Buddhist monuments noticed by Fa-Hsien at Sarnath. *Journal of Indian History*, Vol. 59, 1981 : 87-96.

2714. **Malandra, Geri H.**
The Mahabodhi temple. *Marg*, 40, No. 1 : 9-28.

2715. **Mitra, Debala**
Buddhist monuments. Calcutta, Sahitya Samsad, 1980.

2716. ______.
Buddhist vestiges in Orissa : A survey. In A.N. Tiwari, ed., *Orissa Review : Monument Special*. Bhubaneswar, Govt. of Orissa, 1976 : 31-54.

2717. **Mitterwallner, Gritli Von**
Two stupa basements of Mathura of the 4th and 5th centuries A.D. In Anna Libera Dallapiccola, ed., *The stupa : Its religious, historical and architectural significance*. Wiesbaden, Franz Steiner Verlag, 1980 : 72-89.

2718. **Pant, Sushila**
The origin and development of stupa architecture in India. Varanasi, Bharat Manisha, 1976.

2719. **Rath, Asoka Kumar**
The Buddhist remains in the Cuttack district of Orissa. *Journal of the Andhra Historical Research Society*, Vol. 27, 1961-62 : 155-163.

2720. **Sinha, B.P.**
The Mahabodhi temple. *Indian Journal of Buddhist Studies*, Vol. 4, No. 2, 1992 : 42-68.

2721. **Srivastava, Alakhdeva Prasad**
Nalanda ki sathapatya kala. *Journal of the Bihar Puravid Parisad*, Vols. 7-8, 1983-84 : 255-261 (Hindi).

MUSIC, DANCE AND DRAMA

2722. **Choudhary, Mantosh Chandra**
Glimpses of music and dance from Indian epigraphical records. *Indian History Congress Proceedings*, Session 44, 1983 : 697-704.

2723. **Iravati**
All female theatre : As depicted in ancient Indian literature and art. *Puratan*, Vol. 7, 1989 : 18-28.

2724. **Joshi, N.P.**
Prachin Bharatiya vina. *Nagari Pracharini Patrika*, Vol. 54, Nos. 2-3, samvat 2006 : 120-131 (Hindi).

2725. **Kala, S.C.**
The vina in Indian art. *Sanskriti Darshan*, No. 4, 1991 : 62-67.

2726. **Kuppuswamy, Gowri and Hariharan, M.**
Royal pattronage to Indian music. Delhi, Sundeep Prakashan, 1984.

2727. **Lath, Mukund**
Reflections on the vina in Gupta coinage. *Journal of the Numismatic Society of India*, Vol. 39, 1977 : 114-123.

SCIENCE & TECHNOLOGY

2728. **Agarwal, Urmila**

Non-rusting of the Meharauli iron pillar at Delhi. *Journal of the U.P. Historical Society*, New Series, Vol. 5, pt. 1, 1957 : 37-38.

2729. ______.

On the non-rusting of the Meharauli iron pillar. In M.C. Joshi and S.K. Gupta, ed., *King Chandra and the Meharauli Pillar*. Meerut, Kusumanjali Prakashan, 1989 : 14-15.

2730. **Bhattacharyya, Tarakeshwar**

A forgotten chapter of the history of ancient Indian astronomy. *Journal of the Ganganatha Jha Research Institute*, Vol. 13, 1955-56 : 81-117.

2731. **Chakravarty, A.K.**

Astronomical and calendrical evidence in early Indian inscriptions. *Journal of the Asiatic Society*, Vol. 30, 1988 : 18-30.

2732. **Fergusson, James**

On the art of the Delhi Iron Pillar. In M.C. Joshi and S.K. Gupta, ed., *King Chandra and the Meharauli Pillar*. Meerut, Kusumanjali Prakashan, 1989 : 12-13.

2733. **Gibbons, Donald F.** and **Ruhl, Katharine C.**

The metallurgical technique of the silver "plate with figures", Gupta period. *Ars Orientalis*, Vol. 11, 1979 : 177-182.

2734. **Jha, Parmeshwar**

Aryabhata I : His School. *Journal of the Bihar Research Society*, Vol. 55, 1969 : 102-114.

2735. **Lal, B.B.**

On the metallurgy of the Meharauli Iron Pillar. In M.C. Joshi and S.K. Gupta, ed., *King Chandra and the Meharauli Pillar*. Meerut, Kusumanjali Prakashan, 1989 : 22-58.

2736. **Pande, I.C., Shukla, V.D.** and **Srinivasan, M.S.**
Geology in India. *Prajna*, Vol. 7, 1962 : 40-64.

2737. **Pandey, V.G.**
Non-rusting of the Meharauli iron pillar. *Journal of the U.P. Historical Society*, New Series, Vol. 7, pt. 2, 1959 : 80-84.

2738. ———.
On the non-rusting of the Meharauli iron pillar. In M.C. Joshi and S.K. Gupta, ed., *King Chandra and the Meharauli Pillar*. Meerut, Kusumanjali Prakashan, 1989 : 16-20.

2739. **Pant, G.N.**
Bharatiya talwar-udbhav evam vikas. *Maru Bharati*, Vol. 12, No. 2, July 1964 : 54-68 (Hindi).

2740. ———.
Studies in Indian weapons and warfare. New Delhi, Army Educational Stores, 1970.

2741. **Saran, Santosh** and **Singh, Ravindra N.**
History of science and technology during Gupta period. New Delhi, Prachi Prakashan, 1994.

2742. **Smith, V.A.**
On the iron pillar of Delhi. In M.C. Joshi and S.K. Gupta, ed., *King Chandra and the Meharauli Pillar*. Meerut, Kusumanjali Prakashan, 1989 : 3-11.

2743. **Upadhyaya, G.S.**
Metallurgy in ancient India. *Prajna*, Vol. 3, 1959 : 240-245.

2744. **Williams, Joanna**
On the art of the Meharauli Iron Pillar of Delhi. In M.C. Joshi and S.K. Gupta, ed., *King Chandra and the Meharauli Pillar*. Meerut, Kusumanjali Prakashan, 1989 : 21.

AUTHOR INDEX

KEY-WORD INDEX